Integrating Southern Europe

Integrating Southern Europe presents a stimulating comparative analysis of the position of Spain within the European Union and within the global political economy. It combines a historical perspective – looking at the Spanish political economy throughout the twentieth century, with an analysis of the process of democratization in Southern Europe and of Spain's increasingly trans-European outlook.

The author uses the distinctive theoretical insights of the Amsterdam School of International Political Economy to illuminate the case of Southern Europe. He traces the progression of a transnational power configuration between social forces and the emergence of transnational concepts of control, arguing that these factors together with the transnationalization of civil society were of paramount importance in the smooth transition from dictatorship to democracy in the 1970s and in the subsequent integration of Southern Europe into the European Community in the 1980s.

The book should be of great value both to those readers whose primary interests are in International Political Economy, and to students and scholars of Spanish Politics who will find this a revealing, thoughtful and serious contribution to the literature.

Otto Holman is Senior Lecturer in the Department of International Relations and Public International Law at the University of Amsterdam.

Integrating Southern Europe

EC Expansion and the Transnationalization of Spain

Otto Holman

London and New York

First published 1996
by Routledge
11 New Fetter Lane, London EC4P 4EE

Simultaneously published in the USA and Canada
by Routledge
29 West 35th Street, New York, NY 10001

© 1996 Otto Holman

Typeset in Times by LaserScript, Mitcham, Surrey
Printed and bound in Great Britain by
Mackays of Chatham PLC, Chatham, Kent

All rights reserved. No part of this book may be reprinted or
reproduced or utilized in any form or by any electronic,
mechanical, or other means, now known or hereafter
invented, including photocopying and recording, or in any
information storage and retrieval system, without permission in
writing from the publishers.

British Library Cataloguing in Publication Data
A catalogue record for this book is available from the British Library

Library of Congress Cataloguing in Publication Data
A catalogue record for this book has been requested

ISBN 0–415–12441–7

Contents

Illustrations vii
Acknowledgements ix

Part I Theoretical perspective

1 Introduction: global political economy and the transition to modernity 3
   Introduction 3
   Interstate dependency and the globalization of the crisis of Fordism 7
   International or Atlantic Fordism 16

Part II Historical perspective

2 The making of contemporary Spain: socio-economic and political
     modernization in the twentieth century 33
   Introduction 33
   The peculiarities of the Spanish case 35
   Prelude: late industrialization and the authoritarian solution 42
   Signs of Leviathan: *Franquism and the revolution from above* 52
   *In search of hegemony: state–civil society configurations in
     post-Franquist Spain* 61
   Conclusions 65

Part III The Socialist decade (1982–1992)

3 Operation Europe: the hegemonic project of the PSOE 73
   Introduction 73
   Social democratization and the rise of the Spanish Socialist party 75
   The constituent elements of the Socialist project 77
   Factional strife and the disintegration of a project 84

vi *Contents*

*Operation Europe: still the 'cardinal and transcendent
    thought'?*   91
Appendix   95

4 The NATO referendum and beyond: from great power ambition
   to small power reality   96
   Introduction   96
   Continuity and change under Socialist rule   97
   The NATO referendum of 1986   100
   *The second phase of the Europeanization of Spanish foreign
       policy*   114
   Epilogue: Programme 2000 and the rhetoric of Euro-Socialism   121

5 Socialist economic policy and European integration: the
   internationalization of domestic politics   125
   Introduction   125
   Structural imbalances and Socialist macro-economic policy   128
   External restraints and Socialist economic policy   136
   *The impact of full EC membership on macro-economic
       policy-making and industrial restructuring*   147
   International priorities and domestic protest   162

6 Merging into Europe: private bank capital and the Socialist
   government   166
   Introduction   166
   Private bank capital and the making of a national bourgeoisie   167
   Los siete grandes   175
   *The Socialist government and private bank capital: co-operation
       and confrontation*   179
   Appendix   198

7 Conclusions and epilogue   200
   Spain's road to modernity   203
   The failure of the project   207
   The Europeanization of Spain's foreign and economic policy   209
   Centres of social and political power in Spain   213
   European union: deepening or widening?   215
   Appendix   217

Notes   218
Bibliography   236
Index   251

Illustrations

FIGURE

1 Implications of a large share of the capital goods industry in the national economy ... 140

TABLES

1 Weak and strong state–civil society configurations ... 39
2 Distribution of total number of 350 seats in Cortes ... 95
3 Real unit labour costs in industry in selected OECD countries, 1975–85 (1975 = 100) ... 129
4 Balance of payments (transactions basis) in million dollars ... 132
5 Merchandise trade: imports (c.i.f.) ... 133
6 'Pessimistic Scenario' (current account deficit, 1989–1992) ... 134
7 Authorized investment in Spain by country of origin (% of total) ... 144
8 European Community convergence indicators (1991) ... 153
9 Criteria satisfied (in December 1991) ... 154
10 Convergence plan 1992–1996: macro-economic projection (% annual change) ... 155
11 Spanish private banks among the 500 largest banking entities of the world (assets) ... 181
12 Spanish private banks among the 100 most profitable banks of the world in terms of net profits before taxes (1987) ... 181
13 Claims on non-residents as a % of year-end balance sheet total of commercial banks in selected European countries (1987 and 1991) ... 198
14 Deposit banks' foreign assets by EC member state (billions of dollars) ... 199

viii *Illustrations*

15 Spanish private banks among the 200 largest banks of the world (1992) 199
16 Results of the elections to the Congress, 6 June 1993 217
17 Sectoral structure of GNP (in %) 228

Acknowledgements

This book, which is an abbreviated and partly rewritten version of a doctoral dissertation presented in 1993, is a product of what has come to be known as the Amsterdam School of International Political Economy. I owe a debt to colleagues and students participating in the research programme of this 'school', and more particularly to Kees van der Pijl, whose theoretical acumen and critical support were of invaluable help. I also want to express my gratitude to Gerd Junne, who generously supervised the writing of the dissertation.

Next to them, I want to thank the following persons: Alejandro Chavarri, Francisco Chavarri, Aad Correljé, Alex Fernández Jilberto, Stephen Gill, Hans Keman, Beate Kohler-Koch, Marcel van Maastrigt, Ruud Mascini, Peter Mason, Angela Mata (ISOC-Madrid), Paul Mattick, Jr., Henk Overbeek, Mariné Sujar Gallardo, Ingeborg Tömmel, and two anonymous reviewers. At Routledge, finally, Susan Dunsmore, Nick Gillard, Clare Wells, James Whiting and Caroline Wintersgill were indispensable in the process of producing this book.

Part I
Theoretical perspective

1 Introduction

Global political economy and the transition to modernity

INTRODUCTION

In retrospect, the study of International Relations (IR) as a scientific discipline has long been characterized by a subdivision into two main areas, especially after World War II: first, the causes of war and conditions of peace; and, second, the international causes of persistent underdevelopment and the exogenous conditions of (economic) growth and (socio-political) modernization. These two fields have been inextricably linked as regards content and global scale ever since the beginnings of European expansion in the sixteenth century, but they have only been treated in conjunction sporadically in textbooks, research projects, or academic publications. In fact, in mainstream IR theory foreign policy relations and international power politics were causally separated from international economic relations and unequal development, and (international) power was separated from (domestic) production.

However, in the course of the 1970s and 1980s growing evidence of the fundamental interrelation between domestic and global developments, and between global political and economic structures, made it mandatory to rethink the basic premises of traditional IR theory. This has been clearly illustrated recently by the concurrence of the global economic crisis of the last two decades and the crisis and eventual demise of the bipolar system of superpower politics, resulting in an unprecedented renaissance of liberal economic and political values.

At the political level, the obvious manifestation of this process of liberalization is the shift from authoritarianism to formal political democracy in a number of developing countries, a process which began in Southern Europe in the 1970s, followed by Latin America in the 1980s. This worldwide process of democratization spread to Eastern Europe in the early 1990s.

4 *Theoretical perspective*

This book is the end result of a period of cumulative study of the process of socio-economic and political modernization in Southern Europe. It covers a period of more than a decade in which changing spheres of interest, subjects of research and theoretical perspectives of the author reasonably reflect the above-mentioned alterations in the broader field of IR theory. An initial interest in the history of Spain, and particularly its long-term decline from global power to a position on the European periphery, culminated in a special focus on developments in the first half of this century: the loss of its colonies in 1898; the period of economic and political isolation in the ensuing period; the failed attempt to establish a democratic political system during the so-called Second Republic (1931–1936); the rise of Spanish fascism; and the domestic causes and consequences of the Spanish Civil War. The subject of research then shifted from the 1930s to the 1970s: why was the transition to democracy after the death of Francisco Franco in 1975 so successful and relatively smooth until 1982, while it had been brutally aborted less than forty years before? It soon became clear that the answer to this question was to be found in the transformative impact that the Franquist dictatorship had had on Spanish society. However, since the study of this period (1939–1975) was initially confined to domestic developments, and international causes were viewed mainly from a traditional state-centric perspective, the answer to this question could only be partial at this stage of the ongoing research.

It was only after the range of this study had been extended to include Portugal and Greece that the need for an alternative theoretical approach became urgent. During the past thirty years, these three countries have shown some remarkable similarities in the timing and content of the processes by which each has experienced an accelerated integration into the European, and world, capitalist system. First, Spain, Portugal and Greece experienced high growth rates in the 1960s and early 1970s, as a result of both economic liberalization and a shift in economic policy. Consequently, these countries increased their shares of total world exports and imports and total production, and narrowed the gap between them and the industrialized countries with respect to GNP per capita.

Second, socio-political developments in Spain, Portugal and Greece in the late 1960s and 1970s were characterized by a process that has been called 'the crisis of the dictatorships' – a movement in the direction of less authoritarian governments – that reached its climax in all three countries at the same time, in the years 1974 and 1975. The subsequent periods of transition were very much the same in each country.

Third, the installation of socialist-led governments in these countries represented a legitimization of the parliamentary socialist alternative for the first time in their histories. The way this happened, especially in Spain and Greece, was illustrative of the way in which not only the three societies but also the socialist parties had changed since the formal establishment of democratic rule. It seemed to be accurate in this context to interpret socialism in Southern Europe not only as a result of the distinct processes of economic and socio-political transition towards the social system dominant in North-West Europe, but also as a political tendency and movement which itself was subject to fundamental changes.

Fourth, and closely related to the previous point, it was striking that these 'socialist' changes were characterized not by spectacular social reforms but, rather, by the moderate impact that they had on socioeconomic policy. The way in which these parties have played a leading role in the so-called 'internalization of international austerity' is astonishing. The latter phenomenon is apparently to be explained by reference both to internal power structures, the basis on which these governments have obtained their political legitimacy, and to the restraints that the capitalist world economy imposes on these countries.

Finally, in the field of foreign policy the post-authoritarian governments in Spain, Portugal and Greece were progressively oriented to Western Europe, with formal membership of the Common Market as an ultimate goal. This aspect of their development explicitly contained the combination of the two processes of industrialization and 'social-democratization'. In fact, at this stage of the research it appeared that a comparative analysis of the political and socio-economic developments in Spain, Portugal and Greece would have to take the European aspirations of these countries as a primary, albeit implicit, point of departure.

In comparing these different processes of modernization, democratization, and internationalization two important questions come to mind: to what extent are the transitions to democracy in the three Southern European countries interrelated, and can they be explained on common grounds, both in terms of timing and content? This introductory chapter attempts to explain the similarities between Spain, Portugal and Greece from a global perspective. In doing so, and in transcending the rigid power politics approach inherent to mainstream IR theory, stress will be laid on the *transnational* dynamics of global (and European) integration and its class content, seen from the perspective of the postwar globalization of capitalist relations. In fact, it will be claimed that an answer to the above questions is not possible without reference to the fundamental changes at the level of production, in the field of power relations, and in the ideological sphere. Such an integrated approach, which aims at bridging the gap between structure and agency, as well as at transcending the so-called level of

6 Theoretical perspective

analysis problem and the ongoing question of external versus internal determination, may provide the beginnings of an understanding of global processes. It is the analysis of concrete post-World War II processes, of which the transnationalization of production is certainly one of the most important, that enables us to transcend the theoretical and methodological problems related to, for instance, the neo-realist approach. In particular, the tenacious view that the nation–state is still the basic, if not the only, actor in international relations must be questioned.

In order to understand social change in one particular region or country, one has to grasp the dynamics of social and political action within the context of state structures, on the one hand, and the dynamics of state action within the context of world order structures, on the other. In order to come to terms with this double movement, the power of transnational capital in both its behavioural and structural form is proposed here as a mediating force (see Gill and Law 1989; Gill 1990). Before proceeding to elaborate on what we call the transnational perspective in IR theory, we will review part of the relevant literature that has tried to explain socio-economic modernization and political transition in Southern Europe from an international perspective. We will mainly focus on the so-called interstate dependency approach (here represented by the work of Nicos Poulantzas and Alain Lipietz). The next section presents an alternative approach. One of the constituent parts of what we will call Atlantic (or international) Fordism, i.e. the internationalization of productive capital, has fundamentally changed the global context in which national governments and social actors are operating. Particularly after this system of Atlantic Fordism entered a severe crisis in the 1970s and 1980s, and in a setting of global neo-liberalism, the rising power of internationally mobile capital has become the primary factor in explaining global, regional, and national dynamics, and has revealed the weakness of approaches which are still based on a traditional, state-centric perspective.

This section introduces a second mediating concept, the notion of comprehensive concepts of control. This offers us insight into how to integrate the levels of material forces, institutional ensembles, and ideologies, in both a national and a transnational setting. In the context of a continuing process of internationalization of capital, concepts of control eventually transcend national frontiers, cementing a cohesion between social and political forces on an increasingly transnational basis. It will be argued that the integration of Spain, Portugal, and Greece in the global network of transnational production has made these countries, and individual capital based in them, part and parcel of globally operative processes of class formation and increasingly transnational state–civil society configurations.

INTERSTATE DEPENDENCY AND THE GLOBALIZATION OF THE CRISIS OF FORDISM[1]

In discussing the transition from dictatorship to democracy in Southern Europe in the 1970s, we are not only in search of a model that offers 'a clear criterion of historically significant events' (Bhaskar 1979: 47), viz. those that initiate or constitute ruptures in political regimes. In explaining social change, we must go beyond questions as to what the change or what history is about, and focus on how real historical change takes place. In other words, apart from a criterion for the significance of particular events, we need a conceptualization which helps us to understand at least theoretically why these significant events come about.

If society is to be regarded as 'an ensemble of structures, practices and conventions which individuals reproduce or transform, but which would not exist unless they did so' (Bhaskar 1979: 45–46),[2] then it is most likely that there are fundamental contradictions between different structures, practices and conventions within the totality of society, constituting opposite moments of the same process, and, subsequently, conflicts between different groups or individuals. For instance, every society contains a very important conflict between those individuals who want to reproduce society and those who want to transform it. Moreover, if we assume the hierarchical ordering of different structures, practices and conventions, it may happen that individuals act at the same time within different social structures which are not necessarily complementary. So, groups or individuals may transform particular structures while reproducing other structures through the same social activity and at the same time. In a similar way, an individual's activity within a particular structure may conflict with his position and interests within a larger structure. Finally, the following question is of crucial importance: why do some people reproduce or transform society more than others? Obviously, the answer to this question has something to do with the distribution of the structural conditions of social action, but it is also concerned, and to the same extent, with action itself. What is at stake here is the distribution of material capabilities and power, and, for that matter, the relation between economics and politics, between society and the state, between dominant and dominated classes, and between social classes as related to a particular mode of production and domination, on the one hand, and the state apparatuses, on the other.

What does this all boil down to? In a preliminary way, the conclusion can be that social change cannot be explained by reference to either individualist/voluntarist or collectivist/determinist conceptions. In order to avoid structure/agency dichotomies, and to refrain from interpretations of

8 Theoretical perspective

history as mere contingency, we here propose the notion of the power of capital, in both its structural and behavioural forms (Gill and Law 1989: 480).[3] Production and power, or rather, the distribution of material capabilities and the articulation of social and political power at the level of the state, are the primary factors in explaining social change. This is because the unequal distribution of material capabilities and power is itself subject to human agency (and hence subject to continuous reproduction and transformation), and, in generating contradictions and conflicts, to historical change. In the same way, the structural and behavioural power of capital is subject to changes over time. It is our contention here that in particular the contradictions and conflicts resulting from capital–labour relations, relations between sections of the bourgeoisie, and state–civil society relations are essential in explaining social change.

If we assume that national societies are social systems which are not (or, at least, no longer) characterized by the 'fact that life within it is largely self-contained, and that the dynamics of its development are largely internal' (Wallerstein 1974: 347), we must conclude that the external impact on internal structure/agency relations, and vice versa, becomes an essential component in explaining social change. What we apparently need, then, is a model of the activity of states which can be applied both to the relation between national states and the global economic system, i.e., between political action at the national and international level and economic structures at the global level, and to the relation between individual citizens (e.g. politicians, bureaucrats or individual representatives of national bourgeoisies) and the state. In this sense, individual states operate outwardly as actors and inwardly as objective structures. To put it another way, the global system as a social structure is constituted by the action of individual states at the international level, and yet at the same time it is the very medium of this constitution. On the other hand, the state as a social structure is constituted by human agency, and yet at the same time it is the very medium of this constitution. This confronts us, however, with a new problem: how to analyse the interrelation between national societies (as the outcome of human agency) and the global system (as the outcome of 'state' agency). The double role or function of individual states makes them apparently unique in relation to other social actors which operate exclusively at the national level, e.g. national trade unions and employers' organizations. Apart from the fact that this statement is very near to a state-centric approach to international relations, however, it does not offer a suitable solution to the problem of external versus internal determination in the first place. Indeed, it does not explain how real historical change at the global level takes place; it does not help us to understand why historically significant events come about; it does not account for contradictions between world order structures, practices and conventions, or for conflicts between different states or groups of states; it says nothing about the conflicts between those international actors who want to reproduce 'world society' and those who want to transform it; and, finally, it does not answer the question why certain states (or international actors) reproduce or transform world society more than others.

What we need, then, is an additional conceptualization which will help us to understand social change at both the global and national (or regional) levels, which transcends different levels of analysis, and which avoids the structure/agency dichotomy. In the last part of this chapter we will propose such a conceptualization by introducing the notions of the structural power of transnational capital, hegemony, and concepts of control. In doing this, we will show that the national/international dichotomy is no longer a valid one, since postwar processes of transnationalization affect not only capital–labour relations, but also state–civil society configurations.

Before entering upon this subject, let us first return to the basic point of departure: our analysis of the combined processes of modernization, democratization and internationalization in Spain, Portugal and Greece. The following section contains a survey of the most relevant literature. For the purpose of our argument, we will concentrate on two examples of the so-called interstate dependency perspective: the work of Nicos Poulantzas and of Alain Lipietz. In some ways the work of both scholars can be said to mark an advance on, for instance, the comparative politics approach to democratic transition and the world system approach,[4] but it too has substantial limitations.

Poulantzas and the crisis of the dictatorships

One of the few studies of Southern Europe that incorporates an attempt to consider both internal and external factors in explaining similar developments and characteristics of different countries is Nicos Poulantzas' book on the 'crisis of the dictatorships' in Spain, Portugal and Greece (Poulantzas 1976). Although Poulantzas insisted on the primacy of internal factors, he also used such concepts as 'dependent industrialization' and 'dependent type of state'. In his opinion, Spain, Portugal and Greece stand in a relationship of dependence to the imperialist metropolises. Poulantzas' solution to the problem of the relationship between internal and external factors is

> that those coordinates of the imperialist chain that are 'external' to a country
> – the global balance of forces, the role of a particular great power, etc. –

only act on the country in question by way of their internalization, i.e. by their articulation to its own specific contradictions

(ibid.: 22)

In this context, 'internalization' is understood as the 'induced reproduction' of the contradictions of imperialism. What Poulantzas calls the 'imperialist chain' and 'dependency' are two factors determining the structural, sociopolitical and economic transformation of Spain, Portugal and Greece in the 1970s. These countries can no longer simply be placed on the peripheral side of a traditional division between agriculture/industry in the international system. The 'new' dependency, as he calls it, is the result of a process of industrialization generated by foreign, international capital, which dissolves traditional economic organizations and pre-capitalist modes of production in an accelerated way.

Poulantzas tried to explain why the accelerated industrialization of Spain, Portugal and Greece had little to do with the classical image of underdevelopment. That is, the traditional idea of a class alliance between big landowners, on the one hand, and, on the other, a *comprador* bourgeoisie which is weakly rooted in the national economic structure and functions as a direct commercial and financial intermediary for the penetration of foreign capital, becomes modified. Alongside this *comprador* bourgeoisie, which is still defined as 'that fraction whose interests are entirely subordinated to those of foreign capital, and which functions as a kind of staging-post and direct intermediary for the implantation and reproduction of foreign capital' (ibid.: 42), an industrial, 'domestic bourgeoisie' has come into existence in Spain, Portugal and Greece, which is structurally subordinated to the power bloc of foreign and *comprador* capital, but increasingly attempts to escape from this domination by eventually entering into an alliance with the labour movement. The fall of the dictatorships in Spain, Portugal and Greece, then, is the result of a crisis in the power bloc, weakening the position of the *comprador* bourgeoisie which is the main supporter of the authoritarian regime. The domestic bourgeoisie, on the other hand, successfully reinforces its position by agreeing on democratic transition with the popular forces.

The central question Poulantzas asked is of primary importance here: 'in what way have the so-called "external" factors, the changes involved in the present phase of imperialism, been reproduced and internalized actually within the socio-economic and political structures of these countries?' (ibid.: 41). In the course of his argument, the postwar process within the Atlantic Alliance serves as a model for and is projected on to the developments in Spain, Portugal and Greece, particularly with respect to the relationship between the domestic bourgeoisie (read: Western Europe) and the *comprador* bourgeoisie (read: United States). As in the case of the changing relationship between the United States and Europe in the 1970s, there is an 'emancipation' of the domestic bourgeoisie which produces a contradiction centring on a rearrangement in the balance of power between the domestic and the *comprador* bourgeoisie, in which the latter, however, still exercises hegemony.[5] The problem with this is that, in his analysis of the fall of the dictatorships, Poulantzas could not explain why the (temporary?) coming to power of the domestic bourgeoisie interferes with the interests of the *comprador* bourgeoisie, while at the same time taking place under the absolute hegemony of this *comprador* bourgeoisie. Moreover, in trying to equate the overall relationship between the United States and Europe with what was occurring in the three countries in question, Poulantzas tends to apply his concepts in a rather cavalier manner, disregarding key aspects of the historical situations specific to these countries.[6] This becomes very clear when we look at his idea of the *comprador* bourgeoisie.

In his identification of the *comprador* bourgeoisie with Spanish bank capital, for instance, he explains more about the concept of the former than about Spanish bank capital. Studies of the role of Spanish banking in the formation and development of capitalism have made abundantly clear that the so-called *oligarquía financiera* gained its position as the bastion of Spanish capitalism long before the massive penetration of foreign capital took place in the 1960s (Muñoz 1970; Roldán *et al.* 1973; see also Chapter 6 of this book). Instead of functioning as an agent of foreign (American) capital, Spanish bank capital used co-operation with foreign capital in the 1960s and 1970s to its own benefit, and strengthened its dominant position in the Spanish economy by creating an industrial base of its own. In fact, it was this co-operation which made possible the import of modern technology, the introduction of new forms of industrial organization, a substantial increase in productivity and in the average size of industrial plants, the increasing urbanization together with the subsequent expansion of the domestic market and the introduction of new productive activities and economic sectors. All these economic improvements would not have been possible without foreign capital and technology (see Muñoz *et al.* 1978: 268–269). In this context, the interests of foreign capital and of the Spanish bourgeoisie as a whole have therefore been complementary, and the conflicts between them of secondary importance.

In other words, when the Franquist regime decided in favour of economic liberalization through the Stabilization Plan of 1959, a genuine national (i.e., not domestic) bourgeoisie already existed, characterized by its strong links with the state apparatus. Foreign capital played a decisive role in the modernization and industrialization of the economy, without, however, gaining a dominant position *vis-à-vis* the national bourgeoisie (and notably Spanish bank capital) or exerting direct political influence with respect to the Franquist regime. The internationalization of the Spanish economy between 1960 and 1970 (including the influence of direct foreign investment, the dependence on foreign technology, and the increasing share of foreign trade in GNP) was essential to sustain industrial development. But the opening up towards the world market was also the result of the internal dynamic of the Spanish economy and was in the interests of the national bourgeoisie; it was not the result of unilateral pressure on the part of foreign capital. Although the authoritarian regime stimulated the intervention of foreign capital, this never jeopardized its political independence. Poulantzas' interpretation of the crisis and fall of the Spanish dictatorship as the result of a conflict between a domestic bourgeoisie and a *comprador* bourgeoisie, engendered through the subordination of the latter to foreign capital, is therefore difficult to accept. And, indeed, the same applies to Portugal and Greece.[7]

The French Regulation school: Alain Lipietz

While Poulantzas tried to understand the process of 'independent industrialization' in Southern Europe by analysing the changing 'coordinates of the imperialist chain' in the late 1960s and 1970s, Alain Lipietz has made an attempt to combine the analysis of the Fordist accumulation regime with the changing pattern of the international division of labour in the 1970s and early 1980s. For Lipietz, Fordism is essentially connected with the socioeconomic formations of the old industrial core areas, where it was introduced in order to regulate the long-established relation between wage labour and capital. When speaking of the eventual extension of Fordism to countries in 'the South', Lipietz argues that their problem is 'the *creation* or establishment of the wage-relation' instead of the adjustment of this relation. As a result, the crisis of Fordism in the core countries and the subsequent transfer of production processes to the 'outer periphery' (the so-called Newly Industrializing Countries (NICs)) does not and cannot include the transfer of the Fordist regime of accumulation to its full extent, and is not materialized in a Fordist mode of regulation.[8] Instead of the global extension of Fordism, one should speak of the extension of the crisis of Fordism (Lipietz 1982). In other words, the overall framework of core–periphery relations necessarily excludes the peripheral countries from adopting similar structures to those of core countries. Because Fordism originates in the core and is subsequently imported (or internalized) in some parts of the periphery, an inferior copy of the original regime – 'peripheral Fordism' – is the necessary outcome.[9]

Lipietz warns us not to use labels applying to the 'old division of labour', and particularly the centre–periphery dichotomy, in the analysis of individual states. Instead, he argues in favour of the 'primacy of internal causes': the basic unit of analysis is the socio-economic national formation, which must be studied in its own right rather than in the context of a single world system or 'world regime of accumulation'. At best we may speak of a 'world configuration' of national regimes of accumulation. Nonetheless he adds, '[if] we wish to understand what is happening "in the periphery", we must begin by looking at what is happening in the advanced capitalist world' (Lipietz 1987: 29–30). Thus, though he stresses the primacy of internal factors, he still pays attention to centre–periphery relations within the 'new international division of labour'. These relations

> are not direct relations between states or territories which are caught up in a single process. They are *relations between processes*, between processes of social struggle and between regimes of accumulation that are to a greater or lesser extent introverted or extraverted.
>
> (ibid.: 25)

Here we are confronted with the old dilemma between 'internal' and 'external' determination. 'How can our theoretical analysis recognise the primacy of the "internal" productive process in the colonies, and yet reconcile or combine it with the also determinant "external" exchange and other relations of dependence on the capitalist metropolis?' (Frank 1979: 2–3). This problem of determination or primacy of the internal mode of production and accumulation, on the one hand, and the external relations of exchange and capital flows, on the other, is clearly reflected in the work of Lipietz. Although he seems well aware of Mao's statement

> that external causes are the condition of change and internal causes are the basis of change, and that external causes become operative through internal causes. In a suitable temperature an egg changes into a chicken, but no temperature can change a stone into a chicken, because each has a different basis
>
> (Mao Tse-tung 1977: 28)

it seems that Lipietz applies this principle to the national socio-economic formations of the core but much less so to those in the periphery. In the core states internal class structures and regimes of accumulation subordinate external conditions; inversely, in those states where peripheral Fordism is introduced, internal structures are subordinated to the global 'relations between processes'. Here the external causes, i.e. the crisis in core Fordism and the subsequent internationalization of production, are the basis of change, the internal social struggle conditioning the success or otherwise of the implantation of the intensive regime of accumulation, bloody Taylorism or peripheral Fordism being the only alternative outcomes. It is as if the temperature changes the stone into a disabled chicken. The resulting picture is that the famous 'development of underdevelopment' thesis of André Gunder Frank is turned into an implicit 'underdevelopment of development' thesis.

Several criticisms can be levelled at this thesis. First, Lipietz' implicit analytical distinction between production and accumulation, confined to national socio-economic formations, and international exchange relations may be questioned. It is not that Lipietz denies the internationalization of productive capital. He does say, however, that '[even] if economic interests and transnational ideological pressures do abolish frontiers, it has to be remembered that the form in which those pressures and interests are integrated is still the state form' (Lipietz 1987: 22). Similarly, Lipietz argues that the investments of multinational corporations in peripheral countries, and the subsequent coming into existence of a new international division of labour, are not simply the outcome of the organizational activity of these corporations but, rather, the result of decisions made by the ruling classes of these peripheral countries. I would argue contrary to this view, since the process of class formation itself is part of the growth of transnational capital accumulation, as can be seen in the Atlantic context (see van der Pijl 1984). Indeed, it is the analysis of specific postwar processes, of which the transnationalization of production is certainly one of the most important, that enables us to transcend the theoretical and methodological problems of Lipietz' argument.

This point is related to a second one. Lipietz' analysis of the state reduces its role to the regulation of national processes of accumulation. His interpretation of international relations therefore remains classical and state-centred, though he himself prefers to speak of 'relations between processes'. This cannot hide the fact, however, that the state is viewed as the basic, if not the only, actor in international relations. The tenacity of this view may surprise us in times of transnationalization (of production, but also of civil society, of certain state functions, of ideological structures) and the internationalization of domestic politics.

Third, as we have seen, for Lipietz the notion of the primacy of internal factors only applies to the national social formations in the centre bloc. That is, in the core states internal structures subordinate external conditions.

Inversely, these very internal structures in the peripheral states are subordinated to the global 'relations between processes'. The main aspect of this tendency is the subordination of class analysis in the peripheral countries to the analysis of the imperialist structure as implied by the centre–periphery relations at the international level. Lipietz' analysis of the social struggle and the regime of accumulation in a particular peripheral state is 'built in' to his analysis of the relations between processes, that is, the imperialist structure. The similarity with Poulantzas' approach is striking. A major consequence of this kind of analysis is that, as Arrighi has argued, it favours generalization 'and therefore discourages the concrete analyses of concrete situations . . .'.[10] In particular Lipietz' application of the concept of peripheral Fordism to define the position of Spain, Portugal and Greece, on the one hand, and the Latin American NICs, on the other, in the new international division of labour is illustrative of where such generalization can lead.

This becomes particularly clear when we look more closely at Lipietz' analysis of the process of democratic transition in Southern Europe. In fact, the use of his concept of peripheral Fordism compels him to equate political developments in Spain, Portugal, and Greece, on the one hand, with those in Brazil for instance, on the other: 'the same economic causes [the maturation of peripheral Fordism] have the same effects in the early NICs [Southern Europe] and, ten years later, in the "NICs of the seventies"' (Lipietz 1987: 114). Here Lipietz seems to be inspired by Poulantzas in so far as he uses the concept of 'domestic' (or 'internal') bourgeoisie to explain developments in both the early NICs and the NICs of the 1970s. The emergence of this domestic bourgeoisie coincided with the internationalization of capital, i.e. with the new international division of labour, and resulted in the coming into existence of a 'new social bloc' (composed of the domestic bourgeoisie, a 'new' petty bourgeoisie, and a 'new' working class) which 'necessarily aspired towards the democratic and trade-union liberties enjoyed by the most highly industrialized countries' (ibid.: 115). Apart from the comments already made on the interpretation of Poulantzas, the problem is that Lipietz' generalization cannot account for the striking differences between, for instance, Southern Europe and Latin America as regards their political developments. Why has political democracy become firmly established and consolidated in Spain, for instance, while remaining highly unstable and vulnerable in countries like Brazil?

In the remainder of this chapter, we will argue that two particular developments have made Lipietz' analysis obsolete: the process of socio-economic and political transnationalization in the 1970s and 1980s; and the integration of Spain, Portugal and Greece into the Common Market in the

1980s. Both developments explain the similarities between Spain, Portugal, and Greece, and the differences between Southern Europe and, for instance, Latin America.

INTERNATIONAL OR ATLANTIC FORDISM

In this section we will look more closely at the international economic and socio-political context in which the processes of industrialization and democratization have taken place in Spain, Portugal and Greece. We first outline the basic dimensions of the postwar growth model. Starting from a Gramscian interpretation, we call this complex of interrelated national and international, political and economic features of the postwar growth model international or Atlantic Fordism. This model has three mutually reinforcing dimensions, which are 'superimposed dimensions of reality, where "facts" pertinent to one dimension only acquire their full meaning if they are considered against the background of the other dimensions' (Overbeek 1990: 87).

The first dimension: the adoption of Fordist production methods

First, in its most restrictive meaning, Fordism at the national level originates in the factory through the introduction of new productive methods by individual companies, eventually leading to the macro-economic principle of combined increases in productivity and real wages (that is, the implementation of a macro-economic growth model, based on mass production and mass consumption). The very introduction of Fordism can be partially dependent on external factors, such as foreign technology and capital. That is, the technical superiority of productive forces in particular areas of the world economy can result in the globalization of certain production processes and techniques, and modes of labour organization, through the internationalization of trade and production. Fordism as a mode of accumulation originated in the United States in the interwar years and eventually spread to Western Europe through the postwar internationalization of American capital, 'through the channels of American hegemony' (van der Pijl 1984: 22), but the successful implantation of Fordism within a country is inextricably bound up with the existence of a specific level of socio-economic and political development of that country. This is not to say that exactly the same thing – the internationalization of Fordism as a mode of accumulation – would have occurred without the postwar internationalization of American capital, but it is equally wrong to neglect the historically determined national contexts in which postwar developments

Introduction 17

could occur in the first place. This, among other things, explains the considerable national differences in timing and in content of the eventual emergence and subsequent development of Fordism in the Atlantic area. Materially based on the combination of increasing productivity and real income, Fordism has succeeded in reproducing the capital–labour relation under changing conditions inasmuch as it has resulted in the subordination of the specific interests of both the working class and the bourgeoisie to an overall compromise between their respective interest groups, while preserving the fundamental subordination of wage labour to capital, as functional determinants in the production process. Obviously, the successful implementation of such a social compromise is primarily a matter of historically determined, endogenous factors, such as the level of economic development, the strength of the bourgeoisie *vis-à-vis* the working class, and so on. These nationally determined features explain to a large extent the differences in timing and in content between the introduction of forms of Fordist regulation in, for example, the core states of Western Europe in the immediate postwar period, and in Southern Europe in the 1960s.

In Spain, Portugal and Greece a restructuring of production along Fordist lines was the combined result of domestic (public or private) initiatives and direct foreign investment, producing spectacular economic development during the 1960s and early 1970s. All three countries realized average annual growth rates in this period that were the highest among the OECD countries except for Japan (Tsoukalis 1981: 19ff.). It is striking that for all three countries the year 1960 marks the approximate point of departure of the economic liberalization and opening up to the outside world. Within the context of a rapidly developing and internationalizing world economy, a policy of national economic isolation, or import-substitution, such as was the case in Spain, Portugal and Greece in the 1950s, was no longer compatible with the goal of domestic economic expansion. Economic liberalization, in fact, coincided with a new phase of internationalization of predominantly American capital at the time of the so-called Kennedy Round. In this context, all three economies passed through a radical process of internationalization. Without the heavy influx of foreign capital, and with it the advent of modern and diversified technology, the following period of economic growth would have been impossible. Another similarity between the three countries is the role played by tourism and emigration in their economic development. The concomitant monetary receipts were an important compensation for structural trade deficits.

All three countries saw a combined increase of real wages (average annual rates of 6.38 per cent in Spain, 4.99 per cent in Portugal, and 6.98 per cent in Greece) and 'super-Fordist' average annual productivity rises (5.46 per cent in Spain, 6.81 per cent in Portugal, and 7.51 per cent in

Greece) during the period 1963 to 1973 (Lipietz 1987: 127). They also experienced a radical change in the composition of the labour force. The percentage of workers employed in the primary sector in Greece declined from 57 per cent in 1960 to 29.7 per cent in 1980, in Portugal from 42.8 per cent to 28.3 per cent, and in Spain from 42.3 per cent to 18.9 per cent (OECD 1983, 1984a, and 1984b) in favour of the industrial and service sectors. By this I mean to stress the fact that economic expansion in Spain, Portugal and Greece was associated to a greater or lesser extent with the development of a domestic market, as opposed to a mainly export-oriented development. This crucial aspect of their growth can be seen in the rapid growth of domestic consumption and the resulting change in patterns of consumption, a process that has been described as the gradual rise of 'consumerism' (Pike 1972).

There were three main differences, however, in the content and effect of national Fordism in Southern Europe in comparison with its introduction in the European core in the preceding decades. First, the economic expansion in Spain, for example, rested on a dual structure involving, on the one hand, a relatively small number of large-scale, modernized enterprises with high productivity rates and relatively high real wages, and, on the other hand, numerous small factories and shops that were backward in technology and paid below-average wages. The macro-economic increase of productivity and real wages was almost entirely due to an initial increase in the number of large-scale enterprises, with no spin-off effect whatsoever on the small factories. This further aggravated the dual character of Spanish industrial structures in the course of the 1960s. That is, although Fordism implies the 'rationalization and extension of the class relations of capitalism', it never obtains control over the whole of production (see Cox 1987: 309ff.). Fordist production may eventually become the dominant form, coexisting with other, subordinate forms of organization of production and labour relations, or it may not. In the latter case, a fairly unstable balance between different forms of production (and different forms of social relations of production, for that matter) may persist, leaving regressive and nonproductive forces in society considerable room for socio-political manoeuvre.

Second, the Spanish, Portuguese and Greek economic structures were characterized by a low absolute and relative national specialization in capital goods production and, subsequently, by a low structural coherence of the national productive apparatus. This meant that the ideal–typical conditions on which a continuing spiral of rising productivity and increasing mass consumption is based, i.e., a sufficient increase in productivity in both the producer goods and consumer goods sectors,[11] could only be realized partially within the framework of their national economies.

Third, Spain, Portugal and Greece had become part of the postwar internationalization of capital as receiving countries, without their national capital having yet achieved the strength to internationalize itself. Moreover, within the context of an increasingly international division of labour between core activities such as strategic decision-making and research and development, and peripheral activities such as labour-intensive production (predominantly but not necessarily carried out by vertically integrated multinational corporations), the three economies initially occupied a fairly intermediate position reflected by the 'balanced mix of brain and muscle/ nerve activities' (Arrighi 1985: 275) located in these countries.

The second dimension: macro-economic regulation and the welfare state

The second dimension of Atlantic Fordism refers to the state and its relation to civil society. We are referring here to Keynesianism as an economic policy, with the interventionist state and the 'mixed economy' as its concomitants, on the one hand, and 'modes of social relations of production', on the other (Cox 1987).

Whereas Fordism in its restrictive meaning is characterized by a specific form of organization of production and labour relations, structuring the process of accumulation and eventually leading to a compromise between the main social forces (a compromise based on the combination of increasing productivity and rising real wages), Keynesianism is the reflection of a particular balance of power in economic policy, i.e. a macro-economic, demand-led accumulation strategy (Jessop 1983). In other words, ideal–typical Keynesianism 'implies the use of government to influence and direct decisions made in the private sector' (Wolfe 1981: 54). In those countries in which a strong labour movement existed, a Keynesian economic policy could be effectively pursued in order to 'save capitalism from the capitalists' (ibid.: 51). In most cases social democracy functioned as the obvious political medium of such a policy. Here the structural power of capital seems to be more relevant in explaining macro-economic policy (which itself reflects a particular – though continuously changing – balance of power) than its direct or behavioural power. On the other hand, in those countries without a strong socialist or social-democratic tradition, postwar macro-economic planning implied 'the use of the private sector to influence the scope and activities of government'. In this case we should rather speak of 'counter-Keynesianism' (ibid.: 54). But although counter-Keynesianism 'presupposes an interventionist political authority [whose] economic administration fulfills the expectations of groups or classes that dominate it', the policies of such an authority 'serve to legitimate the authority of the hegemonic power inasmuch as the achievements due to them correspond to the promises propagated within the dominant ideology' (Keyder 1985: 140).[12] That is, even in the cases of counter-Keynesianism, the interests of the dominated groups or classes have to be fulfilled to some extent.

Obviously, neither the above description of Keynesianism nor that of counter-Keynesianism is applicable to the immediate postwar situation in Southern Europe. It is one thing to speak of the social confrontation between dominant and subordinate groups in society, resulting from an unequal division of wealth and income and eventually leading to spontaneous upheavals and strikes in an overall and continuous climate of social unrest but the existence of a well-organized labour movement, institutionalized in strong trade unions and political parties which operate primarily at the political level in order to obtain their goals, is something totally different. It may be clear that the latter situation is characteristic of relatively advanced class societies, a reflection of a particular level of economic and socio-political development on the basis of which a restructuring of production along Fordist lines could take place in North Western Europe in the immediate postwar period. That is, previous industrialization confined within national economic systems provided the economic and socio-political structures within which the introduction of Fordism and the subsequent internationalization of productive capital could be realized during the era which came to be known as the *Pax Americana*. In Spain, Portugal and Greece such basic structures were almost completely absent before World War II. They therefore had to be constructed in an international, Atlantic setting into which the most advanced countries had moved at a new stage of their development. The impact of the postwar industrialization in Southern Europe necessarily had to be a different one from that which the 'old industrial heartland' had experienced previously. One of the most striking examples of this structural deficiency was the absence of considerable middle strata, the so-called new middle classes, on the basis of which social democracy became the obvious political medium of Keynesian economic policy in Western Europe.

Macro-economic, demand-led regulation was thus introduced in Spain, Portugal and Greece under fundamentally different conditions from those in the European core, and imposed from above, within the framework of the state–corporative system of interest mediation. Only after the formal transition from dictatorship to parliamentarism was completed in the course of the 1970s did a genuine social compromise between the various interest groups become possible. In other words, just because the very notion of a mixed economy implies the underlying existence of a social compromise between the main forces in society, and just because the very implementation of a Keynesian economic policy is the result of previous social struggle, the elaboration of this ideal–typical characteristic of international Fordism could only take place after the fall of the dictatorships in Southern Europe. In the next chapter we will elaborate on the transition to democracy, taking Spain as an example. We shall attempt to explain this transition by analysing the articulation of changing class and state structures in state–civil society configurations, and by referring to the historical shift from state corporatism to societal corporatism. It will be argued that a similar analysis can explain developments in Portugal and Greece as well.

For present purposes it is sufficient to state that the economic dimension of Atlantic Fordism, the combined increase in productivity and real wages, was introduced in Spain, Portugal and Greece in the 1960s, generating both an enormous economic expansion and the need for the gradual replacement of authoritarian mechanisms of political integration by more democratic ones. However, the moment this socio-political precondition for further capitalist expansion and continuing control of the dominated classes had to be formally institutionalized in the form of a party system, the economic component was already undermined by the international economic crisis. This produced a very peculiar situation: political liberalization had to be carried out without the material assistance of the economic dimension of Atlantic Fordism, on the basis of which the very need for political liberalization had occurred.

The third dimension: changing world order structures and the power of transnational capital

Raising the discussion to the third dimension of Atlantic Fordism, i.e., the overall political and economic organization of capitalist relations in the Atlantic area, Fordism is characterized by the postwar internationalization of production, the subsequent transnationalization of socio-economic and political relations, and the specific role of the state in this context, both as a point of reference with regard to the political articulation of social relations within its national boundaries, and as an actor in the international system. In order to explain this characteristic, it is useful to introduce the notion of comprehensive 'concepts of control'. This notion is of particular importance for an understanding of the fundamental changes, not only at the level of production and in the field of power relations, but also in the ideological sphere. Such an integrated approach offers us an insight in how the structure/agency and economics/politics dichotomies can be overruled,

22 *Theoretical perspective*

and how we can transcend the so-called level of analysis problem as well as the question of external versus internal determination.

Comprehensive concepts of control

Concepts of control are long-term strategies, formulated in general terms and dealing in an integrated way with such areas as labour relations, socio-economic policies, and the international socio-economic and political order. These concepts serve to organize and safeguard specific interests related to specific social groups or classes. Originating in socio-economic relationships between different sections of the bourgeoisie, and between (sections of) the bourgeoisie and (parts of) the working class, concepts of control must be translated into domestic and foreign policy at the state level to become effective. The rise to hegemony of a particular concept, and its success in representing the specific interests related to it, can be achieved if and only if these specific interests are presented as the 'general interest' (van der Pijl 1984: ch.1; Overbeek 1990; see also Chapter 2 of this book). Hegemony in this sense refers not so much to the extent to which a class or a section of a class 'is able to impose a uniform conception of the world on the rest of society, but to the extent that it can articulate different visions of the world in such a way that their potential antagonism is neutralised' (Laclau 1977: 161). Hegemonic concepts of control are expressions of both the structural and behavioural power of capital, reflecting what Gramsci has called 'Historic bloc'. The state forms the organizational framework within which the elaboration, reproduction, and transformation of specific, ideal–typical concepts of control can take place. Apart from this function as a political platform on which particular concepts can be articulated, the state has to organize and safeguard the interests and hegemony of the bourgeoisie as a whole. The state can accomplish this only when it can take a stand as an autonomous subject *vis-à-vis* the separate sections of the bourgeoisie. This is why, to be hegemonic, a concept of control has to be presented as expressing the general interest, which it partly achieves by incorporating or neutralizing competing visions of the world.

However, the role of the state is not confined to its strict, national character as a political platform. From the moment that the functional forms of capital become internationalized, i.e., when international movements of circulating and productive capital come into being, the material basis will exist for the realization of the political articulation of internationalized concepts of control at the national level. Both the internationalization and internalization of specific concepts of control depend on the pre-existence of historically determined national socio-economic and political structures. In this sense the state forms the political framework within which internationally operating concepts of control can be synthesized with particular national political cultures, attitudes, constitutional arrangements, etc., or, conversely, the very medium through which national, hegemonic concepts of control can transcend national frontiers.

In his analysis of postwar class formation at the international, Atlantic, level, van der Pijl distinguishes two ideal–typical concepts of control, derived from two functional forms of capital – money capital and productive capital (defined by their places in the overall accumulation process), and related to two fractions of the bourgeoisie – bank capital and industrial capital. These are the money capital concept or 'liberal internationalism' and the productive capital concept or 'state monopoly tendency' (see van der Pijl 1984: ch.1).

These two concepts are quite similar to what Polanyi, years ago, called 'the double movement' of two organizing principles in society.

> The one [is] the principle of economic liberalism, aiming at the establishment of a self-regulating market . . . and using largely *laissez-faire* and free trade as its methods; the other [is] the principle of social protection aiming at the conservation of man and nature as well as productive organization . . . and using protective legislation, restrictive associations, and other instruments of intervention as its methods.
> (Polanyi 1957: 132)

These two organizing principles largely overlap with the money capital concept and the productive capital concept as politico-ideological concepts related to economic interests. They are historically reflected in the shift away from the economic liberalism that reflected the nineteenth-century dominance of capital engaged in circulation when this gave way to the dominance of large-scale production in the interwar period. From the moment that productive capital became internationalized, especially after World War II through the internationalization of finance capital (i.e., characterized by its institutional form of the transnational corporation), a synthetic concept came into existence, the concept of corporate liberalism (van der Pijl 1984: 10), forming an integral part of what we have referred to above as international or Atlantic Fordism, i.e., the macro-economic growth model which, at the national level, rested on Fordist production, Keynesian demand management, and an overall compromise between social classes rooted in the extension of public welfare provisions. The globalization of capitalist relations, and especially its Euro-Atlantic articulation, was based on a synthesis between nationally operating and transnational industrial capital, and global financial capital, and on a synthesis between state monopolism and liberal internationalism, i.e., the two ideal–typical comprehensive concepts of control related to different class fractions. In terms of international political domination, this postwar era, which became known as the *Pax Americana*, was characterized by the unquestioned leadership of the United States, which cemented the rudimentary cohesion of an Atlantic, international historic bloc, reflecting a hierarchy of similar, national ensembles of material forces, institutions, and ideologies (see Gill 1993). Here the above definition of hegemony in terms of consensus can be applied to the international system. In the words of Robert Cox, 'world hegemony' means 'an outward expansion of the internal [national] hegemony established by a dominant social class' (Cox 1983: 171/172). It results from a combination of social power and state power. That is, the leading state or states establish a world order based on consensus rather than on coercion, functioning according to general principles that guarantee the continuing hegemony of both these states and their leading social classes by imposing a uniform conception of the world on an increasingly global society, thereby incorporating or neutralizing subordinate states and social classes by offering them particular rewards (or at least the prospect of them).

> In such an order, production in particular countries becomes connected through the mechanisms of a world economy and linked into world systems of production. The social classes of the dominant country find allies in classes within other countries. The historic blocs underpinning particular states become connected through the mutual interests and ideological perspectives of social classes in different countries, and global classes begin to form.
>
> (Cox 1987: 7)

This process of global, or transnational, class formation, which is part of the postwar growth of transnational capital accumulation, has been further developed in the course of the 1970s and 1980s, and has come to include state–civil society configurations. That is, concomitant to the emergence of a 'world economy of transnational production' is the internationalization of the state (see Cox 1987; Picciotto 1991) and the coming into existence of a transnational bourgeois civil society, dividing the international system into a 'Lockeian heartland', on the one hand, and an 'outer rim' of Hobbesian latecomer states with weak civil societies, on the other.[13] We are dealing here with the emergence of a transnational historic bloc, characterized by a hegemonic constellation of transnational material forces, international institutions, and long-term strategies, associated with representatives of national governments and bureaucratic apparatuses, and reflecting the rising structural and behavioural power of internationally mobile capital. The behavioural power of transnational capital is manifested, *inter alia*, in its growing ability to play national governments off against one another with respect to international investment decisions, and in all kind of lobbying activities. Just one of the many examples of the latter phenomenon is offered by the European Roundtable of Industrialists (ERT), a pressure group of the leading transeuropean companies, which played a decisive role in relaunching the process of European integration in the early 1980s (see Sandholtz and Zysman 1989; Holman 1992). 'Perhaps more than in the past,' ERT's vice-chairman Jérome Monod argued, 'business opinions today express a comprehensive world-wide vision of modern society and its problems, a vision which in some ways goes beyond the ideas of our political leaders' (Monod *et al.* 1991: 2). And transnational business is more than willing to impose its opinions on national governments, and, indeed, with increasing success. The structural power of transnational capital, on the other hand, is related to the geographically and economically extended operation of the market mechanisms.

> The movement of large amounts of capital between countries, in the form of direct foreign investment, short-term capital flows and long-term portfolio investment, in response to economic and political conditions, acts to condition, for example, the behaviour of governments, firms, trade unions and other groups. Through the market such structural power is premised upon the greater mobility of transnational capital than its 'national' counterparts. . . . Thus the policies of the state towards the market, towards labour–capital relations, towards the provision of an appropriate social and economic infrastructure, are incrementally recast in an international framework.
>
> (Gill 1990: 113–114)

In other words, national governments are constrained by the policies of other governments and by the investment decisions of transnational capital. Here the notion of the internationalization of the state becomes of particular importance. If we accept that this is 'the global process whereby national policies and practices have been adjusted to the exigencies of the world economy of international production' (Cox 1987: 253), we may recall what was said above about the notion of comprehensive concepts of control. In order to become effective, concepts of control not only have to transcend their origin at the level of sections of the bourgeoisie in such a way that their potential antagonism is neutralized (i.e., the condition of hegemony), but must also be translated into state policy. In this sense, the internationalization of the state can be explained both from external pressures related to the world economy and the internal articulation of hegemonic concepts of control, its mediating force being the process of capitalist transnationalization, and its vehicle the internationalized (supra-)state institutions at the national and international level. As we have argued elsewhere, the European Union forms a paradigmatic example of this phenomenon (see Holman 1992).

Integrating Southern Europe

If we now return to the global context in which the transition to democracy in Southern Europe took place in the 1970s, some important developments have altered the postwar constellation. The world economic crisis of restructuring of the 1970s and early 1980s has been concomitant with the crisis of the bipolar system of superpower politics – that is, the spectacular break-up of Soviet dominance over Eastern Europe and the decline of American hegemony. Moreover, this reshaping of the political world map has been accompanied by an unprecedented renaissance of liberal values in both the political and the economic field. Two obvious manifestations of this upsurge in liberalism, which is both the result and cause of changing class, state and world-order structures, must be distinguished.

First, processes of formal, political democratization have affected individual countries on a worldwide scale, particularly in Southern Europe (in the 1970s), Latin America (in the 1980s), and Eastern Europe. The incorporation of Spain, Portugal, and Greece into the heartland of bourgeois civil society, a process that was the result of the countries' postwar economic internationalization and social modernization, eventually culminated in their integration into the Common Market. For countries like Argentina and Brazil, democratic transition was a mixed blessing. While for Southern Europe the perspective of Europeanization loomed large, the Latin American incorporation into the international credit economy took away a large part of the initial democratic euphoria (see Holman 1993a). The short-term picture for most of the former Warsaw Pact countries shows a combination of regional disintegration and severe economic crisis, eventually leading to the incorporation of some Eastern European countries into the (vicious circle of the) international credit economy, making a comparison between Eastern Europe and, for instance, Latin America highly relevant. On the other hand, the perspective of a renewed regional integration within the context of an enlarged European Union in the medium to long term will make a comparison with the actual position of Southern

Europe of interest. Notably, the effects this will have on economic structures, class relations and state–civil society configurations in Eastern Europe will determine the future stability of democracy in this region.

Second, the crisis of Atlantic Fordism revealed, among other things, the so-called 'contradictions of the welfare state'. In the context of global neo-liberalism, deregulation in the broadest sense of the word became the paradigmatic instance through which the postwar growth of state participation in education, health, pensions, and other social security arrangements was slackened and public involvement itself rationalized and, where possible, externalized through the privatization of state services. It was this context of global neo-liberalism in which the transition and consolidation of the political regimes in Spain, Portugal, and Greece, and the subsequent integration of these countries into the Common Market took place. This global setting determined to a large extent the way in which the historical processes of modernization and 'Westernization' were eventually completed in the 1980s, resulting in the final incorporation of Southern Europe in the Lockeian heartland of transnational production and increasingly transnationalized state–civil society configurations. Let us examine this more closely by recalling the main line of argument in the previous sections.

We have concentrated on the common characteristics of Spain, Portugal, and Greece that have resulted in quite similar developments during the last thirty years. The analysis of structural processes underlying these similarities makes it implausible that they can be explained by either mere coincidence or geographical vicinity, as the proponents of the modernization approach would suggest. This chapter has taken the historical processes of industrialization and social-democratization as points of departure for a more structural and perspectival understanding of the timing and content of these economic and socio-political developments in Southern Europe.

In fact, when speaking of the developments in Southern Europe in the second half of the twentieth century, the combined processes of modernization and Westernization in these countries make it possible to compare them both with each other and with other groups of countries. By modernization we mean relatively autonomous economic, social, and political development, primarily based on historically determined, national factors. By Westernization we mean that this economic, social, and political development becomes increasingly dependent on external developments, and implies to some extent an adoption of Western (European) economic and socio-political structures.

First, economic liberalization and the subsequent period of macro-economic growth based on the combination of industrial mass production and mass consumption were both the result of pre-existing national economic and socio-political developments, and the massive influx of foreign direct investments and technology. That is, the internationalization of Fordist production from the core to Southern Europe formed the context in which a nationally induced economic transformation could succeed; instead of a mere internalization of foreign (American) structures, the introduction of the Fordist mode of accumulation in Spain, Portugal, and Greece signified a gradual adjustment to economic structures operating on the world market.

Second, the formal democratization in Spain, Portugal, and Greece was mainly the result of a social modernization following the introduction of Fordism in these countries. In this sense both the crisis of the dictatorships and the underlying pressure for a shift towards less authoritarian mechanisms of social and political integration were inextricably bound up with the preceding period of economic growth. This is not to propound vulgar economic determinism. In fact, it can be argued that the state corporatist system (which had its roots long before the economic liberalization at the end of the 1950s and early 1960s) was a fundamental precondition of the smooth introduction of Fordism in Southern Europe, and of the subsequent shift towards societal corporatism, as we will see in the next chapter. Here we can confine ourselves to the following proposition: the need for continuous economic growth based on the primacy of private ownership and the market, led first to an economic liberalization and opening up towards the world market and, subsequently, to socio-political modernization and Westernization, two processes that became increasingly inalienable in the course of events. To understand this in greater detail we must consider another phenomenon that characterized the developments in Spain, Portugal, and Greece in the 1960s and 1970s: the internationalization of capital in these countries. To some extent this internationalization formed the link between the overall processes of modernization and Westernization. The more economic development was accompanied by increasing external dependence (on foreign investment, trade, and tourism), the more this development implied an adoption of Western economic and socio-political structures (not least because the alternative, a return to economic and political isolationism, became increasingly incompatible with the ultimate goal of economic growth), and comprehensive concepts of control. The growing economic dependence on Western Europe and the eventual membership of the European Community are an illustration of this point.[14]

How, then, can we relate these developments specific to Southern Europe to the preceding analysis of the hegemonic corporate–liberal synthesis between (international) economic liberalization and (domestic) state intervention, the social compromise between capital and labour based on mass production and mass consumption, and the postwar emergence of an international historic bloc, i.e. the historically specific hierarchy of classes and sections of classes in the era of Atlantic Fordism? Obviously, authoritarian rule impeded the full implantation of Atlantic Fordism, since its very origin had to do with class polarization rather than with class compromise. In order to safeguard the interests of the bourgeoisie as a whole, the hierarchy of classes was imposed from above, leaving no space whatsoever for organized labour. Meanwhile, the hierarchy of class sections became increasingly dependent on the transnationalization of production. That is, the process of class formation in Spain, Portugal, and Greece itself became part of the growth of transnational capital accumulation in the Atlantic context.

How can we relate post-authoritarian developments in Spain, Portugal, and Greece to changing world order structures in the 1970s and 1980s, to declining American hegemony, the crisis of Atlantic Fordism, the emergence of a transnational historic bloc, the rising power of transnational capital, and the relaunching of European integration? As we have seen, one of the main processes underlying the Westernization of Southern Europe has been the internationalization of capital. Not only has this produced a growing integration of the respective economies into the world market, but it has also made the national economic systems more vulnerable to fundamental changes on the world market. In this context, we can state the following: Spain, Portugal, and Greece have attained the 'core position of the previous stage of development of the world economy' at a moment when the world economy has moved on to a new stage of development (see Arrighi 1985: 275). By this we mean that, from the very beginning, the conditions for the full implantation of the corporate–liberal synthesis were in existence (i.e. in order to secure continuous economic liberalization and some kind of social-democratization based on an overall class compromise, the extension of welfare state services, etc.), while the world economy had moved on to a new stage of global neo-liberalism. In a setting of international austerity, characterized by the rationalization and extension of class relations of capitalism 'shorn of all extraneous and precapitalist baggage' (Cox 1987: 309), the transition to democracy in Southern Europe had to take place. It is in this context that we should understand the role of post-authoritarian governments, and particularly the socialist-led ones, in Southern Europe. These governments fulfilled the historical task of consolidating the transition towards a system of interest mediation that is the dominant one in the Western, highly industrialized world, while at the same time being confronted with the rising structural power of transnational capital. A logical step in this double transition was the eventual integration of Greece (in 1981), and Spain and Portugal (in 1986), into the European

Community. Here we have to remember that this formal membership coincided with the project of the European Single Market (to be completed in 1993), and the accelerated deregulation inherent in that project.

In the next chapters we will examine the impact of diverse processes of transnationalization on state–civil society configurations for the case of Spain. It is our belief that we must go back to the state in order to analyse its internationalization, and to provide a proper empirical foundation for a critical theory of IR focusing on transnational class relations. First, we will examine the transition to democracy in Spain, and the coming to power of the Spanish Socialist Party, from a historical perspective. In particular the shift from state corporatism to societal corporatism will be treated here (Chapter 2). Using the notion of comprehensive concepts of control, we will then elaborate on the constituent parts of the socialist hegemonic project, on the basis of which both the socialists' rise to power and their subsequent domestic and foreign policies can be understood. We will argue that this project cannot be grasped properly without reference to the European orientation underpinning it (Chapter 3). Finally, in the last three chapters, we will analyse the foreign policy of the PSOE during the 1980s, its economic policy, and its relations with the stronghold of Spanish capitalism, i.e. private bank capital. In doing this, our constant and primary concern will be to examine whether the socialist project can be interpreted as part and parcel of the globally conceived transnationalization of economic and socio-political relations, and, if so, to which domestic contradictions and conflicts this has eventually led.

Part II
Historical perspective

2 The making of contemporary Spain
Socio-economic and political modernization in the twentieth century

INTRODUCTION

One of the main conclusions we must draw from the analysis in the foregoing chapter is that the processes of democratic transition in Southern Europe cannot be interpreted separately from their historical origins, from the inalienable connection of long-term economic and socio-political developments, and from the global context in which structural changes have taken place in the three countries. In this sense, we analytically distinguished three dimensions: the transforming impact Atlantic Fordism has had on economic structures; the articulation of changing class and state structures in state–civil society configurations; and the impact of changing world-order structures on national economic and socio-political developments.

In the following chapters, the theoretical notion of comprehensive concepts of control will be applied to understand the intrinsic and complex relationship between economics and politics in advanced class societies from an international or global perspective. Two important features of the development of the contemporary international system (and more specifically the Western, Atlantic world) have made it mandatory to rethink this relationship: first, the introduction of universal suffrage and the subsequent consolidation of national political systems that are ordinarily understood by the term 'parliamentary democracies'; and second, the long-term process of the internationalization of capital and the emergence of a transnational bourgeoisie whose characteristics (especially its financial–industrial foundations) have no historical precedent whatsoever. Since World War II these two features have become increasingly intermingled, thereby altering discussions and theoretical insights about the economic basis of political decision-making in a decisive way. In this context the notion of concepts of control has been developed to combine theoretically the relation between

34 *Historical perspective*

economics and politics with the relation between internal and external factors within the Atlantic world.

This raises an important question: to what extent can the theoretical notion of concepts of control be applied to such diverse countries as Japan, Russia, Chile or Spain, countries which to a greater or lesser extent do not share the characteristics of the highly industrialized, parliamentary democracies in the Atlantic area? That is, to what extent do different political systems and different levels of economic development determine the impact of concepts of control in the political articulation of economic interests?

In the remainder of this book we will offer a partial answer to this question by examining the economic and socio-political developments in Spain during the twentieth century in the light of its growing orientation towards the Atlantic world and, more especially, Western Europe. Necessarily, the answer will be partial, because an analysis of Spain does not offer us a blueprint that is applicable to all those countries that show some historical deviation from the 'democratic route to modern society' (Moore 1981). It does, however, give us greater knowledge about the abstract theoretical and the concrete historical significance of the notion of comprehensive concepts of control in explaining socio-political and economic modernization and integration under specific conditions. In other words, the following chapters will examine the validity of extrapolating from the ideal–typical to the a-typical, using Spain as a case study.

In this chapter we will first relate the notion of concepts of control to particular state–civil society configurations. If we accept the view that comprehensive concepts of control are operative in free market economies and liberal political systems, we must distinguish weak state–civil society configurations from strong ones. In applying this distinction to the Spanish case, we will then proceed with an analysis of the historical shift from the oligarchic and clientelist system of late nineteenth-century Spain, characterized by a weak civil society and a weak state incapable of dealing with the social problems related to the incipient industrialization of the Spanish economy to the post-Franquist parliamentary democracy, characterized by the strengthening of both the liberal capitalist state and bourgeois civil society. In particular, the so-called revolution from above under Franquist rule, in combination with the economic liberalization of the late 1950s, are the key elements in explaining the social and political modernization and Westernization of the subsequent years. It is the process of Hobbesian state-building under Franco, and the state-centred economic, institutional, and ideological developments related to it, that have prepared Spain for its full integration into the post-Hobbesian order of transnational production during the 1980s.

THE PECULIARITIES OF THE SPANISH CASE

The Spanish adoption of Western economic and socio-political structures, the so-called Westernization of Spain, occurred at a moment when the international political and economic system had changed substantially in comparison with the nineteenth and early twentieth centuries (and even the immediate post-World War II period). In this sense it is necessary to stress the importance of what some have called 'world time'. By this Anthony Giddens (following W. Eberhard) means 'that an apparently similar sequence of events, or formally similar social processes, may have quite dissimilar implications or consequences in different phases of world development' (Giddens 1981: 167). In the Spanish case this notion of world time must be applied, for instance, to understanding the shift from an estate system to a genuine class society in the course of the twentieth century (and particularly in understanding the dissimilar implications it had in comparison to similar transitions in, for instance, Great Britain and France in previous phases of world development), or to the transition from the authoritarian Franquist state to the liberal capitalist state in the 1970s. Both these long-term developments were, at least partially, determined by the specific moment in world history at which they took place.

The same may be said with regard to the increasing emancipation of Spanish civil society in the 1960s and 1970s, leading, on the one hand, to a fundamental shift in the relation between state and civil society, and, on the other, to the emergence of comprehensive concepts of control aimed at regulating the smooth transition to and consolidation of capitalist democracy (see Chapter 1).

Ideal–typically, we can make a distinction between those authoritarian political regimes in which the formal subordination of civil society to the state is effected either by administrative and legal or repressive means, and liberal democratic regimes in which civil society has achieved a degree of autonomy and self-sustaining cohesion. The emancipation of civil society within particular geographical areas is strongly related to the formal 'insulation' of private economic power and public political and military power, to the successful implementation of some kind of bourgeois revolution, to the predominance of industrial over agrarian class-structures, to societal integration within the context of nation–state building, and to the effectuation and consolidation of capitalist democracies. Concepts of control are related to the division of capital into money capital and productive capital within the framework of the capitalist mode of production, but can perform their mediating role between the levels of production and power only within particular, strong state–society complexes (see below).

...prehensive socialization of the general interest through the ...nnels of civil society is determined by the balance of power ...t classes and sections of classes, the strength and autonomy ...vis-à-vis the state apparatuses, and, particularly after World ... impact of transnational structures of production and power and world order structures on both the domestic class configuration and on state–society relations.

Weak and strong states: the case of Spain

Spanish history from the restoration of the constitutional monarchy in 1875 to the death of Francisco Franco in 1975 and the Socialist victory in the 1982 elections, can be summarized as a long-term shift from oligarchical and elitist rule to liberal democracy. While stressing this rather evident transition, many contemporary observers of modern Spain have attempted to subdivide this period into minor phases or stages of socio-political development (see, for example, Payne 1987).

Instead of adding another, alternative periodization, this chapter is mainly concerned with the underlying developments in Spanish society which have broken the so-called 'vicious circle' (i.e. involving the pattern of a weak state which encourages individualism and particularism, leaving the field open for the so-called *poderes fácticos* – oligarchy, army, and church – who tend to counterbalance any strengthening of the state), and gradually replaced it by a 'virtuous circle' (i.e. a strong state which encourages a civil culture based on socio-political mass participation, strengthening interest groups within civil society who tend to counterbalance excessive state centralism and tend to insist upon a less hypertrophic state) (Tortosa 1985: 20–21). In our view, a weak state is *inter alia* characterized by the virtual amalgamation of political and economic power within an oligarchical ruling class; a class-divided society separating this oligarchic or aristocratic class (or estate) from the dominated classes (or lowest estate); an all-embracing network of patron–client relations serving as a mechanism to contain popular uprisings at an individual level; the absence of nationalism, and more generally a lack of societal vertebration and incorporation; and finally, the fusion of religious, military and political elites resulting in a Predominant position of religion at the ideological level and a strong praetorian tradition. Such a weak state existed in Spain at the onset of the restoration of the monarchy in 1875.

A strong state, on the other hand, does not have to rely on direct or indirect military intervention in domestic politics in order to safeguard regime stability, making possible the effective subordination of the military apparatus to civil institutions. The same applies to religion at the ideological level, giving rise to the formal separation of the Church and the state. At the socio-political level, a strong state is characterized by a formal separation or insulation of economic and political power leading to the emergence of a governing elite which obtains a relative autonomy *vis-à-vis* the social classes at the political level while at the same time safeguarding class domination at the socio-economic level. Finally, a strong state is characterized by a high degree of societal incorporation, making clientelist, oligarchic or authoritarian modes of political domination not only increasingly unnecessary but highly undesirable and contra-productive as well. In this sense, a strong civil society is the concomitant of a strong state. As a matter of fact, it is in this configuration of strong states and strong civil societies that the Gramscian notion of hegemony becomes relevant. In the case of Spain, the formation of such a strong state cannot simply be related to the transition from dictatorship to democracy after the death of Franco in 1975. Some characteristics had developed long before this particular event, while others remain to be developed to their full extent. Still it could be argued that the Socialist project of socio-economic and political modernization in particular, as implemented after the victory of the PSOE in the 1982 elections, must be analysed in the light of the historical formation of a strong state in Spain, and must be seen as a project for further strengthening this very state.

One final point must be made to fully understand this last argument. When talking about strong states, we always have to bear in mind the relative meaning of this notion in respect to the outside world, that is, in comparison with other states. This also applies to a related criterion such as the degree of economic development of a state. A strong state is not only characterized by its relatively developed economic structure. As Wallerstein has stated, 'a state is stronger than another state to the extent that it can maximize the conditions for profit-making by its enterprises [including state corporations] within the world-economy' (Wallerstein 1984: 5). This also includes the position of strength of a state *vis-à-vis* foreign capital operating or aspiring to operate within its territory. In transcending world system theory, however, we have to take into account the double movement of the transnationalization of social relations and the internationalization of the state (see Chapter 1) to give the latter's relative strength in present-day international relations its proper meaning.

The Spanish state was fundamentally weak with regard to its dependence on foreign capital and technology in the early phase of industrialization from 1850 onwards. But what about the protectionist legislation of the 1880s, and more generally the steady rise of economic nationalism after the turn of the century, eventually leading to the creation of state monopolies in such strategic areas as the distribution and commercialization of oil products in the 1920s (see, for instance, Shubert 1980)? And what about the gradual liberalization of Spanish legislation on foreign direct investments after the Stabilization Plan of 1959 (see Martínez González-Tablas 1979), eventually leading to the famous agreement between the Spanish government and Ford España in 1972/1973 (see Muñoz *et al.* 1974; Vellas 1979)? And, finally, how are we to interpret the attempts of the successive democratic governments, especially the Socialist one, to enforce economic modernization and the subsequent internationalization of Spanish capital in the light of full entry into the Common Market after 1992?

In the final analysis, all these examples illustrate the importance of two related problems when talking about 'weak' and 'strong' states: first, every analysis of the strength or weakness of a particular state *vis-à-vis* both national and foreign capital has to be a historical one, in the sense that it ultimately must be based on an analysis of the historical development of the socio-political power structures within that state. The relative strength of a state is thus always inwardly a function of continuously reproduced and transformed inter-class and intra-class structures.

Second, any analysis of the relative strength of a particular state with regard to the outside world (whether it be the world economy or the international state system) necessarily has to take into account the historical changes at the global level. That is, a position of strength at one particular moment in world history may be a position of fundamental weakness at another moment. The loss of control of the Spanish state over its colonies at the end of the nineteenth century was a sign of weakness; the entry into the Common Market in the 1980s, and the subsequent loss of part of the sovereignty of the Spanish state over its territory, is a sign of strength inasmuch as it implies the maximization of the conditions for profit-making by some Spanish enterprises within a world economy of transnational production (see Chapter 5).

This distinction between weak and strong states may be confusing in the context of the discussion of state–civil society relations in recent literature. Strong states are usually viewed as the counterpart of weak civil societies, and vice versa. The problem with this way of defining strong states is its predominantly quantitative character. As a comparative category, strong is measured in terms of the level of bureaucratization, repression and so on, i.e. the general presence of the state in society. As a matter of fact, this view may lead to an a-historical kind of reasoning, inasmuch as it fails to explain why a so-called strong state in the course of events may lose its dominance over civil

Table 1 Weak and strong state–civil society configurations

Civil society	State	Capital	Concepts of control
weak	weak	weak	absent
strong	strong	strong	operational

society. That is, the strength of a state is reflected in its relation to civil society, and therefore it seems difficult to explain how a state may lose its absolute dominance over civil society while maintaining, and even extending, its apparatuses in a substantial way. Moreover, how do we measure the strength of a particular state in a situation in which civil society is virtually non-existent, as was the case in Spain at the end of the last century?

Instead, we should give a qualitative meaning to the strong/weak dichotomy, relating the strength of the capitalist state to the social, economic and political structure it reflects. Development and modernization (which in the twentieth century imply internationalization) are the processes which may in the long run lead to a strengthening of the state. This argument can be illustrated in Table 1.

Applying this scheme to Spain, it may be stated that, on the eve of the restoration, Spanish civil society was virtually non-existent and the Spanish state was extremely weak, not only in international terms, but also in terms of the incapacity of the oligarchical ruling class to articulate different social interests in such a way that their antagonism was neutralized. Conversely, in the 1980s a strengthening of both civil society and the state became part and parcel of the hegemonic project of the Socialist Party, which *inter alia* aimed at maximizing the conditions for profit-making by both domestic and foreign business within the Lockeian heartland of transnational production. The Franquist state (1939–1976) must be seen as a developmental state: its authoritarian, Hobbesian, mode of political domination does not point to its inherent strength but rather to its transitional character.

Socio-political and economic modernization in Spain

As stated above, this chapter is primarily concerned with the structural processes underlying the historical shift from the vicious circle of the Spanish estate system to the virtuous circle of the new parliamentary democracy after the death of Franco, and, in particular, to its consolidation under Socialist rule

40 Historical perspective

in the 1980s. For analytical purposes I shall distinguish five major developments in Spanish society from the Restoration to the present. In doing so, we have to bear in mind that we are dealing with developments which are inextricably interrelated. Moreover, each of the five developments can be divided into two sub-periods; and they are layered in the sense that each first sub-period incorporates the characteristics of the following one in a rudimentary way. As a matter of fact, contradictions in the first sub-period produce an erosion from within and an evolutionary transition to the second sub-period, rather than leading to spectacular ruptures. Not even the Spanish Civil War (1936–1939) represented a fundamental historical break with the preceding period with regard to these five structural processes, although it did produce a rupture in other respects (such as the virtual extermination of working-class representation at the political level, which has never recovered its pre-Civil War dimension or content).

The five major developments in recent Spanish history, then, are divided into sub-periods according to qualitative criteria. This implies that no exact dates (years or intervals) can be given. However, in all five cases it was the period of the Franquist regime which in one way or another represented the transition to modernization and Westernization. The following developments can be distinguished:

1   A transition from a pre-capitalist agrarian economic structure to a predominantly national industrial structure, which became manifest in the first two decades of the Franquist regime; and subsequently, through the internationalization of capital in Spain after the economic liberalization of 1959, the transition from an inward-oriented industrial structure towards full integration into the world market, resulting in an increasingly internationalized economic structure.

2   A shift in the power bloc from a coalition between big landowners, private financiers and the emerging big bourgeoisie in Catalonia and the Basque Provinces, to a coalition between bank capital and national industrial capital in the first period; and a shift from a coalition between Spanish bank capital and national private and public industrial capital to a coalition between Spanish and foreign finance capital in the second period. The latter coalition foreshadows the emergence of a transnational bourgeoisie in Spain.

It should be remembered, however, that both economic internationalization (resulting from the first development) and socio-economic transnationalization have been realized through the entry of foreign capital into the Spanish market, without producing a substantial internationalization of Spanish bank capital or industrial capital itself so far.

3 A transition from an estate system, in which society is divided into an oligarchical ruling class, characterized by a high degree of particularism and the 'primacy of authorisation over allocation' (Giddens 1979: 162), and the dominated classes, characterized by a low degree of organization, the gap between these 'estates' being imperfectly filled by the so-called traditional middle classes, to a polarized class society in which antagonistic class relations, increasingly caught in the setting of a predominantly capitalist mode of production, eventually reach an actual state of civil war. In the second period this polarized class society, under the banner of the authoritarian Franquist state, experienced a high degree of incorporation due to several factors, including the coming into existence of the so-called new middle classes, the gradual revival of civil society, and its subsequent transnationalization.

4 A transition from a state which formally controlled the whole of the Spanish territory (as for instance in its diplomatic contacts with the outside world) but was in fact characterized by the lack of a real national unity, by enormous socio-economic and political regional disparities and by a total absence of any form of national integration (let alone any unifying, national ideology), to a highly centralized, hypertrophic nation–state, implemented and directed from above, using national Catholicism as a unifying national ideology and repressing regional autonomy (without, however, neutralizing the existing regional inequalities). In the second period the excessive degree of nationalism and centralism gradually levelled out, and after the death of Franco it was formally replaced by a system of 'vertebrated regionalism', which is still controlled from above but gives constitutional space to some form of regional autonomy.

5 Finally, a transition from a system of interest mediation which is usually referred to as clientelism (the Spanish variant of which is known as the system of *caciquismo*) to a system of state corporatism during the Franquist era; and, in the second period, a shift from state corporatism to societal corporatism, which formally took place after the collapse of the Franquist dictatorship but had its origins in the 1960s.

Before we embark on an analysis of the Franquist regime and the changes it generated at the institutional level, we will first look at its historical origins. It will be argued that changes at the economic, social, and ideological levels during the restoration period (1875–1923) moulded an increasingly polarized class society in which a traditional economic elite (the so-called oligarchy) had to transfer its direct political power (as cemented by the prevailing system of clientelist interest mediation) to an authoritarian, corporatist state, in which the structural power of capital was strengthened but its direct power weakened, in order to guarantee the survival of an overarching system of private property relations, and to protect it against the revolt of the masses. It is in this context that we must understand the commitment to social harmony under a regime of organic democracy, and, in general, to state interventionism in the economic and social sphere during the Franquist dictatorship.

PRELUDE: LATE INDUSTRIALIZATION AND THE AUTHORITARIAN SOLUTION

In the second half of the nineteenth century, the Spanish economy entered its first phase of, albeit incipient, industrialization. Three phenomena were particularly responsible for this development: the concentration and technological innovation in the Catalan textile industry (which originated in the eighteenth century), the emergence of a metallurgical industry in the Basque Provinces, and the rise of foreign (mainly British and French) direct investment in mining and railway construction.[1] Though these developments were responsible for a considerable degree of industrial growth, and, indeed, laid the foundation for Spain's industrialization in the course of the twentieth century, their consequences for the short and medium term were socio-political and ideological rather than economic.

As for the economic consequences, most contemporary economic historians (both in Spain and abroad) speak of the failure of the Spanish industrial revolution in the nineteenth and early twentieth century.[2] Subsequently, Spain is classified as one of the latecomer states, unable to catch up with developments in the core of Europe during the so-called 'age of industrial revolution', i.e. during the 'long nineteenth century' stretching from the 1780s to 1917 (see Berend and Ránki 1982: 7). However, whereas consensus exists with respect to this 'industrial revolution manqué' (Harrison 1978), its causes have been subjected to different interpretations and have led to a debate among Spanish economic historians. For some, the primacy of exogenous factors has to be stressed: external dependence on trade and foreign capital, and the loss of the colonial empire. For others, endogenous factors are more important in the explanation of the retarded development of Spain: the archaic property relations and the lack of development in the agricultural sector; the budgetary policies of the Spanish state which resulted in high interest rates; the rigid socio-economic and political system in Spain at the turn of the century; a relatively high degree of protectionism; and, in the course of the early twentieth century, the excessive role of the Spanish state in the economy.[3] It would go beyond the scope of this book to enter into this debate in more detail. Here we are primarily interested in the social, political, and ideological consequences of the early attempts to launch industrial development in Spain, i.e. in the consequences of its failure rather than in the causes. Indeed, it will be our contention throughout this chapter that changes in social structure, economic policy, and, generally, in the role of the Spanish state in the economy, as well as the development of integrating ideologies have played a decisive role in the socio-political and economic modernization of Spain, in the formation of capitalist society, and in strengthening state–civil society configurations. Social, institutional, and ideological developments have created the breeding ground on which the combined process of modernization and Westernization, and the subsequent integration into the so-called Lockeian heartland, took place in the second half of this century.

The short-term and medium-term outcome of the incipient industrialization in the second half of the nineteenth century can be summarized by several developments. First it implied a strengthening of the Basque and Catalan bourgeoisie *vis-à-vis* the traditional oligarchy of big landowners of the south and financiers of the centre. Paradoxically, however, this growing strength was accompanied by an increasing dependence on the Spanish state. The Catalan textile industry relied heavily on the domestic market (especially after the loss of the colonies in 1898) and the protection of this home market by high tariff walls. In the words of Raymond Carr,

> throughout their history Catalan textiles were dependent . . . on the purchasing power of the Spanish peasant. . . . Hence the determination of the Catalans to secure this market against cheap English textiles. Protectionism became the creed of Catalonia; the price of Catalan political support for Madrid governments was prohibition of textile imports.
>
> (Carr 1982: 201)

The technical backwardness of the Basque heavy industry (by foreign, and especially English standards, that is) made its representatives prone to some kind of protectionism, and 'turned Basque industrialists into the natural allies of the Catalans' (ibid.: 270). But the Basque heavy industry not only relied on protectionism. Perhaps more important was its growing dependence on government favour and contracts. In part, this difference between the Catalan and Basque bourgeoisie explains the fact that the Catalans were more inclined to opt for regional autonomy, whereas the Basque bourgeoisie increasingly intermingled with the political power centre, i.e. the ruling oligarchy of Restoration Spain, particularly through the process of ennoblement of some of its most important representatives at the beginning of this century (see Harrison 1978: 74/75, and 83–85; on ennoblement in general, see Martínez Cuadrado 1983: 236ff.). This alliance was cemented by the emergence of private bank capital in the Basque Provinces and Madrid, as we shall see in Chapter 6.

Second, the characteristics of the process of industrialization in the second half of the nineteenth century, and particularly its home market orientation, generated a general inclination to import-substitution and continuous pressure from part of the new 'peripheral' industrialists to implement protectionist legislation. In the period from 1890 to 1907 this culminated in progressive tariff walls, and in the final 'triumph of protectionism' (Tamames 1986: 139–141), which with some modifications lasted until the Stabilization Plan of 1959. The debate between protectionists and free-traders dates from the 1830s, and this economic dispute has periodically dominated the Spanish political scene ever since. It would be oversimplistic to reduce it to an opposition between Catalan textile industrialists and Andalusian wine exporters, and between their respective political representatives in Madrid,[4] although this division was one of the most important and continuous ones in the debate.[5]

Particularism in nineteenth-century invertebrated Spain produced an extremely complex landscape of divergent socio-political and economic strategies, based on particular, regional or individual interests. Yet it is possible to draw some dividing lines between albeit heterogeneous social actors, who took up positions on either side in the debate between protectionists and free-traders. In the 1880s and 1890s, the free-trade lobby consisted of Andalusian wine exporters, Cadiz merchants, and the railway companies who believed that trade liberalization would lead to an increase in traffic. Its social composition was, according to Tortella Casares, less homogeneous than that of its adversary, and, more importantly, its influence decreased as the protectionist lobby gained strength in the 1880s (Tortella Casares 1983: 152). It was in this decade that European agriculture entered a crisis as a result of cheap agricultural imports from outside Europe. This caused a widespread pressure on national governments for protection. In Spain the powerful Castilian cerealists confronted this foreign threat by uniting the protectionist lobby of Catalan and Basque industrialists. In the short run, this lobby succeeded in implementing a protectionist trade policy in the 1890s (see Carr 1982: 394; and Moral Santín et al. 1981: 28–30; on Castilian cerealists, see also Sánchez-Albornoz 1985). In the medium term, the triumph of protectionism and the continuous pressure of both the Catalan and Basque bourgeoisie led to a gradual change of the State to economic matters. The official conception of Spain as a free-trade economy, exploited by foreign mining, railway and finance companies, destined to supply the tables and furnaces of the advanced world with foodstuffs and raw materials, gradually gave way to the vision of an autarkic capitalist economy.

(Harrison 1978: 86)

Finally, the incipient industrialization and the subsequent implementation of progressive protectionist legislation not only changed conceptions and visions, but increasingly called for an active role and participation of the state in the formation of a capitalist society. This was, first, because state intervention in and regulation of the productive structure became necessary in order to create 'missing' industries under conditions of economic nationalism, on the one hand, and to avoid overproduction in protected sectors, on the other (Carr 1982: 395). However, the role of the state in economic matters increasingly extended to the social sphere, inasmuch as the rise of Spanish capitalism in a context of autarky had to deal with a central paradox. Industrial production was primarily aimed at a domestic market still characterized by a predominantly agrarian structure; the momentum of modernization of this agricultural structure was very slow, at least until the early years of the present century (see Tortella Casares 1985; Prados de la Escosura 1988: 95ff.; and Maluquer de Motes 1987: 73ff.); and industrial exports slackened due to the high costs of a relatively backward manufacturing system, which kept domestic prices high and thus domestic consumption low. And yet, continuous accumulation of productive capital depended to a considerable extent on the purchasing power of a population which by and large lived under miserable conditions in a predominantly agrarian economy. Ongoing industrialization under conditions of economic nationalism compelled the creation and development of a domestic market and, hence, rising wages. 'Here then lay the nub of the question. How can the purchasing power of an overpopulated agricultural country, where agricultural improvement is difficult, be raised?' (Carr 1982: 400). Big landowners who were reluctant to invest in the modernization of their production, and who were even more opposed to the improvement of the living conditions of their labour force, thus hampered the ambitions of Basque and Catalan industrialists who themselves were incapable of increasing productivity, and who were less prepared to raise industrial wages (in the case of the Catalans this was even more true because of the influx of migrants from the south and the subsequent abundance of cheap labour, see Pike 1973: 43). In the course of the first decades of the present century, this picture became still more complex as a result of the organization of the working class in trade unions and political parties. In this context of stagnating industrial modernization and growing opposition of the dominated classes, the state had to extend its role as arbitrator between an incipient Spanish capitalism and the outside world (through the mechanisms of economic nationalism) to a role as arbitrator between agricultural interests and industrial interests (through direct state intervention in the productive structure) and, indeed, between the Spanish bourgeoisie as a whole and an emancipating working class (eventually leading to the authoritarian solution of state corporatism during the Franquist dictatorship). Here the ideological consequences of the process of industrialization in the second half of the nineteenth century are of particular importance. In fact, it can be argued that the economic changes of this period (in conjunction with the slow but steady social transformation, the triumph of protectionism, and the Great Disaster of 1898) generated a set of ideas at the turn of the century, aimed at regenerating Spain, whose influence was felt far into the 1930s, and perhaps beyond. In essence we are dealing here with the final outcome of the '*europeizar* vs. *españolizar*' debate, on the one hand, and the debate between Spanish conservatives and liberals on the solution of the so-called social problem (or social question), on the other. We also deal with the authoritarian enforcement of a compromise between two apparently irreconcilable worlds, at the expense of the particular social interests related to them, its constituent elements being economic nationalism, state interventionism, and state corporatism, and socially reflected in the gradual shift from an alliance between landed classes and financial capital to an alliance between financial and industrial capital, on the one hand, and the eventual extermination of organized opposition of the dominated classes, on the other. While originally developed as a critique of existing forms of socio-economic and political domination (i.e. oligarchic rule, and quasi-parliamentarism based on clientelist mechanisms of societal integration), the movement of Spanish regenerationists eventually became, to a greater or lesser extent, the intellectual source of most of the major authoritarian and proto-fascist currents in Spanish politics during the first half of the present century. As such, it laid the ideological foundation of both the authoritarian solution to the social problem and the subsequent modernization and Westernization of Spain from 1960 onwards.

Spanish regenerationism and the social problem

To a certain extent the '*españolizar* vs. *europeizar*' debate at the turn of the century not only reflected the dilemma of Spanish society at the crossroads of traditionalism and modernity, but also marked the politico-ideological contours of future strategies to prepare Spain economically and politically for a renewed integration – under different conditions, of course, and in a totally different international setting – into global (and particularly European) structures. When talking about Hispanicization (*españolización*) as a tendency in nineteenth-century Spain, I am not referring to those claims according to which Spain historically and culturally does not belong to Europe. As Fernando Morán rightly points out, in this sense no two Spains ever existed (Morán 1980: 289ff.). In general, the European antecedents of modern Spain and its vocation to participate in the political construction of Europe never raised any doubts among leading thinkers and politicians. In fact, ever since the Reconquest, Spanish politics always took shape within an European setting. What is commonly meant, then, by Hispanicization as opposed to Europeanization is the reluctance among Spanish conservatives to exchange their traditional values and norms for the ideas of the European 'enlightenment'. The direct result of this so-called *casticismo* (or traditionalism) was twofold: first, at the socio-political level the adaptation of Spanish institutions to those of the rest of Europe was obstructed by Spanish conservatives who firmly believed that the introduction of some kind of democratic system would undermine the 'traditional social stability and political cohesion' of Spain's *ancien régime* further (Preston and Smyth 1984: 25). For them Europeanization not only meant social and political modernization, but in the end also implied a menace to their privileged position in the distribution of power. Second, at the economic level the question whether Spain would modernize and adapt its economic structure along capitalist lines or remain a predominantly agrarian and traditional society was met with a similarly motivated opposition by the Spanish oligarchy: the large-scale introduction of materialism, capitalism and economic liberalism in the end would endanger its socio-political and economic interests. Its fear of massive industrialization and competitive capitalism was related to the implication of substantial rises in national purchasing power, and, hence, the creation of some kind of consumer society. Industrialization, they argued, would necessarily imply the transformation of large segments of the Spanish working classes into individualistic capitalists who sooner or later would translate their economic liberalization into political demands for greater influence in the decision-making process (see Pike 1971).

Its opponents in the debate had a much more ambivalent or even contradictory way of looking at the question of capitalist modernization and Europeanization. While attacking the dominant, socio-political position of the oligarchy and the clientelistic system on which its power was based, at the same time these 'Europeanists' feared the rebellion of the lower classes as inherent, as they thought, to their becoming capitalists. This particular point of view can be illustrated by introducing two intellectual movements in Spain at the turn of the century, whose members shared an affinity with the politically marginal urban middle classes (i.e. small merchants, professional classes, etc.): *Krausismo* and *regeneracionismo*. To some extent, both movements were characterized by an elitist spirit: while aspiring to the common good, and particularly to the good of the non-oligarchic classes, they never intended to create an alternative socio-political system in which the people itself could play a significant, participatory role in the attainment of this common good (see Tuñón de Lara 1982).

Spanish Krausism was named after the German philosopher Karl Christian Friedrich Krause (1781–1832), and originally inspired by his 'harmonic rationalism', which in turn was based on the work of Kant (see López-Morillas 1981: ch.2).[6] In the course of its development, and especially after the foundation of the Institute of Free Education in 1876, it became the cradle of a typical mixture of political liberalism and social reformism. On the one hand, Krausism became the 'first attempt (on the whole unsuccessful, because French influence was easily available and traditionally better understood in Spain) to turn the Europeanizing intellectuals away from French models towards Anglo-Saxon (educational) methods' (Carr 1982: 470). The smooth functioning of capitalism in a liberalized political system required that it be confined to a non-oligarchic elite. In general, a rather paternalistic view of the masses, which were regarded as politically under age, was accompanied by a flirtation with liberal political and economic practices in Great Britain. On the other hand, social reformism was integrated into the Krausist project, *inter alia* through the creation of the Institute of Social Reforms in 1903; capitalist development, it was argued, required state intervention in social matters in order to guarantee the smooth and harmonious transition to a non-oligarchic bourgeois society. It was in this context that Spanish Krausism at the turn of the century entered into contact with reformist Socialism in Spain and abroad (with the German *Verein für Sozialpolitik* and the British Fabian Society, for example) (see Guillén 1990: 90–91).

This particular combination of economic and political liberalism and social reformism can be illustrated by the work of the liberal Krausist (or Krausist institutionist) Gumersindo de Azcarate (1840–1917). He believed in a liberal, democratic state form, as advocated by the non-oligarchic middle classes, in which political parties and public opinion would play a major role. Political parties should defend in the first instance the 'national interest', and not their so-called 'party interest'. The national press should be the instrument *par excellence* with regard to the expression of public opinion (see Tuñón de Lara 1982: 65ff.). As a matter of fact, Azcarate did not advocate any direct participation of the masses at the political level in the short term; popular interests should be channelled and to a certain extent sustained from above by an educated, political elite. In the long term, a national education programme would help to emancipate the spirit of the masses, teaching them the benefits of class harmony as embedded in an organic, corporative social structure. State interventionism in social matters should be aimed at the common good and the national interest, creating a harmonious but hierarchical model of social relations, on the basis of which Spain as a nation could recover from the colonial disaster of 1898 and experience true social, economic and political development. In a sense, the 'compromise between Socialism and individualism' (Pike 1971: 124) of which Azcarate dreamed was characteristic of the corporatist mould in which many ideas of *Krausismo* were cast at the turn of the century.

Very much the same can be said of the work of another well known contemporary, the regenerationist Joaquín Costa (1846–1910). In severely criticizing '*Oligarquía y Caciquismo*' as the actual form of government in Spain (Costa 1984: ch.1), he expressed perhaps as no other the sentiments of the Spanish middle classes. From *Krausismo* he took the idea of the primacy of society against the state (Perez de la Dehesa 1984: 9), its interests being suppressed by the particularist and clientelist political system. Like Azcarate, Costa attacked the parliamentary system of the Restoration period as a mere facade, *caciquismo* being the so-called 'real constitution'. Unlike Azcarate, however, he rejected the alternative of political liberalism and democracy as a means to economic modernization, even in its restrictive, elitist meaning inherent to liberal Krausism. In fact, Costa's political programme has been characterized as 'pro-dictatorial' or 'pre-fascist' (Tuñón de Lara 1982: 90) inasmuch as his latest work included such propositions as the creation of a national party and allusions to the necessity of a 'presidential regime' and an 'iron surgeon'. As Manual Tuñón de Lara rightly points out, Costa (like the bulk of the regenerationists, for that matter) confused the cause (a backward agrarian structure, the economic and political power of a traditional oligarchy and its professional political apologists) with the consequence (*caciquismo*, pseudo-political parties of notables, corrupt and non-representative parliamentarism). He therefore attacked parliamentarism as such, corrupt or not, and political parties, oligarchic or non-oligarchic. Only a strong authoritarian leadership could guarantee the transition to non-oligarchic bourgeois capitalism, based on the modernizing spirit of the urban middle classes. Finally, Costa shared with liberal Krausists like Azcarate and regenerationists like José Ortega y Gasset a general reluctance to include the masses in his

50 *Historical perspective*

project of Spanish regeneration. Frederick Pike summarizes this particular stand as follows:

> The masses, if allowed to participate privately in the gains of national economic development would disrupt the development process; for as they came into possession of economic power they would demand a share of political power and thereby jeopardize the complex development mechanism which only an elite could operate.
>
> (Pike 1973: 35)

Here we have the ingredients of an authoritarian solution to the social problem, which were originally intended to constitute an alternative to the existing political system of the Restoration, but eventually became the ideological inspiration of most future attempts to reconcile the tendencies of Hispanicization and Europeanization. It was the social background of the Spanish conservatives (oligarchy and peripheral bourgeoisie) and the ideas of Spanish liberals (Krausism and, especially, regenerationism) which came to dominate the political landscape of Spain after the collapse of the Restoration monarchy in 1923. In returning to the three interrelated consequences of the incipient industrialization introduced at the beginning of this section, we can now provisionally conclude the following:

1 The original difference between regenerationists and the Spanish oligarchy centred around the question of economic modernization and political domination. The position of the Restoration oligarchy can be summarized as 'Hispanicization in the means and in the ends'. That is, big landowners and their apologists in the political centre of Madrid were fiercely opposed to the use of European economic and political methods to resolve the problems of Spanish society at the turn of the century. Only the return to traditional values could guarantee their privileged position. This obviously implied that they, by and large, also resisted modernization as such, i.e. not only as a method but also as an ultimate goal, and hence the continued isolation of Spain from developments in the rest of Europe. In this sense, large segments of the oligarchy could accept the triumph of protectionism and the turn to economic nationalism.

2. The emerging industrial bourgeoisie in Catalonia and the Basque Provinces took a rather ambivalent stand in the debate between traditionalists and regenerationists. On the one hand, they were, of course, not opposed to capitalism. On the other hand, however, they still relied heavily on the state for protection against foreign competition. In fact, as Pike argues, they

did not think in terms of expanding production so much as of acquiring monopolistic control over a limited market. For them, moreover, the way to wealth lay not through technological innovation and the competitive spirit but instead through accommodation and arrangements with those who wielded political power. Thus politics, rather than the market place, was seen as providing the best means for getting ahead economically.

(Pike 1973: 23)

In the short term, this position of fundamental weakness made it more easy for the traditional oligarchy to continue its strategy of cooptation rather than confrontation *vis-à-vis* the peripheral *nouveaux riches*.[7]

3 The position of Spanish regenerationism can be summarized as 'Europeanization in the means and Hispanicization in the ends'. That is, most regenerationists, as exemplified by the ideas of Costa, opted for some kind of economic modernization following the European capitalist model, to be realized by a bourgeois revolution from above, but without assimilating the Western socio-political and ideological models or their inherent tendency to mobilize the masses. Traditional Spanish values and hierarchical socio-political structures were to prevent Spain from falling into the hands of either individualism and materialism or Communism, both ideological systems which were seen as un-Spanish. As Ortega y Gasset put it: '*Eadem sed aliter*: the same things, only in another way' (Ortega y Gasset 1984: 14). But the regenerationists were not able to turn their ideas into direct political action during the period of Restoration monarchy due to the omnipotence of the oligarchic and clientelist system.

The underlying contradictions of the Restoration, then, came fully to the fore in the two decades after its collapse, i.e. during the period 1923 to 1943. A political system in which particularism was the rule, in which economic and political power were amalgamated, and in which national integration was virtually non-existent; an economic system in which sustained industrial development in terms of innovation and diversification was hampered by an archaic structure of predominantly agrarian production that impeded a substantial rise of domestic purchasing power; and a social system in which class division increasingly became the primary force of change as organized labour gained momentum and, through the import of left-wing strategies, raised the ideological debate to unprecedented levels: these were the most important features of Spanish society in the early twentieth century. In this situation, class polarization became the principal threat to existing power structures. At the same time, the historically specific hierarchy of classes and sections of classes impeded the elaboration of social philosophies like Krausism into comprehensive concepts of control, expressing bourgeois hegemony and approximating the general interest. Here the Spanish state came to play a decisive role. The authoritarian solution to the so-called social problem was the only alternative to a 'war of movement' (Gramsci 1983) in a situation in which civil society was undeveloped, i.e. without self-sustaining cohesion. Regenerationism, then, provided the method, i.e. authoritarian, non-oligarchic rule, on the basis of which the 'national interest' could be implemented from above and vested, particularistic interests eventually subordinated to a more comprehensive project. Next to Costa, José Ortega y Gasset was perhaps the most influential intellectual of this persuasion. For him, the essence of particularism was that each social group 'stops feeling itself as part of a greater whole, and as a result stops sharing the feelings of the rest'. Incorporation or 'totalization' then referred to the inverse process, by which social groups who were formerly separate were eventually integrated as parts of a greater whole (Ortega y Gasset 1984: 58–59). He clearly alluded not only to the social problem, but also to the regional problem inasmuch as he viewed the centrifugal tendencies of the Catalan and Basque industrial bourgeoisie as highly particularistic. The regeneration of a socially and regionally invertebrated Spain was only to be attained by force, by a 'great historic surgery' (ibid.: 41).

SIGNS OF *LEVIATHAN*: FRANQUISM AND THE REVOLUTION FROM ABOVE

After the export-led boom during World War I, as a result of which the Spanish economy experienced an industrial expansion of considerable proportions, the Restoration regime entered its final crisis, eventually leading to the 'solution by force' that Ortega y Gasset had propagated: economic crisis, social unrest, an inclination among the Basque and Catalan big bourgeoisie to break with the system of cooptation (particularly after discussions were reopened with respect to the viability of economic nationalism), and a defeat in the Moroccan Wars. These were all factors which contributed to the military *coup d'état* of 1923 under the leadership of General Miguel Primo de Rivera. This *pronunciamiento* was evidently inspired by the ideas of the leading regenerationists. This was most clearly the case with respect to Costa's political programme, since the new dictator thought of himself as the incarnation of Costa's iron surgeon (see Ben-Ami 1983: 72). The dictatorship was not a long-lived one: in the course of the

1920s, all the major forces that initially supported the coup turned their back on him.[8] It took almost another decade before the revolution from above, the real surgery, could start under the leadership of another general, Francisco Franco. As Raúl Morodo states, Franco was the personification of a successful attempt to revise the 'pre-fascist and corporatist' experiment of the 1920s under new conditions (Morodo 1984: 346). Unlike Primo de Rivera, Franco did not fail to embed his regime in society through a complex, institutional network of state corporatist arrangements, and unlike his dictatorial predecessor (and, to some extent, inspirer) Franco succeeded in obtaining a relatively autonomous position *vis-à-vis* the particularistic interests of the preceding epoch. This provided him with an adequate institutional backbone, strong enough to keep him in power over a long period of time, and with a sufficient degree of flexibility to adopt his policies to changing (national and international) circumstances, as can be illustrated by the shift from autarky to economic liberalization at the end of the 1950s.

As previously indicated, in all five of the major developments during the twentieth century the period of the Franquist dictatorship played a decisive role in changing directions and priorities. In a crude and perhaps even oversimplified way, it may be argued that in the decades leading up to the Spanish Civil War, politics were heavily determined by the so-called social question. That is, all the main issues of domestic and foreign policy and of economic policy were dealt with from the perspective of the increasing tensions and struggle between the social classes. At the same time, this period was characterized by an increasing inability to find a structural solution at the political level to this social question, something that became apparent during the Second Republic (1931–1936). As Hugh Thomas stated,

> politicians are the expression of public moods which are the masses' collective dreams. The republic really fell for the same reasons that upset both the dictatorship and the restoration monarchy: the inability of the politicians then active to resolve the problems of the country within a frame generally acceptable, and, on the other, a willingness, supported by tradition, of some to put matters to the test of force.
>
> (Thomas 1977: 194)

At the onset of the Civil War, a situation existed in which no possible political strategy could harmonize conflicting interests, nor could any ideological discourse even approximate to the general interest. In this context the Franquist regime came to power after a bloody class war. From that moment on the social question was resolved by force and repression, providing a framework of social harmony and peace in which all issues of domestic and foreign policy could be subordinated to the objectives of economic development and modernization. In this sense, the advent of the Franquist regime marked a shift from the primacy of socio-political issues to the primacy of economic issues in general state policy.

This does not mean, however, that the political ruling class of the Franquist regime was able to resolve the economic problems of Spain within a generally acceptable framework. The 'general interest' was imposed on the dominated classes (and to a certain extent also on the different sections of the bourgeoisie) from above, through the mechanisms of state corporatism. In the course of events, and as a result of the internationalization of capital and the subsequent transnationalization of Spanish civil society, an additional shift took place from the primacy of domestic policy to the primacy of foreign (i.e. European) policy. This 'internationalization of domestic policy' took place in conjunction with the historical shift from the vicious circle inherent to the Spanish estate system, to the virtuous circle that came into its own after the death of Franco, and more particularly in the 1980s under Socialist rule. First, however, there is more to be said about the system of interest mediation known as state corporatism, and its subsequent transition to a system of societal corporatism in the 1960s and 1970s.

The concept of corporatism

In the case of Spain, the concept of corporatism is applied to both the system of interest mediation under Franquist rule and the tripartite consultation between the democratic governments, the trade unions UGT and CCOO, and the employers' organization CEOE in the post-Franquist era (see for example Martínez Alier 1985; Giner and Sevilla 1984; and Pérez Díaz 1984, who describes the first two decades of Franquism as 'palaeocorporatism').

Obviously, the main difference consists of the fact that under Franquist rule corporatist arrangements were imposed from above in a repressive and coercive way. Though the harmonization of interests became a general principle of organization for society (even affecting student organizations), this authoritarian mode of interest mediation was primarily directed at managing social and political conflict, i.e. at 'conditioning the development of the social forces in struggle' (Foweraker 1987: 57), through the hierarchical, non-representational and exclusive institutionalization of labour relations (establishing as such an authoritarian 'mode of social relations of production', see Cox 1987). In Spain, this took the concrete form of the

Vertical Syndicate within the Franquist organic state (see, for example, Amodia 1977: ch.6; and Valdueza 1982). In other words, these corporatist arrangements were characterized by the primacy of vertical mechanisms of political integration, while (neo-)corporatism after Franco evolved through a voluntary arrangement between the state, the trade unions and the employers' organization, and thus stressed the primacy of horizontal mechanisms of political integration. Moreover, the ideological legitimation of both corporative arrangements by the political ruling class differed. While under Franco the goal of social harmony and peace was legitimated by references to the disasters of the Civil War, and democracy, materialism, and individualism were blamed for all evils, in democratic Spain tripartite socio-economic co-operation aimed at consolidating the process of democratization in the first years after the death of Franco (resulting *inter alia* in the famous *Pacto de Moncloa* of October 1977, see Chapter 5), and was eventually legitimated by reference to international economic competitiveness, integration into the Common Market, and sustained economic growth in the first years of Socialist rule.

From state corporatism to societal corporatism

Taking the process of transition from dictatorship to democracy in Spain into account, we could interpret the eventual fall of the dictatorship as a mere formal act in a structural development from 'state corporatism' to 'societal corporatism', taken as two sub-types of corporatism.[9] We are concerned here with an institutional shift/transition from a predominantly vertical to a predominantly horizontal system of interest mediation, inextricably bound up as ideal types with the transition from an economically backward and authoritarian state to an economically developed democratic welfare state.

> Societal corporatism appears to be the concomitant, if not ineluctable, component of the postliberal, advanced capitalist, organized democratic welfare state; state corporatism seems to be a defining element of, if not structural necessity for, the antiliberal, delayed capitalist, authoritarian, neomercantilist state.
> (Schmitter 1974: 105)

The use of Schmitter's distinction, however, calls for some caution.

First, it suggests an ideal–typical sequence of stages, elaborated from the experiences of highly developed nation–states and subsequently applied to countries in which transitions to democracy have taken place in recent years, such as those in Southern Europe and Latin America (see O'Donnell and Schmitter 1986). This approach tends to focus on the intrinsic characteristics of state and societal corporatism, conceived in isolation (see Foweraker 1987), without being able to explain fully the historical shift from one form to another. Explanations remain ideal–typical and static, in the final result being detached from the assumed interrelation between the historical sequence of corporatist stages and the stages of socio-economic and political development within a particular nation–state.

Second, both the erection of state corporatist forms of interest mediation and the subsequent transition to societal corporatism cannot be explained exclusively by endogenous factors or developments. The strategic initiative of the Franquist state to implement a system of state corporatism must be explained both from the polarization of class relations, the incapacity of the former regimes to resolve the social problem within a generally acceptable framework, and the progressive elaboration of reactionary ideologies, which in one way or another found their roots in the debates at the turn of the century; and, at the ideological level, from the international context in which it took place. Corporatist practices in fascist Italy, the predominance of corporatist ideologies within the Catholic Church at that time, and, in general, the anti-liberal, anti-democratic, and totalitarian spirit that swamped Europe in the inter-war years, all clearly influenced (and gave ideological direction to) the authoritarian, state corporatist project of the Franquist state. After World War II, Spain was confronted with a fundamentally hostile environment, impeding the entrance of Spain into Western economic and politico-military alliances. This international isolation confirmed the new order of things in Spain, and particularly the excessive degree of state interventionism in the social and economic sphere during the period of autarky.[10]

The economic liberalization at the end of the 1950s, finally, was both the result of endogenous factors, of which the disequilibrium of the economic structure, rising inflation, balance of payments crises, a fear of increasing social unrest, and a progressive remodelling of the government in favour of the so-called Opus Dei technocrats (and to the detriment of Falangists and representatives of the military apparatus) were the most important ones; and exogenous factors such as the growing external pressure of the United States from the early 1950s on, the signing of the Treaty of Rome and the establishment of external convertibility for most of the Western European currencies, Spanish membership of the institutions of the Bretton Woods system and the Organization for European Economic Co-operation, the subsequent role of these international organizations in influencing the elaboration of the Spanish Stabilization Plan of 1959 (which was moulded on the successful French Stabilization Plan of 1958), all contributed to an ideological reorientation of the regime with respect to international economic policy matters, and to the economic liberalization and subsequent internationalization of the Spanish economy (see *inter alia* González-González 1979; Clavera *et al.* 1978: ch.4; and Viñas *et al.* 1979: ch.6–8).

It is important to note that the opening up of the Franquist regime, led by the Opus Dei technocrats who entered the government in 1957, was initially an economic one, leaving the institutional framework of state corporatism and its ideological underpinning largely intact. In the words of a leading member of the Opus Dei, it implied 'europeanization in the means and hispanicization in the ends' (quoted in Pike 1972: 42), a characterization which echoed the old regenerationist propositions. In the context of the late 1950s and 1960s this meant a doctrinal shift towards both liberal internationalism and continued, though less excessive, state paternalism and authoritarian rule. Paradoxically, as a direct consequence of this economic liberalization, a structural transformation of Spanish society took place which eventually resulted in increasing popular discontent and, more particularly, increasing discrepancy between a societal demand for democracy and the vertical socio-political structures of the authoritarian state.

The development of the Vertical Syndicate can illustrate how state corporatism channelled the transformations in Spanish society through state institutions and corporations that showed a remarkable capacity to adapt to changing circumstances, especially in the field of labour relations (see for example Maravall 1978: chs. 2–4; and Valdueza 1982). This Syndicate was created to control and order the whole of national production according to vertical lines of command. Already in the 1940s syndical elections were held at the factory level, and at the local, provincial and national levels, though the electorate became smaller and less representative as the posts to be filled increased in importance. Initially, the hierarchical lines from the Ministry of Labour downwards were far more important. During the liberalization and internationalization of the Spanish economy in the 1960s, this Syndicate provided the space for collective bargaining and the organization of the labour force 'from below', a space which was in due course filled up by the Spanish Communist Party through the so-called *Comisiones Obreras*. These workers' commissions infiltrated the Syndicate through the syndical elections at factory level, and eventually came to play an increasingly important role in decentralized negotiations on production and labour conditions. Their landslide victory in the 1966 syndical elections was met by severe repression in an ultimate (but, in the end, unsuccessful) attempt by the Franquist regime to prevent the movement of autonomous workers' representation from turning into a national movement of democratic opposition. As Foweraker puts it,

58 Historical perspective

> it was the *representational form* of the Syndicate which created the political space for the early organization of the commissions and moreover catalysed their later growth into a national movement . . . , and indeed it was the corporatist strategy of the regime which opened its own institutions to colonization by the autonomous organizations of civil society. Franco was hoist by his own petard.
>
> (Foweraker 1987: 64–65)

More generally, the economic liberalization generated a fundamental transformation of Spain at the economic, social, and eventually also political levels, thereby eroding the state corporatist foundations of the Franquist state from within. The progressive loss of legitimacy of the regime at the end of the 1960s and early 1970s was not only reflected in increasing popular discontent and organized opposition, but also, and more importantly, in a changing attitude of the economic elites. These elites had traditionally benefited most from the authoritarian system, but began increasingly to extricate themselves from the regime once they perceived a turn to democracy as the best way to continue their class dominance under changed socio-economic conditions. It is in this context that we can understand the smooth transition from state to societal corporatism after the death of Franco. This transition contributed to the stable character of the general process of democratization (see below).

Third, a static and a-historical distinction between state and societal corporatism may result in quite erroneous conclusions as to the transition from the former to the latter. To return to what we have referred to as world time, a shift from state to societal corporatism in Spain in the 1970s may have different implications or consequences from an apparently similar shift at previous moments or phases in world history in other states. The formal implementation of societal or neo-corporatist arrangements in the post-Franco years took place in the setting of global economic crisis, internationalization of austerity and the general advance of neo-liberalism in the Western world. This international context determined the margins and the ideological content of the successive state initiatives to reach tripartite agreements. One could no longer depend on a successful trade-off between increasing real wages and rising productivity, as in the immediate post-war period, or on Keynesian state intervention in the economic sphere (on the basis of which the social compromise in the liberal democracies of the Atlantic core had come into existence). As a matter of fact, the formal liberalization of Spanish civil society from state oppression took place in an international context in which a fundamental, cyclical shift was taking place in the relation between state and civil society, a shift reflected in the replacement of the postwar corporate liberal synthesis by global neo-liberalism. This implied that the Spanish political ruling class, if it wished to avoid a recurrence of the hegemonic crisis of the democratic regime during the Second Republic, had to resolve the problems involved in a smooth transition to democracy within a generally acceptable framework, in an international economic context of crisis, and without being able any longer 'to put matters to the test of force'.

At this point in our argument we must return to the notion of concepts of control. Applying this notion to the Spanish case, we can easily detect two main divergences from the general picture. First, the productive capital concept (or the principle of social protection, for that matter) did not come into existence as a reaction to a pre-existent dominance of the money capital concept (or the principle of economic liberalism). If there is a sequential order, it is the other way round: the plea for economic liberalization in the 1950s, led by the technocrats of Opus Dei and resulting in the opening up of the Spanish economy in 1959, was directed against the excessive state monopolistic tendencies in the first decennia of Franquist rule.

Second, the system of interest mediation specific to Franquist Spain played a decisive role in the way the two organizing principles in society, i.e. social protection and economic liberalism, were elaborated, reproduced and transformed in that country. To explain this second point we have to recall another concept which has already been introduced, that of hegemony.

As indicated, concepts of control are long-term strategies related to particular sections of the bourgeoisie and presented as the general interest in order to become hegemonic. A class or class section is hegemonic, 'not so much to the extent that it is able to impose a uniform conception of the world on the rest of society, but to the extent that it can articulate different visions of the world in such a way that their potential antagonism is neutralised' (Laclau 1977: 161; see also Chapter 1). In this sense there is an important difference between dominance and hegemony: hegemony refers to the capacity of a class or class section to take into account the interests of other classes or class sections in the formulation of its specific interests as the general one.

Apart from this ideological, strategic implication of the notion of hegemony, it is also necessary to refer to its institutional and structural meaning. Robert Cox has made a useful distinction between institutionalization and the use of plain force. These are counterparts, inasmuch as the former tends to minimize the latter.

60 Historical perspective

Force will not have to be used in order to ensure the dominance of the strong to the extent that the weak accept the prevailing power relations as legitimate. This the weak may do if the strong see their mission as hegemonic and not merely dominant or dictatorial, that is, if they are willing to make concessions that will secure the weak's acquiescence in their leadership and if they can express this leadership in terms of universal or general interests, rather than just as serving their own particular interests. Institutions may become the anchor for such a hegemonic strategy since they lend themselves both to the representations of diverse interests and to the universalization of policy.

(Cox 1986: 219)

Hegemony, then, refers to a certain degree of institutionalization and to the capacity of the dominant class to ideologically represent diverse interests without obstructing its own particular interests or material position within the prevailing power structure. In other words, hegemony refers to the degree to which civil society has obtained an autonomous position *vis-à-vis* the state. Hegemonic concepts of control are comprehensive strategies, originating in civil society and using the state as their political platform. In this way we can distinguish hegemonic concepts of control from state corporatism. Both are ideological expressions of social harmony aspiring to represent the 'general interest', and both rely on an ensemble of institutions as the anchor for such strategies. Concepts of control, however, ideal–typically are operative in a state–civil society configuration 'in which civil society has achieved a degree of autonomy and self-sustaining cohesion, relegating the state to a minimal, executive role for the hegemonic bourgeoisie' (van der Pijl 1988: 8). State corporatist arrangements, on the other hand, are necessary in a state–civil society configuration in which no such self-sustaining cohesion of civil society is yet realized, either because of a high degree of particularism or because of extreme class polarization. In the process of Hobbesian state-building, institutional development is pre-eminently state-centred in a continuous attempt to curtail intra-elite conflict and to repress popular uprising or mere organized opposition. The distinction between state and societal corporatism is thus useful for an additional reason; the latter being a transitory form of interest mediation from one particular state–civil society configuration to another, from domination to hegemony. And, as we have indicated in the previous chapter, in Spain this shift from state to societal corporatism coincided with a transition from an international historic bloc in the setting of Atlantic Fordism to a transnational historic bloc in the setting of global neo-liberalism.

IN SEARCH OF HEGEMONY: STATE–CIVIL SOCIETY CONFIGURATIONS IN POST-FRANQUIST SPAIN

In the case of post-Franco Spain, the terms on which democratic policy-making had to take place did not favour a mere platform function of the liberal capitalist state. The death of Franco produced a political impasse, in which, on the one hand, the staunchest supporters of continuation ('Franquism without Franco') opted for a mere cosmetic reform from within the old regime, while the left-wing democratic opposition pleaded for a democratic break with the past (*ruptura democrática*). By far the largest part of the Spanish bourgeoisie objected to both alternatives (see for instance Pérez Díaz 1987). The left-wing option for a democratic break might, it was feared, generate additional pressures to break with existing socio-economic power structures as well. By all means possible, this detested scenario had to be prevented in the first place. On the other hand, the alternative of the so-called Franquist 'bunker', a moderate reform from above without subverting the fundaments of the Franquist state, was rejected for not being far-reaching enough.

This last point can be explained, among other things, by one of the most important features of socio-political development and modernization after 1939: the coming into existence of a single 'national' upper class. As Giner and Sevilla Guzman have stressed, Franquism 'finally created one single ruling class, and finally put an end to the traditional clashes between the different local interests of each sectorial or regional ruling class' (Giner and Sevilla Guzman 1980: 209). In contrast to these authors' conception, however, I am not referring to the creation of a national ruling elite whose common interests have a neutralizing effect on sectional differences. Instead, I refer here to the modernizing impact of the authoritarian Franquist state on the earlier particularistic mentality of the dominant social actors (Catalan and Basque industrial bourgeoisie, Andalusian landowners, Madrid financiers). Under Franco, different sections of the bourgeoisie learned to translate their particular interests into comprehensive and national formulations, appealing to the general (national) interest. They learned that the forming of coalitions around single, comprehensive projects would improve their ability to continue their 'structural power' beyond Franquism. What is more, they grouped their coalitions around ideological projects that were originally formulated in the upper echelons of the state in order to provide Franquism with its necessary political legitimacy. This included the principle of social protection that was originally defended by the movements of Krausism and social Catholicism at the turn of the century, then fiercely rejected by the oligarchy; and the principle of economic liberalism that finally put an end to the long-lived 'triumph of protectionism'. It was the synthesis of both principles after 1959 that eventually convinced the Spanish bourgeoisie of the compatibility of continued economic growth and social leadership with internationalization and rising purchasing power of the masses. In other words, the Franquist era generated an increasing social cohesion of the Spanish bourgeoisie on ideological, strategic grounds, which resulted not only in the articulation of different projects in such a way that their potential antagonism was neutralized (leading to the final solution of the so-called social problem and to the reconciliation of the previously incompatible positions in the debate on Europeanization versus Hispanicization),[11] but also in an increasing preoccupation among the Spanish bourgeoisie with the more general process of policy-making, reflected in the elaboration of comprehensive concepts of control. In Chapter 6 we will argue that the emergence of bank capital at the turn of the century, and its subsequent concentration and centralization, made it the very pivot of this social cohesion.

In itself this fundamental feature of the Franquist era was not enough to drive the Spanish bourgeoisie to reject the cosmetic reform proposed by the 'bunker' after the death of Franco. It did, however, create the objective basis on which 'the hegemonic classes ... would begin to try to extricate themselves from the [Franquist] regime and turn in search of a new political formula for their continued domination' (ibid.: 210–211) once they found the authoritarianism of the Franquist regime unacceptable in their own situation under changed socio-economic and political conditions. The elaboration of comprehensive concepts of control, as a 'new political formula', and the formation of a historic bloc were, however, obstructed from the beginning, because there was no self-evident social cohesion *between* separate classes, let alone any natural, historically developed willingness within the labour movement to co-operate with the Spanish bourgeoisie, a situation which was aggravated by the international economic crisis. As a result, in the immediate post-Franco years the Spanish bourgeoisie had to rely heavily on the capitalist state to obtain its two fundamental objectives: democratic transition and continued class domination.

The centre-right UCD (*Unión de Centro Democrático*), which won the first parliamentary elections after the death of Franco (in 1977; see Appendix), could fulfil this role. Recruiting its party leaders from the moderate cadres of the old regime (for instance, among many others, Prime Minister Adolfo Suárez), this party could guarantee both socio-economic continuity and political democratization as no other could. The method it used has come to be known as *ruptura pactada* (negotiated break), meaning the continued negotiation of the path to democratic consolidation with the left-wing and other members of the democratic opposition. To this end, several neo-corporatist, extra-parliamentary arrangements were made with the most important economic-interest organizations. This negotiated transition to democracy in conjunction with corporatist arrangements succeeded, and received such nationwide support (especially from part of the labour movement), mainly because of a constant fear of a reaction by the army. Under these conditions, the new liberal state could not be relegated to a minimal, executive role for the bourgeoisie, and could not serve as a mere political platform for the articulation of hegemonic concepts of control. Instead, it had to take an active, initiating role in order not to repeat the errors of the Second Republic. In referring once more to the above quotation from Hugh Thomas' *The Spanish Civil War*, the ability of the UCD politicians (and especially Suárez) 'to resolve the problems of the country within a frame generally acceptable' determined the course of events in a decisive way.[12]

To return to our theoretical point of departure, an additional remark has to be made: comprehensive concepts of control transcend the strict, national political framework, operating both within and across national frontiers, only in so far as, and because, class formation becomes transnational in character. In this respect the role of the capitalist state is not confined to its strictly national character as a political platform. From the moment that the functional forms of capital become internationalized, i.e., whenever international movements of circulating and productive capital come into being, the material basis will exist for the political articulation of internationalized, transnational concepts of control at the national level. Both the internationalization and internalization of specific concepts of control depend on the pre-existence of historically determined national socio-economic, institutional, and ideological structures. Accordingly, the emergence of a transnational bourgeoisie by way of the internationalization of the circuits of productive capital and money capital is the combined result of forces operating at the international and national levels. In this sense, the capitalist state is the obvious political framework in which the alternation of comprehensive concepts of control takes place in conjunction with changing social relations of production and changing world order structures, or conversely, the very medium through which national, hegemonic concepts of control can transcend national frontiers. However, in a world economy of increasingly transnational movements of circulating and productive capital, the executive role of the state can be partly transferred to international organizations or quasi-state structures at the regional (or supranational) level; the growing importance of the institutions of the European Union is a clear example of the latter.

If we apply these general remarks to the Spanish case, and if we characterize the 'transnational bourgeoisie' as that internationally operating bourgeoisie whose global, transnational interests not only exceed but also tend to neutralize the specific and exclusively national orientation and articulation of its economic interests at the political level, we must conclude that the internationalization of capital during the second phase of Franquism (i.e., after the economic liberalization in 1959) did not create a transnational bourgeoisie of Spanish origin. That is, economic internationalization has been realized through the entrance of foreign transnational capital into the Spanish market, without producing a substantial internationalization of Spanish bank capital or industrial capital itself until recently. This particular feature has resulted in close co-operation between foreign and national capital, based on mutual interests, but without changing the predominantly (not to say exclusively) national orientation of the Spanish national bourgeoisie in terms of investment decisions. Of course, the increasing external dependence on trade with Western Europe in particular did generate an outward-looking mentality in the Spanish business community, but it did not generate a cosmopolitan view on domestic politics. The internationalization of the Spanish economy had still to be interpreted from a national perspective. Indeed, it must be argued that only after the Spanish Socialist party took power in 1982 did things change in a radical way, leading to an internationalization of domestic policy, to the benefit of some and the detriment of others. As a matter of fact, this change took place in conjunction with a historic shift in the origin of direct foreign investments in Spain: from a predominance of American foreign investments to a predominance of West European and, more specifically, West German foreign investments. In this context, the growing importance of trade with Western Europe did not yet imply, in the 1960s and 1970s, a growing global, transnational perspective among the Spanish bourgeoisie. It did, however, indicate the direction and orientation of its future transnationalization.

In order to appreciate the historical significance of the hegemonic project of the PSOE, we have to return to the period of the Franquist dictatorship. We may borrow the simplified but useful set of distinctions Pollack makes between 'a series of competing ideologies of modernization' during this period. Pollack distinguishes a non-democratic–nationalist ideology, which can be identified with the first, autarkic phase of Franquism (1939–1959); a non-democratic–internationalist ideology, related to the internationalization of the Spanish economy after 1959, inspired by Opus Dei, which did not call into question the authoritarian political system; and a democratic–

internationalist ideology, which was adopted by the main anti-regime opposition through most of the Franquist period (Pollack 1987: 131). Characteristic of this last ideology was its internationalization through democratization stand. Total modernization and integration into the Common Market required a previous transition to a democratic political regime. This was also the position of the UCD government in the immediate post-Franco years, and, for that matter, of the Spanish bourgeoisie. The ideology of modernization of the PSOE can be summarized as democratization through internationalization, an ideology reflected by the internationalization of domestic politics after 1982, and, even more importantly, by the transnationalization of Spanish civil society. It is in these terms that both the Socialist stand in favour of Spain's continued membership of NATO, and its efforts to integrate Spain into the EEC, must be interpreted.

The Socialist hegemonic project will be dealt with in more detail in the following chapters. It should be remembered that this political party was one of the first organizations of group interests of Spanish civil society to experience a process of transnationalization in the real meaning of the word, long before it came to power. There can be no doubt about the decisive influence of the Socialist International, and in particular of the German SPD, on the ideological formation of the party's leadership (Felipe González being a case in point, not least because of his personal relationship with Willy Brandt), the spectacular deradicalization of the PSOE in the 1970s, and the direction of the party's foreign policy objectives, not to mention the financial support the PSOE received from its sister parties.[13] One of the most important consequences is that the current party leadership has developed a global (West European) perspective from which it interprets domestic politics and economics. The only way for Spain to become an internationally respected and politically and economically powerful nation, it is argued, is to think and act internationally. In the following chapters we will analyse the constituent elements of this plan in terms of its strategic objective: Europeanization in the means and Europeanization in the ends.

CONCLUSIONS

In this chapter we have attempted to analyse the historical shift from the weak clientelist state and the oligarchic power relations underpinning it to the liberal capitalist state in post-Franco Spain, characterized by its progressive adoption of Western socio-economic, institutional, and ideological structures. Mouzelis has examined these 'intricate, shifting relationships between clientelistic and class political organizations during the process of capitalist growth' in the case of Greece. Clientelist elements, he argues, are to be found to a greater or lesser extent in every political system. The extent to which these elements are manifested depends on the level of development of a country. Political conflict tends to have a predominantly class character in social formations where the capitalist mode of production is both dominant and widespread in the economy. Clientelistic elements do not disappear completely in the process of capitalist development, but are gradually replaced by an increasingly dominant class structure.

> When capital has ceased to operate exclusively in the sphere of distribution and has a large-scale entry into that of production (agricultural and/or industrial), one finds (a) a widespread process of social and political mobilization as the rural periphery loses its self-contained character (through the development of national markets, communication networks, education, etc.) and the working masses are inescapably drawn into the political process; and (b) the emergence, within the context of parliamentary regimes, of favorable conditions for the development of formal organizations (political parties, trade unions) which try more or less successfully and autonomously to articulate and promote the collective interests of the dominated classes, i.e. of the urban and rural direct producers.
>
> (Mouzelis 1978: 476–477)

Thus, the introduction of wage labour and the separation of the direct producer from his means of production (associated with the coming to dominance of the capitalist mode of production) are related to the development of class consciousness and organization, which tend to replace vertical mechanisms of political integration by horizontal ones. When this happens, 'conditions are favorable for the decline of personalistic politics and the all-pervasive clientelism always associated with it' (ibid.: 477).

In Spain, however, the clientelist system of the Restoration regime did not give way to class-based parliamentarism as a result of evolutionary transition, i.e. at some moment during the process of economic growth. It was the opposition of the Restoration oligarchy to the full introduction of capitalism, in combination with the mobilization of the dominated classes, that made an authoritarian solution to the social problem a necessary precondition for continued class dominance by the Andalusian landowners and the Basque and Catalan bourgeoisie. However, in relegating their direct political power to the Hobbesian state, the dominant classes lost their control over the direction of state intervention and their capacity to constrain the process of capitalist development.

State corporatism, then, created the conditions for the eventual transition and consolidation of democracy in Spain. Forced upon the social classes by a bloody class war, this authoritarian mode of interest mediation not only saved capitalism from revolutionary counterforces through physical extermination and severe repression, but also offered the institutional framework for the deepening of capitalist relations of production (and a total restructuring of the Spanish economy). Paradoxically, by implementing this very framework, the dictatorship set in motion its own internal erosion and prepared its own collapse. To understand this, we first have to refute the characterization of democratization as the turning over of state functions to the institutions of an incipient but reinforcing civil society, as if civil society and the state were separate spheres, and the strengthening of the one necessarily implied the weakening of the other.

One of the determinants not only of the transition to democracy as such, but also of its very success in the long run, was the coalescence of this political project with dominant concepts of control, or 'modes of economic behaviour', in the ranks of the bourgeoisie. When opting for democracy, the Spanish bourgeoisie developed a clear perception of the nation's role in present and future economic and political relations at the global level.

In this sense it is important to note that the liberalization and opening up of the Spanish economy in the 1960s, and the subsequent internationalization of capital in Spain, generated an outward-looking mentality in the Spanish business community, which for obvious reasons was first and foremost directed at Western Europe, notably at integration into the Common Market. All the same, in order to realize this option Spain had to establish democratic politics, an additional reason for the Spanish bourgeoisie to support democratic transition. During the period of transition, especially after the Socialist party had come to power, this European option was confirmed as the only realistic alternative for Spanish capital. The increasing transnationalization of the Spanish economy in conjunction with its growing orientation to the Common Market formed an important reason for the successful transition and consolidation of democracy: this was as important as the impact of the Franquist 'revolution from above'. In fact, from the perspective of the Spanish state–civil society configuration in the 1970s and 1980s, these two phenomena cannot be separated.

During this period Spanish civil society has obtained a relative strength, i.e. it has achieved a certain degree of autonomy and self-sustaining cohesion *vis-à-vis* the state. In order to understand this fully, we may use one of the Gramscian conceptions of civil society, quoted in the editors' introduction to the chapter on 'State and civil society' in the *Prison Notebooks*.

> Between the economic structure and the State with its legislation and its coercion stands civil society. . . . The State is the instrument for

conforming civil society to the economic structure, but it is necessary for the State to 'be willing' to do this; i.e. for the representatives of the change that has taken place in the economic structure to be in control of the State.

(Gramsci 1983: 208)

The editors rightly state that Gramsci in effect is here equating the notion of civil society with 'mode of economic behaviour'. In Spain, the 'representatives of the change that has taken place in the economic structure', i.e. the Spanish Socialist party in co-operation with the transnationalized, Europeanist bourgeoisie, have effectively used the Spanish state for 'conforming civil society'. On the other hand, the Spanish bourgeoisie still depended on the Spanish state with regard to the policy needed to prepare Spanish business for full competition in 1992. The Socialist policy of industrial reconversion and modernization, on the one hand, and anti-cyclical macro-economic adjustment, on the other, implies 'the use of government to influence and direct decisions made in the private sector' (Wolfe 1981: 54). If a state is stronger than another state to the extent that it can maximize the conditions for profit-making by private, domestic and foreign, business, our evaluation of the strength of the Spanish state will also depend on the degree to which it succeeds in neutralizing demands of the trade unions and in giving direction to the modernization of Spanish industry within the context of the Lockeian heartland of transnational production.

In Gramscian terms, this 'Europeanization', as an alternative to political isolationism and mercantilism, has been the mediating force in the historical transition from the economic corporate level of consciousness to the hegemonic level of consciousness,

bringing about not only a unison of economic and political aims, but also intellectual and moral unity, posing all the questions around which the struggle rages not on a corporate but on a 'universal plane', and thus creating the hegemony of a fundamental social group over a series of subordinate groups.

(ibid.: 181–182)

The option of European integration materialized through the links between the Spanish bourgeoisie and its European counterparts has united the economic and political aims of the principal social groups, thereby creating the framework for the 'universalization' of Spanish politics, while preserving bourgeois hegemony. In the context of this 'European consciousness',

Spanish social democracy fulfils the political task of making transnational capitalism more acceptable to the subordinated classes.

The acceleration of the process of European integration in the second half of the 1980s, itself a concomitant to changing world order structures, has furthermore reinforced the need for Spain to adapt its economic and socio-political structures to those prevailing in the most advanced member states. The transferring of resources from Northern European countries to the South has been and will be an essential factor in making this process of modernization a success, as will be shown in the following chapters.

Part III
The Socialist decade (1982–1992)

3 Operation Europe
The hegemonic project of the PSOE

> A great nation needs in order to live and develop a cardinal and transcendent thought to orient it ... Once this orientation is established, there must be subordinated to it in the first place the foreign policy of the state; ... and to its foreign policy the nation's domestic policy must in turn be subordinated ... For us the ideals of the great Hispano-American patria must encompass this thought, this orientation.
> (Sánchez de Toca 1898)[1]

INTRODUCTION

In Spain the death of Francisco Franco in November 1975 was the prelude to a process of democratic transition, involving the principal governmental and oppositional forces and strongly supported by trade unions and employers' organizations. This resulted in the final consolidation of democracy when the Socialist party (PSOE) obtained an absolute majority in the 1982 elections.[2]

The so-called '*ruptura pactada*', and the concomitant shift from state corporatism to societal corporatism, is the reflection of a process of societal modernization, which in turn is strongly related to industrial development. At the politico-ideological level, social democracy has played an essential role in this relatively smooth transition towards parliamentarism and societal corporatism. By social democracy, then, we do not refer to the role of particular social and/or political forces in the first place, but rather to the institutional and ideological articulation of a change in the general pattern of social relations, gradually reconciling previously incompatible and strongly antagonistic class positions. This totality of changing social relations of production (i.e. in the course of the process of capitalist socialization), institutional adaptation (i.e. the shift towards societal corporatism), and the emergence of an 'ideological community' based on a nationwide consensus between the main social and political forces, which we shall call the process of social democratization, served as the framework in which the Socialist party could come to the fore.

As a result of the modernization of Spanish society during the last two decades of the Franquist dictatorship, for the first time in the history of Spain increasing social unrest primarily took the form of disaffection with the political system and not that of a political struggle aimed at the overthrow of the socio-economic system. The political deradicalization that underlaid this development implied a decreasing need for authoritarian, vertical political structures, originally designed to contain social conflicts. In other words, at the beginning of the 1970s a situation was created in which, both as cause and consequence of the political deradicalization of large sections of the population, an increasingly strong political awareness and involvement developed, and with them an increasing need for new, institutionalized forms of organization. In this context, parliamentary democracy gradually became a realistic alternative to the existing authoritarian state form, not least because socio-political opposition no longer directed its efforts against the system in general. Only the formal political structures were marked out for destruction, while the socio-economic structures could remain largely intact (or, at any rate, were not brought up for discussion by the majority of the opposition).

This is the context in which the politico-institutional developments after the fall of the Franquist dictatorship in 1975 must be understood. That is, already prior to these changes, a process of profound social transformation had laid the foundations on which a modern party system could be established; the formal start of the transition process (including the legalization of political parties) constituted 'merely' a necessary condition of its continuation (as, indeed, did the death of Francisco Franco). In this sense, also the breeding ground of the Spanish Socialist party is to be found in a historical development, i.e. the process of social democratization, which revealed itself *inter alia* in a change in the electoral composition of Spanish society.

The next section contains a survey of the main developments and events that contributed to the landslide victory of the Spanish Socialist party in the 1982 elections. This is followed by an analysis of the constituent elements of the party's hegemonic project. In stressing the coherence of this project we will momentarily abstract from the contradictions underlying it. In the following section we will deal with the most important of the continual intra-party conflicts, i.e. that between the so-called Guerristas and the neo-liberals. The final section includes a short introduction to the following chapters on foreign policy and socio-economic policy, and on the Socialist party's strategy with respect to the Spanish business community, notably bank capital. All three chapters are intended to elaborate on specific elements of the hegemonic project, its contradictions, and the conflicts it generated both within the ruling party and within Spanish society.

SOCIAL DEMOCRATIZATION AND THE RISE OF THE SPANISH SOCIALIST PARTY

One of the most important social changes within Spain in the last twenty-five years is the spectacular depopulation of the rural areas. Massive external migration, particularly to North-Western Europe, internal migration, and urbanization were characteristic of this process (see Tezanos 1989a: 77ff.; King 1984). Inasmuch as this rural exodus (which in some cases led to a total depopulation of traditional rural communities) was caused by centripetal movements of industrialization and bureaucratization (centred on the largest cities at the regional and national level), it also had a radical impact on the composition of the labour force, and on social stratification. The total percentage of workers employed in the primary sector sharply declined in the 1960s and 1970s, while the percentage of people employed in industry and the service sector changed in the opposite direction. Perhaps of even more importance was the impact on social stratification. Particularly as a result of new forms and possibilities of upward mobility, and of higher requirements for education in the light of economic modernization, a rise of the so-called new middle classes could be observed in the course of the 1960s (Baklanoff 1978: 18–19). Occupational groups such as modern managers, technicians, civil servants, white-collar workers, but also workers in the modern and better-paying industrial sectors became part and parcel of this new social stratum. In one of the early studies of consumerism in Spain, it was estimated that in 1970 these, broadly defined, new middle classes already included more than 50 per cent of the population (Pike 1974: 180; see also García San Miguel 1980: 213ff.). Although differences of opinion exist with respect to their actual dimensions (depending on how narrowly this social stratum is defined, i.e. to what extent the so-called labour aristocracy is included), all the relevant publications agree on the substantial increase of these occupational groups in the social composition of the Spanish labour force (see for instance Gunther *et al.* 1988: ch.5; and Tezanos 1989a).

These transformations, and in particular the changes in social stratification, may explain the growing importance of the PSOE. Political and sociological studies have shown that the increasing electoral success of this party in the late 1970s and early 1980s was largely due to the additional support it received from occupational groups other than the traditional labour force. In the parliamentary elections of 1977 and 1979, the PSOE and the centre-right UCD were the only two parties that obtained electoral support from all the major social strata. In the 1982 elections a part of the electorate which had formerly supported the UCD switched over to the PSOE (and another part to the right-wing Partido Popular). Moreover, the same investigations have made clear that the Spanish Socialist party obtained grassroots support which in certain respects was a reflection of this new social stratification. That is, both the party's electoral support and its affiliation increased to the extent that it succeeded in incorporating large segments of the new middle classes.[3] Or as José Felix Tezanos puts it, 'the changes in the sociological profile of the PSOE are the logical consequence of the intense transformations that have taken place in Spanish society during the last decades' (Tezanos 1989b: 479).

In short, the Socialist party established itself electorally on the dividing line between two traditionally hostile social classes and ideologies, and thereby politically narrowed the gap that had already been bridged socially. It is, however, important to remember that any analysis of the breeding ground of the PSOE does not in itself explain its ultimate electoral victory in 1982. It does show the fundamental social changes that have resulted in an electoral upheaval; but it cannot answer the question of why and how this party could, and actually did, take advantage of this new situation.

In addition to the above-mentioned social and electoral changes in Spain, two other factors largely contributed to the Socialist party's victory. In the first place, the party that had governed previously went through serious crises. It is no exaggeration to say that the strength of the PSOE is partially due to the weakness of its centre-right predecessor (and, indeed, of the parties to the Left and Right of both the PSOE and UCD). At the end of the 1970s the Union of the Democratic Centre (UCD) was torn by severe factional strife. The rivalry between various factions escalated when in 1981 Prime Minister Adolfo Suárez tendered the resignation of his cabinet and soon afterwards turned his back on the UCD. His successor, Leopoldo Calvo Sotelo, proved to be incapable of reconciling the contending factions. After two 'families' left the party, Calvo Sotelo also resigned. The 1982 elections showed dramatically that the UCD had lost its electoral support (see Appendix) (see Huneeus 1985; Caciagli 1986, 1989).

In the second place, the striking moderation of its objectives provided the PSOE with an increase in its domestic electoral appeal. This took place in the course of the second half of the 1970s. During the 27th party congress in 1976, the PSOE, at that time still illegal, presented itself as a Marxist and democratic mass party, and officially rejected every attempt to realize reforms within the framework of the capitalist system. The indirect involvement of PSOE in the institutional transition from dictatorship to parliamentary democracy, however, made it necessary to compromise with other parties. Apart from this, an important section of the party leadership of the the PSOE took the view that a one-sided concentration on the working class would impede the party's electoral growth. Accordingly, at the extraordinary party congress of 1979, Marxism was given up as the central guiding principle and a more moderate course was set. In the course of events leading to the PSOE's own 'Bad Godesberg', transnational linkages with sister parties were of paramount importance. In particular the advice of Willy Brandt (as president of the Socialist International since 1976) was decisive in the deradicalization of the Socialist party's programme. During the electoral campaign of 1982 (under the slogan 'por el cambio') the PSOE tried to address as large a share of the electorate as possible. The planks in the party platform included a continuation of the moderate sociopolitical reforms, decisive anti-crisis measures (such as curtailing inflation and unemployment), the introduction of the forty-hour week, and the reorganization of public finances. With regard to foreign policy, the PSOE pleaded for the entry of Spain into the Common Market and promised to organize a referendum on NATO membership (see Share 1985).

THE CONSTITUENT ELEMENTS OF THE SOCIALIST PROJECT

Once in power after the 1982 elections, the PSOE was confronted with several objective constraints on its ability to develop an alternative comprehensive project.

In the first place, the new Socialist government was faced with a situation of international economic crisis and the so-called 'internationalization of austerity policy', which did not allow for an incentives policy in one particular, and highly dependent, country. As a matter of fact, the Spanish Socialists learned from the experiences of the Mitterrand government in France and the PASOK government in Greece, both elected in 1981 on a platform of economic stimulation. Right from the start of its first term of office, the PSOE began to implement a policy of adjustment characterized by the priority of deflation over employment. Initially this policy was supported by the Socialist trade union UGT and institutionalized by regular tripartite consultation. However, in the course of events, and especially after the second victory of the PSOE in the 1986 elections, the Spanish economic picture improved considerably. A boom in foreign investment, a substantial decrease in the rate of inflation, rising corporate profits, and even an increase in employment were all factors which paradoxically resulted in increasing socio-political tensions between the Socialist government and the trade unions. These reached a climax in the general strike of December 1988 and led to the final break-up of the so-called concerted action between the PSOE and the UGT. The increasing pressure by the trade unions to improve the economic conditions of the labour force, and more generally their plea for a *giro social* in the general policy of the PSOE, were met by reluctance on the part of the government to change the basic premises of its economic policy (see Chapter 5).

Second, when it came to power the new Socialist government had to take into account the continued presence and influence of the so-called '*poderes facticos*', the '*de facto* powers' (the Spanish business community, especially the large private banks, the army, and, to a lesser extent, the Catholic Church). In fact, it can be demonstrated that the party leadership anticipated this socio-political reality even before the PSOE took office in 1982; this in part explains the gradual deradicalization of the party's political objectives during the late 1970s. Characteristic of the position of the PSOE in this respect was a statement made by Felipe González on the eve of the 1982 elections: 'I will be satisfied if we now implement a bourgeois reform, through which democracy can be stabilized, making it possible for my children to realize a genuine socialist programme in the future' (cited in *Keesings Historisch Archief* 1982: 706). Initially, the absolute majority of the PSOE in parliament was received with great reticence (and in some cases even with overt hostility) by a considerable part of the *poderes facticos*. In due course it became clear, however, that they had nothing to fear from Spanish Socialism in the 1980s, and were in fact even better off. As Pedro Toledo, the former president of one of the largest Spanish private banks (Banco de Vizcaya), had repeatedly stated, 'the Right would have done things worse than the Socialist government' (*Tiempo*, 21 March 1988).

Third, in the field of foreign policy the Socialist government was faced in 1982 with a contradictory situation. On the one hand, a nationwide mass consensus existed in Spanish society as to the desirability of full entry into the Common Market. From Left to Right, all social and political forces favoured the formal Europeanization of Spain, although major differences existed over the future direction the process of European integration would have to take, and the role Spain could play in it. At the same time considerable reluctance prevailed on the part of some member states (especially France) with regard to Spanish membership in the near future. On the other hand, a large part of the Spanish population fiercely opposed Spanish membership of NATO, while at the same time the governments of the

United States and other NATO member states displayed great eagerness, forcing the Socialist government to remain in NATO. Spain's continued participation in NATO was finally approved in a national referendum, held in 1986, and formal entry into the EEC took place on 1 January 1986, the result of successfully linking the two memberships, neutralizing opponents at home and abroad (see the next chapter).

Finally, from the start of its first term of office the party leadership of the PSOE was well aware of the uncertain future of the party's absolute majority in parliament. A deficient party organization, limited membership, and militant support in comparison to the electoral base of the party (see Caciagli 1986: 231), made the Socialist party highly vulnerable to the unsteady behaviour of the Spanish electorate, or at least it could not guarantee stable electoral support over time, as was shown by the dramatic loss of votes by the UCD in the 1982 elections. In order to avoid such a situation and to increase the institutional and electoral stability of the PSOE, the party elite opted for a dual strategy, making use of both old and new methods.

The party's 'dual strategy'

In the first place, the PSOE continued an old tradition, dating back at least to the Franquist state, in attempting to accomplish a societal embedding of the party by using the state apparatuses, a case of what Lyrintzis has called 'bureaucratic clientelism'.

> Bureaucratic clientelism . . . consists of systematic infiltration of the state machine by party devotees and the allocation of favours through it. It is characterized by an organised expansion of existing posts and departments in the public sector and the addition of new ones in an attempt to secure power and maintain a party's electoral base. When the state has always played a central role in both economic and political development, it is very likely that the parties in government turn to the state as the only means for consolidating their power, and this further weakens their organisation and ideology.
>
> (Lyrintzis 1984: 103–104)

This strategy of bureaucratic clientelism was carried through by the so-called 'Guerristas' within the party elite (named after the vice-secretary general of the PSOE, and the former deputy Prime Minister, Alfonso Guerra) who almost completely controlled the party executive. It resulted in what some have called the enormous difference between the 'institutional power' of the PSOE and its 'social presence' (see Sotelo 1984: 48).

That is, the Socialist party's lack of strong national organization was compensated by its growing primacy in the state institutions.

In the second place, in order to maintain its political hegemony the party elite carefully elaborated the constituent elements of the 'catch-all' strategy on the basis of which the PSOE had obtained absolute majority in the 1982 elections. Once in power, an ideological offensive was carried through, aimed at presenting the comprehensive hegemonic project of the PSOE as the only possible one, the only way to realize what was seen as essential for the future of Spain: the country's modernization and Europeanization. Each part of the government's domestic, social, and economic policy was presented and legitimized by reference to the necessity of adjusting Spanish socio-economic and political structures in the light of future membership of the EEC, and, after 1986, by stressing the implications of the magic year 1992 (the end of the transition period with regard to Spain's entry into the Common Market, and the creation of the Single European Market).

The hypothetical policy options of the PSOE

Theoretically, in the course of the 1970s and early 1980s three alternative and to a large extent mutually exclusive policies stood at the disposal of the PSOE party elite, with respect both to the elaboration of its successive electoral strategies and to the implementation of a comprehensive socialist policy after 1982.

From a strictly hypothetical point of view, the PSOE could have opted for a policy of disassociation, implying the suspension of the negotiations with the European Commission and the withdrawal of Spain from NATO. Needless to say, such a programme would probably have prevented the PSOE from obtaining an absolute majority, apart from the fact that the resulting political and economic isolation of Spain could only have been based on a vision of global relations that could be labelled as 'Eurosclerosis' (*El País*: 20 November 1988), a vision totally contrary to the existing nationwide Europeanist mood at the time.

Alternatively, assuming the European destiny of Spain, the PSOE could have opted for socio-economic state intervention and a Keynesian expansionist policy at home (aiming at the social protection of man and nature), while accepting the conditions of free trade within a single West European market. As we have indicated above, the Spanish Socialists did not implement such a policy of stimulation, partially because they anticipated its negative macro-economic effects (see also Chapter 5). Moreover, and this increasingly became the predominant legitimation of the adjustment policy adopted (as entry into the Common Market was realized in 1986 and a conjunctural upswing of the world economy took place in the course of the 1980s), reference was (and is) made to the necessary modernization of the Spanish economy from an archaic capitalist and protectionist system to a highly competitive one without frontiers. To this end a tight monetary policy was carried through, in combination with a reduction of public spending to curtail government deficits, and a so-called 'industrial conversion' aimed at restructuring or closing down inefficient or uncompetitive traditional industries while developing high-tech industries. The mentors of this economic policy were known as the 'technocrats' or 'neo-liberals' of the PSOE, headed by superminister Carlos Solchaga (Finance and Economy), forming together with the above-mentioned Guerristas the most influential 'families' within the Spanish Socialist party.

A third option would have been the PSOE's choice of *laissez-faire* and economic liberalism at home together with politico-military protection under the banner of American hegemony within the Western Atlantic alliance. In fact, this policy was the one best represented by the neo-conservative Partido Popular (the former Alianza Popular), embodying the neo-liberal and Atlanticist current in Spanish politics. It is interesting to take a look at the links this party maintained with the so-called *'derecha económica'* (the economic Right), especially in comparison with the PSOE's links with other sectors of the Spanish business community. Partido Popular was predominantly tied to businessmen from real estate, insurance, and the finance sector (see *El Independiente*, 17 February 1989: 5). The party had privileged relationships with the most reactionary of the seven largest banks, Banco Español de Crédito (Banesto) and, to a lesser extent, Banco Central and Banco de Santander (see also chapter 6).

The final outcome: the hegemonic synthesis

Bearing in mind the hypothetical options open to the PSOE when it aspired to power, we may now summarize the constituent elements of the party's hegemonic project, part of which only became clear and took definite shape during the first years of office after 1982. The 'catch-all' political strategy of the Spanish Socialists consisted of a comprehensive compromise between elements of the above-mentioned potential policies, its constituent elements being the following:

1 A 'socialization' of the party achieved by the use of its power in the state institutions to increase the institutional and electoral stability of the PSOE ('bureaucratic clientelism'), an effort organized and directed by the 'Guerristas'.

2 An internationalization of domestic and foreign politics, which not only comprised an interpretation of national, economic problems from a global, transnational vantage point (global interdependence determining the specific content of the crisis management pursued), but also a global, non-particularistic vision of international politics, reflected, for instance, in the foreign policy of the PSOE towards Central and Latin America (and the Middle East), which is increasingly moulded in an European setting.
3 Full integration into the Common Market, with an attempt to play a dominant role in the construction of a European Political Union, which is interpreted in the light of a transnational, European counter-offensive against global neo-liberalism.
4 Spain's remaining in NATO, albeit under special conditions, attempting to strengthen the European (Mediterranean) pillar of NATO from within.
5 An attempt to neutralize the excessive influence of the *poderes facticos* (army and Spanish bank capital) on domestic politics through a comprehensive plan of transnationalizing (part of) Spanish civil society and some elementary state functions in the field of security policy. In this regard, NATO membership was intended to shift the function of the Spanish army away from a repressive and predominantly national one (as it was during the Franquist dictatorship), to an international security one (a case of what can be called the 'internationalization of security policy' in Spain). In addition, full membership of the EEC would change the attitude of the Spanish business community from a predominantly nationally orientated one to a transnational, European one.
6 Finally, an attempt to neutralize excessive economic demands from part of the trade unions by forcing through continued tripartite negotiations on the general direction of Socialist economic policy.

It was this hegemonic project (which, in Spain, has been frequently referred to as *Felipismo*), comprehensively relating such areas as labour relations, socio-economic policies, and the international socio-economic and political order, which, at least in its initial formulation, differed in a fundamental way from 'global neo-liberalism' (as can be shown by a comparison with, for instance, the Thatcherite policy in Great Britain, see Overbeek 1990) in respect of its social origins, its socio-economic and political content, and, most importantly, its European orientation.

In discussing the implementation of *Felipismo* in Spain, however, we must stress the growing contradiction between the constituent elements of the hegemonic project elaborated for national political purposes, represented by the Guerristas in the party apparatus, and still caught in a

Hobbesian configuration; and those constituent elements of the hegemonic policy directed at incorporating Spain in the Lockeian heartland of transnational production, represented by the neo-liberals in the Socialist government. In the course of the 'Socialist decade', and particularly after 1985, this contradiction between societal corporatism at the national level and economic liberalism at the European level was resolved to the benefit of the neo-liberals in government, as we will see.

The accelerated liberalization of the Spanish economy and the externally induced modernization of the economic structures as a result of Spain's integration into the EC were the levers of this shifting emphasis, and the main causes of the progressive internationalization of domestic politics under Socialist rule. However, it is important to note that, in constructing the monetarist elements of the desired adjustment policy, the Socialists never lost sight of the productive capital vantage point. In order to understand this point fully, one has to remember the important but excessive role the Spanish state traditionally played in controlling the process of economic development in the course of the 1960s and 1970s, not only through politico-economic intervention but also through state ownership of industrial capital. In order not to become a structural constraint on further capitalist development, state interventionism had to be rationalized and public spending had to be curtailed, in the interest, first and foremost, of private national and foreign large-scale enterprises. EC membership formed the perfect legitimation of this policy, but also forced Spanish public and private industrial capital and bank capital to restructure and concentrate their activities, and to increase international competitiveness in the face of the free movement of goods and capital.

It has to be emphasized, however, that this policy served more than the particular interests of the transnational bourgeoisie in Spain. The comprehensive strategy of social modernization that accompanied this policy of macro-economic restructuring strongly appealed to the (at least subjectively experienced) interests of the new middle classes. In this sense, the politically articulated social compromise was presented as the general interest inasmuch as it was extended to the new middle classes, excluding *de facto* all those workers in the traditional industrial sectors who became the victims of this forced restructuring and modernization.

This programme could be successfully implemented as long as it continued to have a strong appeal for the new middle classes. That is, as long as their interests as a social and electoral target group, i.e., democratic consolidation and economic modernization, could be observed in general terms. The victims of this programme were all those workers in the lower strata of society who could not accept that democratization was carried through at the expense of their employment and purchasing power, which in some cases fell below subsistence level. For them, 'Socialism' implied economically what authoritarianism had implied politically: the seizure from above of their castles in Spain.

FACTIONAL STRIFE AND THE DISINTEGRATION OF A PROJECT

Before entering into discussion of some of the most relevant constituent parts of the PSOE's hegemonic project in more detail (i.e. its foreign and economic policy, and its relationship with Spanish bank capital) we must further correct the impression of harmony and consensus implied in the above description of the 'Felipist' policy. The Socialist party's strategic objectives were at times fiercely attacked from outside the party, as we shall see in the next chapters, and they were also subject to continuous intra-party conflict between different tendencies. Both the way in which the principal objectives were to be achieved, and, indeed, the objectives themselves, were a constant source of factional strife. This started in 1974 when the old party leadership in exile, the so-called '*históricos*', was defeated by the young guard of militants who had been active in the clandestine, anti-Franquist opposition within Spain, and who were not susceptible to the anti-Communism of those who still wanted to keep the memory of the Second Republic alive. The resolutions adopted by the reborn Socialist party at its first congress held in Spain after forty years of Franquism, in December 1976, represented a 'Bad Godesberg in reverse' (Gunther *et al.* 1988: 74): for the first time in its history the PSOE redefined itself as a Marxist party, which sought the 'suppression of the capitalist mode of production through the conquest of political and economic power, and the socialization of the means of production, distribution and exchange by the working class' (quoted in Maravall 1982: 150), and *inter alia* aimed at nationalizing the largest private banks and companies. In the following years a conflict came to the fore between the so-called '*críticos*' and '*felipistas*', which centred on the future ideological course of the PSOE, and particularly the role of Marxism in it. Already in May 1978, the secretary general of the PSOE, Felipe González, declared himself openly in favour of the elimination of the term 'Marxism' from the party manifesto, shortly after the Communist leader Santiago Carrillo had done the same with 'Leninism' (see Gunther *et al.* 1988: 168ff.; see also Nash 1983: 40ff.; and González Hernández 1989). Obviously, it was the catch-all electoral strategy of the *felipistas* that motivated this attempt to convert the PSOE ideologically into a reformist, social democratic party. After the 1979 elections, as a result of which the PSOE only slightly improved its presence in parliament, it took an extraordinary party congress in October of the same year to finally confirm the unquestioned leadership of González, and his right-hand man Alfonso Guerra. From that moment on, the PSOE progressively modified its ideology and deradicalized its electoral platform. It is important to remember that this programmatic shift was in part inspired by the German SPD, personified by the strong personal influence of Willy Brandt on González.

After coming to power in October 1982, the party leadership's continuous self-identification as a harmonious group of people united in one single, coherent project could not hide the underlying tensions and open conflicts between representatives of the party apparatus and members of the government. To some extent the internal cohesion of the new ruling party was based less on the strategic objectives of *Felipismo* than on the authoritarian leadership of Felipe González and Alfonso Guerra, the hierarchical structure of decision-making within the party, and the almost complete control of the party organization by the Guerristas. Only one group of militants, the politically marginal Izquierda Socialista (the 'Socialist Left'), was formally accepted as a critical 'sector' within the PSOE. In the course of the Socialists' second term of office, and particularly on the eve of the 32nd party congress in 1990, this picture of ostensible consensus dramatically changed as personal and factional differences were increasingly brought into the open. As a reaction to this, the top echelons of the party began to speak rather euphemistically of different 'sensibilities' within the PSOE (see for instance the interview with Felipe González in *El País*, 9 December 1990). In May 1991, a publication of the party's Sistema Foundation (presided over by Alfonso Guerra) for the first time reported four, more or less competing, 'sensibilities' (Escudero 1991; see also *El País*, 24 May 1991). These were as follows:

1 A reformist political orientation, centred on the Guerristas and the party apparatus, which 'was and still is the backbone of Spanish Socialism'. This orientation has endowed the PSOE with an 'anti-dogmatic flexibility' and a great capacity to adapt itself to changing political circumstances (Escudero refers to the abandonment of Marxism and the change of the party's stand in favour of NATO membership), and has been the main source of programmatic inspiration with respect to the Socialist project of 1982 (particularly its stress on progressive, social modernization). Moreover, it has been responsible for the maintenance of internal party discipline (limiting the divulgence of the inevitable tensions between the Socialists in government and those in the party apparatus, i.e. between the 'logics of conduct' and the logics of the Socialist

project, as much as possible) and the successful election campaigns. In the course of the 1980s, these latter virtues of the reformist political orientation had also become its inherent weakness. First, the party's hierarchical and centralized decision-making and the control from above of the (appointment and functioning of) party representatives in the institutions at state, regional and local level curtailed intra-party democracy, and increasingly hindered new initiatives and, in general, political creativity. Second, and related to its 'anti-dogmatic', electorist strategy, this orientation was unable to reformulate the Socialist project with an eye to the future.

2 A rationalist economic orientation, centred on the technocrats in the Socialist government and headed by the Minister of Economics and Finance, Carlos Solchaga, which has directed the economic modernization and the 'supra-national integration' of Spain, on the one hand, and contributed to the transcending of traditional socialist dogmas with respect to the planification of, and state intervention in, the economy, on the other. Its shortcomings are threefold. First, this orientation is responsible for the deterioration of the relationship between the PSOE and the trade unions. Second, it has put too little emphasis on the promotion of a proper national, industrial basis. Third, it has shown an excessive indifference to the political costs of the economic adjustment measures it thought necessary to implement.

3 A radical democratic orientation, centred on militants like the ex-Minister of Education (and the successor to the late Francisco Fernández Ordóñez as Minister of Foreign Affairs in 1992), Javier Solana, the ex-minister José María Maravall, and the president of the Autonomous Community of Madrid, Joaquín Leguina. Though this tendency aims at deepening 'political liberalism as the basis of democratic Socialism', its main concern has been the promotion of intra-party democracy, and, hence, the curtailment of the influence of the Guerristas.

4 Finally, an orientation of renewal (*orientación renovadora*), centred on people like Escudero himself, who have developed the party's '*Programa 2000*' (see pp. 89–90). It aims at giving the reformist political orientation a new impetus inasmuch as it attempts to reformulate the Socialist project, and to renew the Socialists' objectives for the future.

In the following section we will concentrate on the most constant personal confrontation and factional strife within the PSOE, i.e. that between Alfonso Guerra and Carlos Solchaga, and between the so-called Guerristas, on the one hand, and the technocrats in the successive Socialist governments, on the other.

The party versus the government: Guerristas against 'social liberals'

According to Manuel Escudero, the four above-mentioned 'sensibilities' in the PSOE are by no means irreconcilable. In fact, the proximity of the orientation of renewal to the Guerristas, and the understanding between proponents of the radical democratic orientation and the technocrats, may lead to a greater degree of pluralism and a political debate on the future of Spanish Socialism to the extent that the 'radicals' and 'renewers' are able to bridge the gap between the two main factions. Developments in the late 1980s and early 1990s, however, did not suggest an increasing willingness to compromise, or an emerging consensus of opinion with respect to the way in which the party's and the government's strategic objectives are to be achieved.

From the very start of the first Socialist mandate, internal conflicts over the contents and general direction of the government's social, economic and foreign policies existed, though they were rarely exposed to the outside world. This was mainly because the 'neo-liberals' (who liked to call themselves 'social liberals') were initially much less assertive than the Guerristas, who not only controlled the party apparatus but also occupied the second most important seat in the government. The balance of power between the Guerristas and neo-liberals in favour of the former was clearly indicated by the forced resignation, in 1985, of the Minister of Economics and Finance, Miguel Boyer, after a prolonged confrontation with vice prime minister Alfonso Guerra. The immediate cause was the failed attempt of Boyer to increase his power in government. In the context of a reshuffle of the Cabinet, he claimed the post of second vice-premier, to be created next to that of Alfonso Guerra, and the creation of a homogeneous team of ministers and state secretaries in the field of economics and finance, consisting of specialists sympathetic to his ideas of economic adjustment. Both demands were directed at rationalizing and centralizing decision-making on economic matters, and at curtailing the public deficit without interdepartmental competition (between, for instance, agriculture or industry, on the one hand, and economics and finance, on the other). In overplaying his hand, Boyer prepared his own defeat. It was the opposition of Guerra to an omnipotent 'superminister' that finally led to the replacement of Boyer by Carlos Solchaga (see Lomana 1987: 217).

Though this example seems to indicate that the main issue at stake was the distribution of power rather than the incompatibility of different ideologies, some additional remarks have to be made in order to understand the continuation of the conflict between Guerristas and technocrats after Boyer had left the government. It has been frequently reported that Guerra did not interfere in matters of economic policy, and that he agreed on the general direction of the economic adjustment policy. In fact, he was less concerned with or interested in international economic integration and the mechanisms and instruments of economic restructuring and modernization (which he by and large viewed as necessary and inevitable), than with domestic politics and the securing of a stable power base for the Socialist party. In this sense it is not accurate to interpret the continuous Guerra–Boyer/Solchaga confrontation as a mere Left–Right one, expressing an ideological collision between the syndicalist/socialist orientation and the neo-liberal one. The pragmatist Guerra always outstripped the dogmatist Guerra. That is why the sometimes contradictory public statements by Guerra and his continual confrontation with the technocrats always had two things in mind: first, to prevent the 'Solchaguistas' from becoming too powerful, and, hence, to maintain the capacity to impose the primacy of the party apparatus over the government if necessary; and, second, to compensate for the electorally less attractive economic measures, and to guarantee the smooth functioning of the mechanism of 'bureaucratic clientelism'. As to the latter, part of the public spending of the central government had to be diverted to the party's own use, inasmuch as the financing of regional and local projects was intended to meet clear electoral purposes; in this respect an additional contradiction existed with the government's goal of curtailing public deficits. More importantly, however, it was the underlying contradiction between a strategy of consolidating hegemony at home, *inter alia* through the mechanism of neo-corporatist interest mediation, and a strategy of integrating Spain's ruling class into an essentially transnational power configuration that was at stake in the recurrent confrontations between Guerristas and Solchaguistas.

In the course of the second half of the 1980s things were gradually changing in favour of the Solchaguistas in government. First, the relaunching of the process of European integration through the neo-liberal 1992 project increasingly gave legitimacy to the austerity measures of the Spanish technocrats. Second, the economic upswing after 1984–1985 gave them a lot of prestige, both inside and outside the Socialist party. Third, the dominant position of the Guerristas in the party apparatus came increasingly under pressure as a rising number of leading party officials urged pluralism and open debates. Fourth, a couple of private and political scandals further weakened the position of the Guerristas (thereby indirectly strengthening the position of the neo-liberals) and, most importantly, forced Alfonso Guerra to resign as vice-premier in January 1991.[4]

The 31st party congress in January 1988 was perhaps the last manifestation of the way in which the tandem González–Guerra had managed to hide the latent contradictions in the 'Socialist family' during the first years of Socialist rule. In his opening speech to the congress, González fiercely defended the economic policy of his government, asserting that 'economic growth is socialism' (*El País*, 23 January 1988). At the same time, leading party executives announced a 'new phase in the Socialist project' and a '*giro social*'. In an interview with *El País*, for example, Alfonso Guerra summarized the basic elements of this new phase: the fundamental importance of strong and sound relations with the Socialist trade union UGT, the 'socialization of wealth' and a 'compromise of solidarity', the defence of a mixed economy and the promotion of public enterprise, and, finally, the control of the technocrats: a situation in which technocrats take political decisions and politicians are left with the technical details had to be reversed, and the basic criteria for political decision-making had to become social ones in the years ahead (*El País*, 22 January 1988). The main function of this discourse was clear from the onset: it did not mark the start of a change in policy, but was merely intended to prevent the increasing tensions between the Socialist government and the UGT from becoming the central issue during the party congress, and to prevent the 'neo-liberal' tendency from being implicitly recognized as the best representative of the future orientation of Spanish Socialism.

During the 32nd party congress of November 1990, then, the factional differences came openly to the fore. It was in the course of the preparatory phase that Carlos Solchaga started an offensive against the Guerristas and their dominant position in the party's highest authority between congresses, viz. its federal committee, and in the executive committee. Some of the members of both bodies had to be re-elected by the party congress, and Solchaga not only demanded his own entry to the party executive, but also that of some of the adherents to the so-called radical democratic orientation, and, in short, a greater pluralism in favour of the liberals and to the detriment of the Guerristas. This attempt dramatically failed since the latter succeeded in closing ranks and asserting their power. Solchaga even concluded that 'Alfonso Guerra and the party apparatus have won the congress' (*El País*, 12 November 1990).

A second outcome of the 32nd party congress was the final approval of the *Programa 2000*. The preparatory work was started just after the second electoral victory of June 1986. A large group of party militants and sympathizers, with a general emphasis on members of the academic community, were invited to contribute to 'an effort of collective reflection', and to a prospective study of Spanish society at the turn of the century, and the role of the Socialist party in it. The formulation of a comprehensive

Socialist project inherent in this study was coordinated by Manuel Escudero and resulted in the so-called *Manifesto of the Programme 2000* of 1991. In the next chapters we will elaborate on the main components of this Programme. Here it is important to note that the 'effort of collective reflection', which was presented as an open debate not only incorporating the major tendencies within the party but also reflecting the embedding of the PSOE in Spanish society, in reality proved to be another example of the growing discrepancy between the Guerristas and the technocrats, and between the neo-liberal policies implemented by the latter and the socialist rhetoric of the party apparatus (see Elorza 1990). Though it was intended to neutralize the internal confrontations by projecting the achievement of the party's social goals into a remote future (thus implicitly recognizing the inevitability of continuing the general course of the economic policy actually pursued in the short term), its coordination by militants of the Guerrista persuasion and the strong involvement of Guerra himself in the final editing of the Programme exposed the whole enterprise to severe criticism. Already at an early stage of the elaboration of the Programme 2000, various Solchaguistas had commented that 'we are concerned with the analysis of today's problems, instead of making sketches of the future', whereas militants of the party's left-wing spoke of a diversion aimed at preventing debates on the real issues (see *Mercado*, 15 January 1988). Criticized by both the right-wing and left-wing of the PSOE, the initiators of Programme 2000 felt obliged to defend themselves against charges of rhetoric and the abuse of power. During the presentation of the Programme in early 1990, they chose to attack the government's economic policy. In clearly referring to Solchaga, Manuel Escudero, for example, indicated that the success of the party's ideological renewal would depend on the effective control of certain 'conservative positions' (*El País*, 2 March 1990).

In the months following the 32nd party congress, the intra-party conflicts reached a climax. In January 1991, Guerra was forced to resign as vice-premier. The subsequent governmental crisis was finally resolved by Felipe González in March: he ignored the wish of Solchaga to become the new vice-premier but he did offer him the coordination of the complete socio-economic sector, including the Ministries of Agriculture, Social Security and Employment, Health, and Infrastructure; he appointed the former Minister of Defence, the Catalan Narcís Serra, as vice-premier;[5] and, in general, he decided to reshuffle the Cabinet in favour of the Solchaguistas (who now controlled the major part of public spending) and to the detriment of the Guerristas (see *El País*, 12 March 1991: 17–23).

OPERATION EUROPE: STILL THE 'CARDINAL AND TRANSCENDENT THOUGHT'?

The most important consequence of the governmental changes in early 1991 was the formal separation of power between the party apparatus and the Socialist government, a precondition for the further integration of Spain into the European heartland of transnational production. The Guerristas were no longer able to control the technocrats from within the government; this in turn confirmed the primacy of short-term macro-economic crisis management over long-term 'socialist' strategic objectives, and, indeed, put an end to the uneasy compromise between those who at least rhetorically wanted to implement some kind of social reform and those who favoured 'instrumental rationality'. In essence we are here dealing with the 'why' as opposed to the 'how', the latter being primarily posed in the following way: how to sustain economic growth, how to adapt national economic structures to an open, European environment, and how to obtain the necessary economic convergence with the most advanced European economies? It would be wrong, however, to equate the 'why' of the Guerristas with an attempt to formulate a proper Socialist discourse. We should rather speak of an 'instrumental ideology', inasmuch as the answers to these questions were instrumental in two senses: it formed an electoral instrument inasmuch as it added, albeit rhetorically, a social component to the economic adjustment measures; and it formed an instrument of power politics as it was used to impose the primacy of the party over the government. In the course of 1991, the Socialist government reasserted its autonomy *vis-à-vis* the party apparatus.

It is important to note that the growing intra-party tensions, and particularly their escalation in the second half of the 1980s and early 1990s, coincided with the relaunching of the process of European integration, first through the signing of the Single European Act in 1986, and second through the preparation of, and eventual agreement on, the creation of a European Political Union in December 1991. Both the Europe '92 project and the phased creation of a European Monetary Union functioned as external levers in the progressive move towards the primacy of macro-economic adjustment over, *inter alia*, social policy, and hence in the strengthening of the technocrats in government *vis-à-vis* the Guerristas in the party apparatus. In the course of this 'technocratization' of policy-making, the original coherence of the Socialists' hegemonic project, and the very foundations on which the hegemony of the PSOE was based, were eroded. Ironically, the declining hegemony of the Socialist government took final shape in the course of the pre-election year 1992, during which the original euphoria of European unification turned again into Euro-pessimism, and the prospect of crisis-induced disintegration became a very realistic one.

'A great nation needs in order to live and develop a cardinal and transcendent thought to orient it,' wrote Sánchez de Toca at the close of the last century (see the quotation at the beginning of this chapter). He referred to the great Hispano-American patria as potentially encompassing this thought, or orientation. Almost a century later, at the conclusion of the Socialist decade, we know that Spain experienced a long-term process of economic, social, and political modernization, and, as a result of this, full integration into Western (and increasingly European) structures of economic and political co-operation. We also know that Spain did embark on incorporation in the heartland of world capitalism instead of developing closer ties with Latin America. And it was the Socialist party which most explicitly tried to regenerate the Spanish nation through the formulation of 'a cardinal and transcendent thought to orient it'. The ideals of European unification encompassed this thought, this orientation. Once this orientation was established, the main components of Spanish foreign policy were subordinated to it, as we shall see in the next chapter. And the 'nation's domestic policy' became subordinated to the Socialists' European project, as will be shown in Chapter 5. However, the rise to hegemony of this particular orientation depended on the extent to which the Spanish Socialists could articulate different visions of the world in such a way that their potential antagonism was neutralized (see Chapter 1). Initially, both the Spanish labour movement and the largest part of business supported the Socialist policy and succeeded in neutralizing their potential antagonism. In the course of the second half of the 1980s, and in part as a reaction to the 'extended relaunching' of European integration, however, overt opposition, first by labour (Chapter 5) and then by national capital (Chapter 6), exposed the inherent contradictions of 'Operation Europe'.

In this context, the intra-party conflicts between the technocrats and Guerristas, and their final settlement, point to one of the most important paradoxes during the Socialist decade. They show the continual and eventually abortive attempt to reconcile national socio-economic interests (i.e. labour and part of Spanish business) with enhanced internationalization, and to synthesize a left-wing, populist discourse with an increasing externally induced need to implement a pragmatic austerity policy aimed at macro-economic convergence with the most developed economies of the EC.

In the next chapters we will deal with three constituent elements of the European project of the Spanish Socialists: their foreign policy; their socio-economic policy; and their relationship with the Spanish business community, particularly bank capital. On the one hand, we will continue the line of reasoning set out in the present chapter: besides an analysis of the original goals, their relative importance as coherent parts of more comprehensive policy-making, and the subordination of domestic politics to the government's European project (as part of the so-called internationalization of the Spanish Lockeian state in a transnational European configuration) during the 'Socialist decade', we will consider the conflicts between different party factions, and between the Socialist government and some elements in civil society with regard to the different domestic implications of this comprehensive project. In Chapter 4 we will argue that the subordination of traditional foreign policy objectives to the 'cardinal and transcendent thought' of European unification seemed the least problematic, since nationwide consensus with respect to the European vocation of Spain was firmly established in the course of the 1980s. Until the consequences of the Maastricht Treaty came to the fore, the only conflict that arose over the general line of foreign policy was related to Spain's membership of NATO. Once this conflict was settled after the referendum of 1986, agreement among the principal political and social forces on the general foreign policy orientation was the rule. In the following chapter on economic policy, it will be shown that conflicts arose on its general, and, as the left-wing opposition argued, increasingly neo-liberal direction: first and foremost with the Spanish trade unions, and second within the Socialist party itself between the so-called technocrats, on the one hand, and the party apparatus, on the other. Finally, in Chapter 6 the conflicts between the Spanish government and segments of Spanish bank capital will be dealt with. In particular the Socialist strategy to concentrate public and private banks as part of the European strategy initially met with great opposition from the most traditional sections of the Spanish bourgeoisie.

Another thread of reasoning in the next chapters is related to the supposition of Spain's increasing incorporation in the Lockeian heartland of transnational production, the internationalization of important state functions, and the progressive transnationalization of Spanish civil society. In the next chapter, this will be illustrated by the shift from traditional, state-centred, power politics to the embedding of foreign policy objectives in a European setting. The modifications in the Spanish security and defence policies are cases in point. In the chapter on economic policy the stress will be *inter alia* on the rising structural power of transnational capital and its constraints on the policy autonomy of the Socialists in the field of macro-economics. Moreover, the industrial policy which was implemented to adapt Spanish business to an increasingly competitive environment, and the active promotion of a European dimension and outlook by national public and private capital will be dealt with. In the chapter on banking, this line will be continued in so far as the Socialist strategy with respect to mergers is to be explained in terms of the more comprehensive attempt to create a strong, competitive, transnational business of Spanish origin. This last chapter on Spanish banking also attempts to offer a mirror image of the process of modernization as described in Chapter 2. In analysing the emergence and subsequent development of private bank capital in the course of the twentieth century, two additional objectives are set: one is to explain the decisive role Spanish bank capital as a whole has played in the long-term transition of Spain from an isolated, backward country at the end of the nineteenth century to an integrated part of the Lockeian heartland of transnational production at the end of the twentieth century; the other is to explain, through an analysis of the long-term fragmentation of bank capital, the different positions of individual private banks in the forced process of concentration and centralization during the late 1980s.

APPENDIX: RESULTS OF THE ELECTIONS TO THE CONGRESS, 1977–1989

Table 2 Distribution of total number of 350 seats in Cortes

	1977	1979	1982	1986	1989
UCD	165	168	11	–	–
PSOE	118	121	202	184	175
AP/CD/CP/PP	16	9	107	105	107
PCE-PSUC/IU	20	23	4	7	17
CDS	–	–	2	19	14
PDC/CiU	11	8	12	18	18
PNV	8	7	8	5	5
OTHERS	12	14	4	12	14

UCD	Unión de Centro Democrático.
PSOE	Partido Socialista Obrero Español (and Socialistes de Catalunya).
AP/CD/CP/PP	Alianza Popular in 1977; Coalición Democrática in 1979; Coalición Popular in 1982 and 1986; and Partido Popular in 1989.
PCE-PSUC/IU	Partido Comunista de España and the Partit Socialista Unificat de Catalunya in 1977, 1979, and 1982; and Izquierda Unida in 1986 and 1989.
CDS	Centro Democrático y Social.
PDC/CiU	Pacte Democràtic per Catalunya in 1977; and Convergència i Unió in 1979, 1982, 1986 and 1989.
PNV	Partido Nacionalista Vasco.
OTHERS	In 1989: Herri Batasuna, Partido Andalucista, Unión Valenciana, Eusko Alkartasuna, Enskadiko Ezkerra, Partido Aragonés Regionalista, and Agrupaciones Independientes de Canarias.

Sources: Gunther *et al.* 1988: 402; Amodia 1990: 296; *El País*, 28 May 1991.

4 The NATO referendum and beyond
From great power ambition to small power reality

INTRODUCTION

In the previous chapter it was argued that the ideals of full participation in the process of European integration encompassed the 'cardinal and transcendent thought' on which the Socialists oriented themselves in formulating their hegemonic project. Convinced that the course of Spanish history had been decisively influenced by developments in other parts of the European continent (see, for instance, Morán 1980: 292), and confronted by major changes at the global (and European) level, the only alternative for Spain was to accelerate its ongoing Europeanization. Only by actively participating in, and eventually giving direction to, the process of European, economic and political, unification could the promotion of essential national interests be guaranteed.

It is important to remember that the socialist decade coincided with the reactivation of the process of European integration. The final negotiations between Spain and the EC, and its formal entry on 1 January 1986, took place in conjunction with the presentation of the Commission's White Paper and the signing of the Single European Act (SEA) in 1986. This implied that the conclusion of the period of transition would coincide with the scheduled completion of the internal market on 1 January 1993. After becoming an EC member, negotiations were started on a comprehensive revision of the Treaty of Rome, eventually leading to the signing of the Treaty concerning the European Union (the so-called Treaty of Maastricht) on 7 February 1992. Spain obviously played a secondary role in the initiation and conclusion of both developments. In fact, from a traditional state-centric view of foreign policy, it could be argued that it entered the chess game of European political and diplomatic relations as a small power, not being able to promote its foreign policy objectives in the final agreements in a substantial way.

This discrepancy between the Socialists' ambitions and the reality of Spain's playing second fiddle in European affairs was one of the principal grounds on which the neo-liberal economic policy was legitimized during the socialist decade, as we will see in Chapter 5. Economic convergence with the leading economies was seen as a necessary precondition to active participation in the redefinition of the role of Europe in world affairs. In the field of foreign policy this reasoning raises some important questions: how is the Europeanist orientation of the PSOE to be reconciled with the pro-NATO position of the Socialist government in the 1986 referendum? In general, what is the stand of the Spanish Socialists on the ongoing debate between 'Atlanticists' and 'Europeanists' with respect to the future direction of the process of European integration? To what extent are the traditional foreign policy objectives of Spain subordinated to the 'cardinal and transcendent thought' of European union? What role is played by the intra-party confrontations between Guerristas and technocrats in the formulation of the Spanish European policy? Finally, to what extent does the European orientation of the González government still reflect elements of the traditional party ideology? This chapter is an attempt to formulate an integrated answer to these questions.

CONTINUITY AND CHANGE UNDER SOCIALIST RULE

Spanish foreign policy since World War II has been characterized by a constant emphasis on seeking recognition as an equal partner in international affairs. This foreign policy goal initially took the form of trying to end the international isolation that resulted from the Spanish support of the Berlin–Rome axis (see Portero 1989). The cold war at the end of the 1940s and early 1950s made its realization much easier, important bilateral contacts were established, and membership of the United Nations was assured, but participation in the Western Alliance was impeded on several occasions. NATO membership was refused, Spain was excluded from the Marshall Plan, and deliberately left out of the negotiations which would eventually lead to the creation of the EC.

In the 1960s this search for international recognition was gradually transformed into an attempt to neutralize the international image of a socio-politically and economically backward country, a struggle for respectability which went beyond mere formal recognition. To some extent, Franco's Spain always remained an outcast with respect to international decision-making. For Franco, one way to deal with the continuation of this relatively isolated position of Spain during the 1960s was to refer now and then to the importance for Spain of its historical ties with Latin America

98 The Socialist decade (1982–1992)

(see *Pensamiento Político de Franco* 1975: part II, 765–835). Spain as the '*madre patria*' of the great family of Hispano-American nations seemed to serve the goal of periodically compensating for the Spanish inferiority complex with respect to the outside world. Meanwhile, it was the opening up of the Spanish economy, the internationalization of capital and the subsequent process of socio-economic and political modernization that were in the end responsible not only for the growing orientation towards the EC, but also for the gradual international recognition and self-acceptance of Spain as a Western nation.[1]

Under the PSOE government some of the traditionally autonomous and main foreign policy objectives of Spain[2] were viewed as inextricably bound up with, and even subordinated to, the country's European orientation. An illustration of this is given by the military strategic component of Spain's foreign policy. That is, under Socialist rule Spain was finally integrated into the Atlantic Alliance. All the same, the Socialist government did not view this entry into NATO as a foreign policy aim in itself. It was seen as a pragmatic step on the way to an independent European security policy; the strengthening of the European pillar within NATO could precede, and even form a necessary precondition to, the subsequent establishment of a legal and institutional framework for a truly European defence community. Even the Western European Union (WEU), of which Spain became a member in 1988, was initially seen as a kind of surrogate with respect to this ultimate foreign security objective.

Other illustrations of this Europeanization of Spanish foreign policy during the 1980s are offered by the changes in the so-called special relationships of Spain with Latin America and the Middle East. These relationships were increasingly subordinated to the country's involvement with Europe, and in particular to the European Political Co-operation (EPC).

In the second place, the priority of European integration is inextricably bound up with the fact that economic factors became extremely important with respect to the formulation of comprehensive foreign policy objectives. Especially after 1982 this phenomenon resulted in an increasingly close connection and strong reciprocation between domestic and foreign policies. The growing economic dependence of Spain on the countries of the Common Market did not fail to have its impact on the formulation of Spanish foreign policy aims, but it is equally correct to state that its logical consequence, i.e. the entrance into the EC on 1 January 1986, has been (and still is) the principal motive force behind the accelerated modernization of the Spanish economy. In this sense, it seems correct to argue that the domestic (economic) policy of the Socialist government has become the continuation of its foreign policy aims and ambitions. In other words, the internationalization of the state, as such part and parcel of the process of transnationalization, has resulted in the internationalization of domestic policy, on the one hand, and the domestification of foreign policy, on the other. The two processes are sides of the same coin: the transnationalization and Europeanization of Spain.

In the third place, an important and constant element in the foreign policy of Spain since World War II, the continual search for international recognition, was altered in a fundamental way: the Socialist government moved away from the strictly defensive strategy of the Franquist dictatorship, strongly related to internal political motives, to an offensive strategy, grafted on to international political ambitions. The aim of the PSOE was to make Spain one of the leading nations in Europe, and to be at the centre of European developments. If the Socialist government succeeded in this ambitious objective, so it was argued, then it would not only be able to convert the more progressive elements of its own foreign policy into general European policy within the framework of the EC, but it would also be much easier to realize other aims, such as a common security policy.

With respect to the realization of these aims and ambitions, in the medium term, however, the González government depended on the achievement of its economic adjustment policy. The extent to which Spain was able to keep up with the more developed and economically powerful member states would be both the basis and precondition for the realization of the ambitious (and offensive) elements in the Europeanist policy of the PSOE. The degree of success was in turn inextricably bound up with the way in which the Spanish economy would adjust to the consequences of the end of the transitional period (as laid down in the Treaty of Accession between Spain and the EC) and the creation of the Single European Market after 1992. And this was, finally, in part dependent on the way in which the Spanish government would be able to maintain some kind of social dialogue with the major trade unions (see Chapter 5).

In the remainder of this chapter both the subordination of foreign policy objectives to the general European project and the growing importance of economic rationality in decision-making during the Socialist decade will be illustrated by an analysis of the continuities and changes in Spanish security policy, and an analysis of the Spanish position in the 'extended relaunching' of European integration in the late 1980s and early 1990s.

We will first take a closer look at the programmatic deradicalization of the PSOE, exemplified by the changing position of the party leadership with respect to the role of Spain in the Atlantic Alliance, and eventually leading to the government's pro-NATO stance in the national debate preceding the referendum of 1986. In the section on p. 114, the main, non-security, elements of the Socialists' European policy will be treated: we will first consider the Spanish presidency of the EC in the first half of 1989, and, second, the role of Spain in the process of European unification in the late 1980s and early 1990s. In this section we will deal in particular with the consequences of full EC membership for the reformulation of the Socialists' European policy objectives. Finally, an epilogue will focus on post-Maastricht developments and the growing discrepancy between the government's ambitions and the country's economic realities (Blaisse 1991). It will be stated that the strategic objectives of the Socialist ruling party have been increasingly subordinated to the pragmatism of short-term crisis management, and that Operation Europe has merely become the legitimation of economic restructuring and macro-economic austerity, the latter becoming goals in themselves, serving the short-term interests of important sections of Spanish and foreign capital, while paying mere lip service to traditional social goals.

THE NATO REFERENDUM OF 1986

The post-World War II incorporation of Spain into the Western security system was concomitant with the emergence of the cold war and the subsequent termination of the political isolation of the country and its regime. It took the form, however, of a bilateral pact with the United States, on the basis of which Spain received financial and military aid and the United States obtained the right to use military bases on Spanish soil (see Viñas 1981; Marquina Barrio 1986: 498–574; 1989: 49ff.). These agreements, the so-called '*Pactos de Madrid*' of 1953, were renewed in 1963, 1970, 1976, 1982, and 1988. According to Antonio Marquina Barrio, since the 1953 pacts every renewal signified a progressive reduction of the American presence in Spain and growing Spanish control over the military bases, particularly in the 1970s and 1980s (Marquina Barrio 1989: 71). On the one hand, this development reflected the fundamental shift in the role of the United States in the international system, the decline of US hegemonic leadership, but it also reflected the long-term transformation of Spanish foreign policy objectives from an acceptance of absolute American hegemony, based on internal political and military strategic grounds, to a reorientation on Western Europe, based on politico-economic considerations. This restructuring of Spanish foreign security priorities resulted in higher aspirations to become a full member of NATO and the EC, aspirations which became even more pronounced after the death of Franco in 1975. As a matter of fact, both memberships were increasingly linked during the process of democratic transition, not only by the UCD governments, but also by the member states of both NATO and the EC: integration into NATO was presented as the key to membership of the EC.

After the death of Franco, it took some years before the gradual 'multilateralization' (Rodríguez 1988) of Spanish security policy was formalized. It has been said that Adolfo Suárez, the first UCD prime minister, was reluctant to pursue entry to NATO (see Sarasqueta 1985: 43–44). After his resignation in 1981, the next government of Leopoldo Calvo Sotelo made the rash decision to enter NATO. The haste with which this step was taken is to be explained by the imminence of general elections and the anticipated victory of the PSOE (see Tusell 1988: 14–15). In the words of Calvo Sotelo:

> I suspected that the decision [to join NATO] would be particularly difficult for a government in which sectors of the left were certain to participate, possibly at high levels . . . The decision to commit Spain to an Atlantic Alliance would not be easy for a government (or a coalition) of the left, though such a government might accept it as a *fait accompli*.
> (quoted in Pérez Royo 1988: 20; see also Calvo Sotelo 1990: 123–141)

Indeed, events happened as planned, but only after the Socialist leadership had taken great pains to explain to the Spanish population its shift from an anti-American, neutralist stand in the security debate to a pro-NATO position in the 1986 referendum.

'¡OTAN, de entrada, no!'

In 1976, in the early days of his leadership of the PSOE, Felipe González argued that NATO was nothing but a military superstructure introduced by the US with no other reason than to guarantee the survival of the capitalist system. Ten years later, on 4 February 1986, he pronounced himself before parliament in favour of NATO membership, and he stated that breaking off ties with the Atlantic Alliance would cause a 'trauma' with unpredictable consequences (see *Cambio* 16, 17 February 1986). In the nationwide debate that preceded the referendum of 12 March 1986, a great deal of stress was laid on this alleged inconsistency, as if the PSOE leadership in general, and González in particular, had changed their opinion all of a sudden. In reality, and notwithstanding the public statements of party officials, the PSOE had slowly but surely deradicalized its political platform on international security issues.

The foreign policy of the PSOE was formulated for the first time in the so-called 'Transition Programme', which was approved during the 27th congress of the party in December 1976. Four basic directions were outlined in this document: recovery of territorial independence and integrity (a clear reference to the military presence of the United States); participation in the process of European construction; solidarity and co-operation with the Third World; and struggle for world peace, justice and progress (see Barbé 1981: 171; and especially Garcia i Segura 1986a: 63–69). More specifically, the dismantling of all foreign military bases on Spanish soil had to carried out, the relations with the United States had to be radically reconsidered, no Alliance treaty or military relation was to be accepted without the explicit approval of the Spanish people, and a policy of active neutrality had to be implemented.

> As a political and economic imperative, a democratic Spain cannot stay outside the construction of a united Europe which overcomes an obsolete nationalism and provides a framework for the development of Socialism, independent of the imperialist powers and in co-operation with the Third World.
>
> (quoted in Barbé 1981: 172)

In this formulation the Europeanist strategy of the PSOE is well summarized. Though this foreign policy objective was to be progressively emptied of social and ideological content in the next fifteen years, it contained the basic premises of the party's project: supra-national Europeanism versus nationalism (in socio-political terms); regionalization versus globalization (in economic terms); and Europeanization versus Atlanticism (in terms of foreign policy and European security issues).

In the course of the following year the initial statements of the 'Transition Programme' were carefully deradicalized, though González continued to speak of Spanish neutrality 'from a military point of view' during the 1977 II Congress of Socialist Parties of Southern Europe in Madrid (Garcia i Segura 1986b: 45). During a parliamentary session on foreign policy issues in September 1977, the then secretary of foreign relations of the PSOE, Luis Yáñez, 'de-ideologized' some elements while quoting literally from the text of the 'Transition Programme': the word 'radically' was left out in the original statement of 'the relations with the United States have to be radically reconsidered'; the phrase 'Europe of the Workers' was changed to 'Europe of the Nations', and terms like 'relations of production', 'capitalism', 'imperialism' simply disappeared.

Moreover, a new element bearing on future NATO membership was introduced: this question could, among other things, be subject to a referendum (see Barbé 1981: 174). The following year, and looking back to the accomplishments of the previous year, the same Luis Yáñez concluded that 'we have moved from the exclusive realization of a foreign policy of the party to the development of a foreign policy of the state . . .' (quoted in Garcia i Segura 1986b: 51). This significant differentiation between a foreign policy of the Socialist party and the official one of the state formed one of the first expressions of the opportunist course the PSOE would progressively follow in the next years, eventually leading to the affirmative position of the Socialist government in the NATO referendum. It also gave the initial impetus to a division within the party between a programmatic and 'pragmatic' wing. As a matter of fact, in the same year (1978) another spokesman of the PSOE on foreign policy issues, and first foreign minister after the 1982 elections, Fernando Morán, criticized the primacy of international power politics in the formulation of foreign policy. 'Without taking into consideration the kind of society we want to construct,' he wrote, '. . . we fall into a short-sighted pragmatism' (*pragmatismo miope*) (quoted in Barbé 1981: 174–175; see also Morán 1980).

In the following years the party's leadership continued to neutralize carefully the most radical elements in the political platform with respect to foreign policy (and security) issues. On the question of possible NATO membership, however, the party remained clear, at least until the end of 1981. In the electoral programme of 1979 it was explicitly stated that the 'PSOE is opposed to the linking of Spain to any of the military blocs, because of the limitation this implies with respect to our independence and national sovereignty' (*España y la OTAN* 1986: 305). The party's 28th congress of 1979 did not deal extensively with foreign policy issues because of the emergence of internal power struggles during the sessions, eventually leading to the consolidation of Felipe González' absolute leadership of the party. The 29th congress of October 1981 repeated once more that 'the PSOE is opposed to the integration of Spain into NATO', but it also stipulated that the NATO membership of Spain (which the Calvo Sotelo government announced in February 1981, and indeed, effectuated on 30 May 1982) would be subject to a consultative referendum if the PSOE stayed in power (ibid.: 312).

In the course of 1981 the PSOE launched a campaign against the decision of the Calvo Sotelo government to incorporate Spain into NATO. In this context the party presented the famous document called *50 Preguntas sobre la OTAN* (October 1981), in which general questions were answered with respect to the functioning of NATO, the relation of Spain with NATO, and the role of the UCD government (*España y la OTAN* 1986: 314–330). Though this document was quite explicit and unequivocal as to the party's opposition, the slogan which accompanied the anti-NATO campaign was rather ambiguous: '¡*OTAN, de entrada, no!*' ('NATO, right away, no!'). According to Javier Tusell, this slogan was, despite its ambiguity, 'interpreted unequivocally as a testimony of pacifism and reluctance to involve Spain in a militarist NATO' (Tusell 1988: 15–16). This may be true, but such an interpretation by the Spanish people is one thing, while the intentions of the party's strategists are another. Pere Vilanova is right in stating that this slogan for the first time suggests that an unequivocally hostile attitude had made way for a critical stance with respect to the conditions under which the integration into NATO would take place (Vilanova 1985a: 15). As a matter of fact, freely translated, the Spanish slogan '¡OTAN, de entrada, no!' also means 'no, not in this way', or indeed, 'not under these conditions' (Vilanova 1985b: 6). In this respect, it is therefore reasonable to conclude that the PSOE had changed its position considerably by the end of 1981, though this change was not yet reflected in official party documents. The consolidation of this new foreign policy with respect to NATO, Vilanova rightly states, would take time, but time was not available since the general elections of October 1982 resulted in an absolute majority for the Socialist party in parliament (Vilanova 1985a: 15).

The 'decalogue' and the conditionality clauses of the NATO referendum

From the above two tendencies must be distinguished: the party's shift from ideology to pragmatism, anticipating its future role as a ruling party; and its anti-NATO rhetoric as an opposition party in the 1981–1982 period. This ambiguity is reflected in the defence sections of the 1982 electoral programme and the deliberate confusion the government created, at least until 1984, with respect to its own position in the debate.

In the political platform of the 1982 elections, it is stated that the 'PSOE reaffirms its philosophy of opposition to the policy of military blocs', but a withdrawal from NATO is not mentioned. Instead, the PSOE will freeze negotiations with respect to the Spanish integration into the integrated military structure, and call a referendum on the issue of membership (*España y la OTAN* 1986: 333).

Only in the course of 1984 did some clarity arise regarding the government's position and the procedures to be followed. Two events are essential in this respect: the 30th congress of the PSOE in December 1984 and, more importantly, the parliamentary debate on the state of the nation in October of that same year. It suffices to treat the latter, because the resolutions of the 30th congress on foreign policy show no breach with the previous statements of Felipe González in October (for the complete text of these resolutions, see *España y la OTAN* 1986: 333–341). This link was explicitly affirmed in the Proposal for a Policy of Peace and Security of December 1985 (ibid.: 361–364).

In the parliamentary debate on the state of the nation, González launched his so-called 'decalogue', a ten-point programme on Spanish foreign policy. It announced the following policies:

1. The maintenance of Spain's membership in the Atlantic Alliance.
2. Spain will not be incorporated into the integrated military structure of NATO.
3. Spain will maintain a bilateral relation with the United States on security aspects, but its military presence on Spanish soil will be progressively reduced.
4. The non-nuclearization of Spain remains an incontestable principle, backed by almost unanimous support in parliament.
5. For the time being, the Non-proliferation Treaty will not be signed.
6. The participation of Spain in the WEU is desirable, though it is necessary to wait for the results of the Spanish integration into the EC first.
7. Given the new status of Spain, the Gibraltar issue needs a definitive solution.
8. The active work of Spain within disarmament forums must be continued and reinforced.
9. The development of a network of bilateral agreements within the field of defence co-operation with other Western European countries will be continued.
10. The Joint Strategic Plan of the Spanish armed forces must be included in the dialogue between the PSOE and the opposition parties in order to establish a consensus within the field of defence as regards its domestic and international dimension.

For the literal text of the 'decalogue' see *España y la OTAN* 1986: 361–363; see also Vilanova 1985a: 20–21; Armero 1989: 173–174; and Pollack 1987: 123.

In the final analysis, this 'decalogue' was intended to pave the way for the referendum, i.e. its content, and to influence its outcome. In the first place the conditions were set forth under which Spain would remain within the Atlantic Alliance (see the clauses of the referendum below). In the second place, a consensus with the opposition was aimed at, which would then give support to the 'Sí' in the referendum. Finally, the international security of Spain was inextricably bound up with the security of Europe, and with the more comprehensive theme of the process of European integration.

In the end, on 12 March 1986, the NATO referendum was held, after a passionate debate both inside and outside parliament. The question and conditionality clauses of the NATO referendum ran as follows:

> The Government considers it in the national interest that Spain remains in the Atlantic Alliance and resolves that established on the following terms:
>
> 1 The participation of Spain in the Atlantic Alliance will not include its incorporation in the integrated military structure.
> 2 The prohibition on the installation, storing or introduction of nuclear arms on Spanish territory will be continued.
> 3 The progressive reduction of the military presence of the United States in Spain will be proceeded with.
>
> 'Do you consider it advisable for Spain to remain in the Atlantic Alliance according to the terms set forth by the Government of the nation?'[3]

The outcome of the referendum was influenced by a couple of factors, of which the call for abstention by the centre and right-wing parties was certainly one of the most important. This resulted in a participation of 59.73 per cent of the Spanish electorate (and hence the very high abstention percentage of 40.27). Some 52.53 per cent voted 'Sí', 39.84 per cent voted 'No', and 6.54 per cent cast a blank vote (*El País*, 13 March 1986).

Explaining the volte-face of the PSOE

The shift from an ideological, anti-NATO and anti-American stand in 1976 to a pragmatic position in favour of remaining in NATO in 1986 has been subject to different interpretations. More often than not, explanations were coloured by the author's personal standpoint in the national debate prior to the referendum.[4]

In attempting to cover the major objective conditions for the Socialists' deradicalization, we may start with the five domestic variables Pollack distinguishes to explain the volte-face of the PSOE: the position of the Spanish Communist party (PCE); the link between the Socialist party and the Socialist trade unions; the degree of ideological commitment of the PSOE; the factional differences within the PSOE and their impact on the 'pragmatic U-turn' on the NATO issue; and, finally, the national economic factors favouring international co-operation and integration (see Pollack 1987: 162–168).

The political landscape after the 1982 elections certainly played an important role (see the Appendix to the previous chapter). The PSOE obtained nearly twice as many seats as the second largest party in parliament, the CP; the former ruling party UCD almost disappeared from the political scene; and the Spanish Communist party saw its representation in the Cortes reduced from twenty-three to four seats. In this situation, the main opposition parties were in no position to influence the Socialist government, or, in the case of the PCE, to press for a negative decision with regard to the Spanish NATO membership. This magnificent point of departure, characterized by a weakened left-wing opposition and a divided right wing, was clearly illustrated by the ambivalence of the Coalición Popular (CP) of Manuel Fraga. In an act of pure political obstruction, he advised his electorate to abstain from voting.[5] This schizophrenia between the party's pro-Atlantic platform and its advice on how to vote showed the impotence of the right-wing opposition, and particularly its incapacity to formulate an alternative to the Socialists' foreign policy project (see also García Cotarelo and López Nieto 1988).

Besides the discussions in the Spanish Cortes, all the major actors in civil society participated in the NATO debate in one way or another. The Socialist Unión General de Trabajadores (UGT) and the Communist Comisiones Obreras (CCOO) adopted a clear stand against Spain's remaining in the alliance. One of the resolutions of the 33rd congress of the UGT (in June 1983) called for a policy of neutrality, and demanded a referendum in which the Socialist government should actively defend Spain's withdrawal from NATO (see *España y la OTAN* 1986: 429). The CCOO had declared itself in similar terms in June 1981, and both trade unions presented a joint 'manifest on peace and the withdrawal of Spain from NATO' in October 1984 (ibid.: 430–432). Like the left-wing parliamentary opposition, however, the Spanish trade unions were incapable of influencing the government's security policy. Declining levels of affiliation (see Pérez Díaz 1987: 233ff.) in conjunction with the impact of the economic crisis of the late 1970s and early 1980s weakened their position *vis-à-vis* the Socialist government in a substantial way (see also chapter 5).[6]

On the other side of the social spectrum, the Spanish employers' association Confederación Española de Organizaciones Empresariales (CEOE) supported the policy of obstruction of the CP, and advocated a 'passive abstention' in the referendum (see Díaz-Varela and Guindal 1990: 253–255). It is interesting to note that the largest private banks, at that time still united in the so-called '*Club de los Siete*', jointly published a statement in favour of Spain's membership of NATO. 'An outcome different from a "yes",' they wrote, 'would have incalculable results on the economic perspectives of the nation.' It has been reported that this joint statement was initiated by those members of the '*Club de los Siete*' akin to the neo-liberals in the Socialist government (particularly Claudio Boada and Miguel Boyer), and reluctantly accepted by others (see Rivases 1988: 37–38). As we shall see in Chapter 6, the different strategies of the CEOE and the '*Club de los Siete*', on the one hand, and the differences within the higher echelons of the Spanish banking community, on the other, were clear examples of a more comprehensive schism of the Spanish bourgeoisie during the Socialist decade.

In the light of the discussion in the previous chapter, we may group together two other domestic variables, viz. the Socialist party's ideological commitment and its division into different factions. As we have seen, the ideological deradicalization and subsequent turn to economic 'pragmatism' had been the subject of continual strife between the Guerristas and the technocrats or neo-liberals, and of continual tension between the party and the government. As long as Alfonso Guerra was a member of government, he mediated between the critical sector of the party (by criticizing and controlling the technocrats in government) and the pragmatists (by explaining and defending the main direction of the government's comprehensive project). This Janus-faced political performance was essential in the process of declining ideological commitment during the late 1970s and 1980s. Guerra carefully prevented the two most opposed factions within the PSOE from becoming too powerful; and in the end he always remained loyal to the unquestioned leader González and to the decisions he took. The central role Alfonso Guerra played during the 1980s, i.e. his guidance of the process of deradicalization, can be illustrated by his position in the NATO debate.

Starting from a tradition of Third Worldism, neutralism and anti-Americanism as the basic, defining elements of the foreign policy orientation of the renewed and rejuvenated PSOE (and of the majority of its militants and grassroots support) during the early 1970s, it was a long road indeed towards full Westernization and towards the multilateralization of Spanish security policy in an Atlantic setting. Many party leaders, including the party's specialists on foreign policy matters, had pronounced themselves against Spain's taking sides in the cold war. Non-alignment was preferable to full participation in the (still) bipolar power structure of the 1970s. Fernando Morán was a case in point. This career diplomat had occupied important positions in the Spanish diplomatic service (Argentina, South Africa, Portugal, England, United Nations) during the Franquist regime, and had been Director General of the Department of Africa and Continental Asia of the Ministry of Foreign Affairs during the first post-Franquist government. He was considered a specialist on Africa and the

Third World, on which he had published several books. Besides his professional career he had been active in intellectual and political movements of the so-called democratic opposition in the 1960s. After becoming a militant of the PSOE, he actively participated in the period of democratic transition, *inter alia* as Socialist spokesman in the Commission of Foreign Affairs of the Spanish Senate and as personal adviser to Felipe González. These activities, together with the publication of his influential *Una Política Exterior para España* (Morán 1980), made him the party's authority on foreign policy issues *par excellence*, and the obvious candidate to become the first Socialist Minister of Foreign Affairs after the 1982 elections.

In his 1980 book, Morán had listed a number of reasons for the rejection of Spain's membership of NATO as unnecessary and even counterproductive (ibid.: 94ff.). Outspoken in his pro-European orientation, he pleaded for the eventual construction of a West European defence system without American participation (ibid.: 144–145), and, in the short term, for a modified neutralism *inter alia* characterized by a strong, independent, national defence system, the maintenance of Spain's territorial integrity, a renovation on more equal terms of the bilateral agreements with the United States, and enhanced military co-operation with Spain's direct neighbours, Portugal and France (ibid.: 121). Spain should adopt an intermediate position between neutralism and Third Worldism, on the one hand and the full acceptance of the Atlanticist option, on the other. By the same token, Spain should try to find a mixture between ideology and pragmatism or realism in the formulation of its foreign policy goals. Finally, only by maintaining its relatively autonomous position in the international system could Spain effectively play a role in the creation of a New International Order in which the existing power blocs would become obsolete (see also Morán 1984).

During the first mandate of the Socialist government, a growing rift came to the fore between the Minister of Foreign Affairs, Morán, on the one hand, and the Minister of Defence, Narcís Serra, Minister of Economics and Finance, Miguel Boyer, and Felipe González, on the other. Initially, Morán seemed to obtain support not only from members of the so-called critical sector in the PSOE (who were still inclined to impose their Third Worldist ideology on the party's leadership), but also from leading figures in government and the party apparatus, such as the Ministers of Culture (Javier Solana), Education (José María Maravall), and Health (Ernest Lluch), as well as Alfonso Guerra (see Rodríguez 1988: 65). Before mid-1984, Guerra had frequently expressed his opposition to NATO membership. In an interview in July 1983, for example, he affirmed that 'Spain must not stay in NATO. It must leave' (*El País*, 17 July 1983). One year later, however, he started to move in the opposite direction. In the same newspaper he stated that 'it would not be fair to affirm that NATO limits Spanish sovereignty and increases the nuclear danger' and that 'the Spanish community had not been hurt by forming part of the political committee of NATO' (quoted in Sarasqueta 1985: 106). In the months prior to the referendum, then, he openly defended the government's decision to ask for a popular vote in favour of remaining in NATO (see Guerra 1986).

With hindsight, it can be established that the two principal leaders of the PSOE, i.e. González and Guerra, carefully coordinated their actions and statements in what came to be known as the strategy of '*la ambigüedad calculada*' (calculated ambiguity) (see Vilar 1986: 169–170; and Morán 1990: 370). Having promised a NATO referendum in the 1982 electoral campaign, González initially expressed himself ambiguously as to the exact date of the referendum and the government's advice on how to vote, while at the same time Guerra continued to produce anti-NATO statements. After González had launched the ten points of the Spanish defence policy programme (the 'decalogue') in October 1984, the government started a propaganda campaign in favour of continued NATO membership, while Guerra began to impose strict discipline on the party. Already in December 1984, during the 30th congress of the PSOE, this resulted in the adoption of an official pro-NATO resolution, albeit against the will of a large number of delegates. In the words of Fernando Morán: 'The atmosphere was clearly hostile to remaining in NATO and even to continuing as part of the Treaty of Washington, but the control by the leadership was, as always, almost iron' (Morán 1990: 384). During the next year, and until the referendum in March 1986, the apparatus succeeded in disciplining the majority of the party militants, while the government tried to present its position as the national interest. One essential step was the removal of Fernando Morán as Minister of Foreign Affairs in the cabinet reshuffle of July 1985. He was replaced by the pro-Atlanticist Francisco Fernández Ordóñez, an appointment that was greeted with approval by NATO representatives who spoke of 'the definite end to Spanish governmental ambiguity with respect to NATO' (quoted in Rodríguez 1988: 66). The final referendum, and particularly the additional conditionality clauses, formed the last step in a strategy of finding sufficient grassroots support for continued membership without completely cutting off the traditional ties with the Left both within and outside the PSOE. That both González and Guerra were well aware of this dilemma is illustrated by the former's statement that 'I cannot let them overtake me on the left', and by the latter's 'to my left the abyss' (quoted in Sarasqueta 1985: 107).

The NATO referendum and beyond 111

As we have seen, apart from the Prime Minister, two members of the Socialist government were particularly in favour of keeping Spain in NATO: both Defence Minister Narcís Serra and Economics Minister Miguel Boyer (and his successor Carlos Solchaga) were among the first to openly defend their pro-NATO stance. Though based on different realities, their aims were very similar: their common goal was 'modernization through internationalization' of the Spanish army and the economic structure respectively.

In the case of Defence Minister Serra, the reality of a still powerful and extremely conservative officer corps played a significant role in his pro-NATO stance. Only one year before the Socialists came to power, on 23 February 1981, the most reactionary elements in the Spanish army had tried to stage a coup against the democratic government (see Preston 1984). Although the army as a whole formally accepted its subordination to the democratic system, this failed attempt proved once again the intrinsically authoritarian spirit of a substantial part of the leading officers. Investigations into the political attitudes of the Spanish army in the 1980s point in the same direction (see Pérez Henares *et al.* 1989; see also Cavero 1990: 265ff.). This explains the efforts of the Socialist government to reform the personal structure of the Spanish army, to reduce the great number of commanders, officers, and warrant officers, to professionalize the military, to reform military training, and, in general, to rationalize and modernize the Spanish armed forces. In this context, the multilateralization of Spanish defence policy was thought to provoke a greater homogenization of the Spanish armed forces with the dominant mentality in the Western armies, and to contribute substantially to a profound modernization (see Pérez Henares *et al.* 1989: 74–75).[7]

Perhaps of even greater importance for the understanding of the government's shift towards full support of staying in NATO was the underlying economic motivation, or rather the link with EC membership which the government constantly emphasized. This interconnection of (European) economic and (Atlantic) military integration had a dual purpose: on the one hand, an attempt was made to trade off staying in the Atlantic Alliance with the much desired integration into the EC, and, on the other hand, participation in NATO was viewed as a necessary precondition to '*europeizar*' the Atlantic relationship (Morán 1990: 371) from within, and as a first step towards the formulation of a common European security policy.

As to the first point, already during the rule of the UCD government the link between both memberships was explicitly made, for instance, by the then Foreign Minister Marcelino Oreja (see Pollack 1987: 155). Spain had applied for Community membership in July 1977 and negotiations were opened with the EC in February 1979. Particularly in the period 1980–1981 these negotiations became increasingly problematic as a result of the crisis of the Suárez government in Spain, the presidential elections in France, and problems within the EC on issues like the Community budget. France succeeded in blocking a quick entry of Spain (and Portugal) making it conditional on the prior settlement of the budgetary problems of the EC and on a reform of the Common Agricultural Policy (see Macdonald 1988: 78–79). In this context, the newly elected Socialist government in Spain (confronted with the 'last minute' decision of Calvo Sotelo to push Spain into NATO and the deadlock in the EC negotiations) made an explicit case out of actively supporting remaining in NATO in exchange for the successful conclusion of the application period. Therefore, the strategy of calculated ambiguity not only made sense for domestic political reasons, but it also became a tool in realizing the main Socialist foreign policy objectives. This explains why it was only after the Fontainebleau European Council meeting of June 1984, during which the budgetary crisis was resolved and a final timetable was set for the formal entry of Spain and Portugal, that Felipe González announced his ten-point defence policy programme. During the referendum campaign in 1985 and early 1986, the Socialist government then reversed the linkage between both memberships: the successful conclusion of the negotiations was used as a carrot to obtain a majority vote in favour of staying in NATO (see Tortosa 1985: 104–105; and Armero 1989: 175–176).

As to the second point, i.e. the Europeanization of the Atlantic Alliance and the eventual development of a proper European defence policy, González explicitly referred during the referendum campaign to the strengthening of the 'European pillar' in NATO as an important reason for remaining in NATO. Rather than withdraw from NATO, an official party document stated, it was necessary 'to work from within NATO in order to ensure that the European nations are masters of their own destiny without submitting themselves to the interests of Washington' (quoted in Pollack 1987: 168). By the same token, the multilateralization of the defence policy under the specific conditions incorporated in the referendum text would guarantee a substantial reduction of the United States military presence on Spanish soil, and hence reduce the bilateral military relationship of dependence.

From 1986 onwards, the Socialist government repeatedly put forward its inclination to Europeanize not only its own defence policy but also to strengthen the European pillar of NATO, though a careful move from an outspoken pro-European attitude towards a more pragmatic compromise stance in international power politics is noticeable. A first example is offered by the initial attitude of the Spanish government towards the

Western European Union, which was seen as a kind of surrogate with respect to the ultimate foreign security objective of establishing a European defence policy within the framework of the EC. In his speech to the European Parliament on 17 January 1989, in which he presented the programme of the Spanish presidency for the first six months of that year, the Spanish Minister of Foreign Affairs, Francisco Fernández Ordóñez, brought article 30 of the Single European Act up for discussion. This article was questioned inasmuch as it reduces the co-operation between the twelve member states in the field of international defence and security to political and economic matters, excluding military ones. If the time is ripe, he argued, 'we must consider the advisability of removing the restrictions article 30 is imposing on our coordination in the field of security'. And, '[the] entry of Spain into the Western European Union is a consequence of the dichotomy as accepted in the Single European Act, a dichotomy which my country would be pleased to see removed' (quoted in *El País*, 18 January 1989).[8]

Another example is offered by a speech of Felipe González before the Madrid plenary meeting of the Parliamentary Assembly of the Atlantic Alliance in October 1991. In direct response to the discussions at the time with respect to the Franco-German defence initiative,[9] González stated that, for Spain, the only viable method was the so-called '*doble gorra*' ('double hat'). By this he meant that the units of a future European army (the so-called 'double-hatted forces') would have to accomplish missions within the framework of both NATO and the WEU. The 'double use' of these units could avoid unnecessary duplication, and thus guarantee the full employment of the limited financial and logistic resources. Once again, we witness an expression of Europeanism of the Spanish government inasmuch as the creation of a European intervention force in order to deal with conflicts and crises outside the NATO area (an idea supported by the United States), was implicitly rejected as not going far enough. If no serious effort was made to develop a proper, common European defence policy, González warned his audience, a breakdown of the process of European unification 'could unchain disintegrating tendencies of renationalization', with a multiplication of alliances based on national schemes as the possible result (see *El País*, 22 October 1991).

A final remark has to be made with respect to the post-referendum period. Two important developments, i.e. the full membership of the EC in 1986 (and the problems of adjustment related to it) and the changes in Eastern Europe after 1989, have moved Spanish security policy to a second plane in the comprehensive foreign policy orientation of the Socialist

114 The Socialist decade (1982–1992)

government. In a context in which first, the Atlantic Alliance had lost one of its most important *raisons d'être* after the collapse of 'real existing Socialism'; and second, an unexpected revival of European integration had been agreed on in the course of the 1980s, starting with the presentation of the Commission's White Paper and the signing of the Single European Act (SEA) in 1986, and followed by two intergovernmental conferences culminating in the Treaty of Maastricht (signed on 7 February 1992); and in a situation in which, in the third place, the Socialist government was increasingly faced with the externally induced pressure to adjust its economic structures to the most advanced member states (see the next chapter), issues of foreign policy coordination at the European level have become subordinated to issues of economic and monetary union. In this sense it is accurate to speak of a second phase in the Europeanization of Spanish foreign policy that extends from the start of the second term in office of the Socialist government in June 1986 to the legislative elections of 1993. The priorities of the Socialist European policy during this period will be dealt with in the following section.

THE SECOND PHASE OF THE EUROPEANIZATION OF SPANISH FOREIGN POLICY

Spain's presidency of the EC during the first six months of 1989 formed the first real test on the long road to the final realization of the European ambitions of its Socialist government. The programme of the Spanish 'semester' was presented by Fernández Ordóñez to the European Parliament on 17 January. Its priorities were so numerous, and presented in such general terms, that many members of parliament regarded the speech of the Spanish Foreign Minister as lacking realism or specificity, and hence as lacking conviction (see *El País*, 18 January 1989; and *El Independiente*, 20 January 1989). All the same, it is possible to categorize the Spanish priorities into three major areas.

The first area of priorities consisted of all those imperative decisions that, independent of the Spanish presidency, would not permit any delay, such as those related to the completion of the European Single Market or the annual fixing of agricultural prices in the framework of the Common Agricultural Policy.

A second area of priorities grouped together all activities relating to the external relations of the EC and to the European Political Co-operation. In addition to an emphasis on the ongoing themes, such as the EC–US trade relations and the formulation of a common approach to the crisis in the Middle East, Fernández Ordóñez paid particular attention to the relationship of the EC with Latin America in his presentation of the Spanish programme. The promotion of a common, European position with respect to the Latin American debt crisis was the avowed priority of the Spanish presidency, but in the end it did not live up to its promise. A Spanish proposal to set up a European Guarantee Fund received a cool reception, particularly from West Germany, Great Britain and the Netherlands; it was referred to the Council of Finance Ministers, where it died a gentle death.[10]

A third and final area of priorities concerned the preparation of the European Council meeting in Madrid in June 1989, during which progress was to be made with respect to the phased creation of a European Monetary Union (EMU) and the drafting of a Social Charter. As in the case of the second area, the Spanish government came to play a minor role in the course of events, both before and during the meeting. In Madrid its role was confined to a mediatory one, in a continuous effort to reconcile the central actors. It was the modest status of small power and newcomer that left Spain no room to come into prominence; it was the leaders of the three major member states (France, Germany and Britain) and the Commission's president Jacques Delors who dominated the process of 'interstate bargaining' in the European Council (see Holman 1989: 632–633). Yet the Madrid summit was the first important opportunity for the Socialist government to formulate and present the constituent elements of its comprehensive European policy. After all, the first step in the relaunching of European integration (i.e. the signing of the Single European Act) was agreed upon without the active participation of Spain. Only in the course of the move from the single market project to the European Political Union, a process in which the Madrid summit played an important, initiating role, could Spain try to influence its direction for the first time. Before entering into the details of this European policy, it is first necessary to consider the more general development of European integration in the period between early 1986 and December 1991.

There is, of course, a clear line to be drawn from the agreement on the SEA in February 1986 to the Maastricht Treaty, although the sequence of integrational events and institutional changes did not take place automatically. That is, the SEA itself did not contain specific further steps towards a European Union.

The project of completing the Single European Market was welcomed by the national parliaments and by both trade unions and employers' organizations because of the growth-generating impact that the removal of non-tariff barriers would have. Even among conservatives and anti-federalists in Britain, the SEA was received with approval, mainly because of its neo-liberal underpinning. In the following years, however, the impact the SEA was to have on the course of European integration (that is, beyond free market competition) became the object of serious conflicts. There were those who thought that the economic growth potential of a Single European Market would be needlessly limited without the creation of a single European currency. The famous 'costs of non-Europe' argument was turned into a 'costs of non-ECU Europe' one. Others believed that the effects of market liberalization (and especially its social and regional impact) would have to be compensated for by a range of measures within the framework of what came to be known as the social and regional dimensions. Fervent federalists, finally, were of the opinion that the completion of a Single European Market and the creation of a European Monetary Union (EMU) were levers that could be used to push the EC towards a European (Political) Union.

These Europeanist projections were represented by the President of the European Commission, Jacques Delors. In his July 1988 address to the European Parliament, he predicted the primacy of functional decision-making at the European level within a period of ten years. The completion of the Single Market, he argued, would necessarily reduce the importance of national decision-making in economic, social and fiscal matters (see Urwin 1991: 240). Delors' most formidable adversary, Britain's former Prime Minister Margaret Thatcher, reacted immediately. In her seminal speech of 20 September 1988 in the European College in Bruges, Thatcher not only advocated the ongoing Atlantic vocation of the European Community, on the one hand, and the widening of the Community, on the other, but she also expressed her fierce opposition to any strengthening of the European institutions. 'We have not successfully rolled back the frontiers of the state of Britain,' she riposted Delors, 'only to see them recognised at a European level, with a European super-state exercising a new dominance from Brussels' (quoted in Urwin 1991: 240; see also Overbeek 1992). This combination of Atlanticism, continental Europeanism, and inter-governmentalism encompasses all the basic ingredients of a comprehensive concept that we have labelled liberal internationalism (see Chapter 1), and formed a constituent element of the hegemonic policy which in Britain became known as Thatcherism (see Overbeek 1990).

But the times had changed, and Mrs Thatcher was not in the same position that Charles de Gaulle had been in more than two decades before. Instead of having a decisive impact on the course of European integration, 'Euro-Thatcherism' was unable to impede further steps in the process of enlarging the role of Brussels, particularly in monetary and social issues. In fact, it took only a couple of years 'to dissolve the British effort to control the Community and to isolate the British government' (Grahl and Teague 1990: 304).

With respect to the gradual realization of an economic and monetary union, the first move was made in Hanover during the European Council meeting in June 1988. The Council decided to assign the task of studying and proposing the specific steps necessary to establish such a union to a committee under the chairmanship of Jacques Delors. The resulting Delors Report of April 1989 outlined a three-stage plan towards an EMU. After the first phase (a greater convergence of economic developments by way of strengthening the coordination of economic and monetary policies among the twelve member states, but as yet without fundamental institutional changes) had been initiated at the Madrid summit in June 1989, subsequent developments superseded it as a blueprint of accelerated monetary integration. In particular, the December 1989 decision to start an intergovernmental conference on EMU, parallel to a second conference on the European Political Union (EPU), made the Delors project far more specific and irreversible, and embedded it in a package deal of institutional reforms affecting economic and monetary as well as foreign policy areas. At least this was the initial motivation behind this 'extended relaunching' of European integration at the end of the 1980s. Developments in Eastern Europe and the subsequent reunification of Germany, it was argued by the staunchest supporters of a deeper (instead of a wider) Europe, made it necessary to act immediately in order to prevent the throwing away of the 'European unification baby' with the 'Cold War bath water'. In particular, the altered role of a reunified Germany in the New European Architecture called for rapid decision-making.

In this context, the Maastricht summit of December 1991 had to decide upon a range of interconnected issues affecting not only the member states' sovereignty in the field of economic and monetary policies, but also, and far more delicately, in foreign policy and defence matters. In returning to the constituent elements of the Socialists' European policy as elaborated and defined in detail after 1986, and particularly during the period between the preparation of the Spanish presidency in late 1988 and the European Council summit of Maastricht,[11] we must first specify the Spanish position in three interrelated debates as to the future direction of European integration: the ongoing debate between 'Atlanticists' and 'Europeanists'; that between those in favour of intergovernmental co-operation and those who support some kind of supra-nationalism; and that between those in favour of a widening of the EC and those who stress the need to deepen the present level of integration first. We shall specify the position of Spain by taking as our point of departure the crucial questions with respect to the European

Political Union that were raised after the signing of the SEA and were provisionally answered in Maastricht.

With respect to the first question – i.e. whether or not a single European currency and a single European Central Bank should be created – decision-making was certainly the least difficult part. Before the actual summit was held, the Dutch presidency reached total agreement among the EC twelve on the main points of monetary unification.[12] Spain had been one of the most fervent supporters of a European Monetary Union ever since the Delors committee was formed in 1988.[13] Several politico-ideological reasons were put forward to explain this stance, but, in the final analysis, monetary integration served as a legitimation of domestic austerity measures, as we will see in the next chapter.

Closely related to this first question is the issue of sovereignty, and the question of whether or not the ultimate goal of the ongoing process of unification should be a federal Europe. The Spanish Socialists were strongly in favour of a European Political Union, i.e. 'a supra-national Union cemented in democratically legitimized institutions' (PSOE 1990: 80). In 1989 this position was firmly established in both the electoral programme for the national elections (PSOE 1989a: 7–9, 75) and the party's European Manifesto (PSOE 1989b: *passim*). This Political Union must be based on a federal structure, in which a strengthening of the EC institutions (the Commission and the European Parliament), and the explicit safeguard of the exclusive competences of the Community in some fields, go hand in hand with the so-called 'shared competences' (*competencias compartidas*) in others.[14] The latter formulation indicates the extent to which the encroachment on sovereignty is still acceptable to the Spanish Socialists, particularly in the field of economic and monetary integration. 'One cedes sovereignty in order to share it,' Felipe González stated in an interview with *The Financial Times*.

> I accept that we are in a D-Mark zone. The difference between there being one day an EC institution to define monetary policy and the reality now is that we depend on the D-Mark, but according to the decisions taken in the Bundestag and not on common decisions shared by all.
> (*Financial Times*, 17 December 1990)

Monetary unification, and the formal cession of sovereignty concomitant to it, are thus the vehicle for compensating a *de facto* loss of autonomous decision-making as a result of existing economic and monetary relations in Western Europe.

In the field of foreign affairs and security, other essential themes to be decided upon during the European Council of Maastricht, Spain has always supported arriving at a Common Policy in order to optimize national objectives. Here again the formula of 'shared competences' is used to clarify the Spanish position. 'As in other areas,' an adviser in the Spanish Prime Minister's office states, 'an integrated European long-term plan is sought which does not entail delegating sovereignty to bodies beyond the control of EC member states, but rather sharing sovereignty in supranational bodies' (Ortega 1991: 68). A Common Defence Policy must include an integrated military structure in which Spain, unlike its approach to NATO, would be able to participate. The WEU must function as the military arm of the EPU, and its forces would have no geographical limits on where they could operate (ibid.: 71).

In all these issues (i.e. monetary union, the strengthening of supranational European institutions, and the development of a Common Foreign and Security Policy) the Spanish government stressed the need to deepen the present level of integration first, before the EC can be geographically enlarged and incorporate new member states. Particularly with respect to the future membership of countries like Poland, Hungary and Czechoslovakia, an additional reason for the primacy of deepening over widening is given. For Spain, the possible accession of Central European countries to the EC, and, more generally, the channelling of foreign (i.e. West European) aid and investment to the area, are perceived as a major threat to the Spanish economy, making socio-economic convergence with other member states more difficult. As indicated above, the acceleration of the process of European integration in the second half of the 1980s has reinforced the need for Spain to adapt its economic and socio-political structures to those prevailing in the most advanced member states. The transfer of resources from North European countries to the South has been and will be an essential factor in making this process of modernization a success. This is why the so-called New European Architecture and its consequences for the process of European unification generated great fears, whether realistic or not, among Spanish politicians and industrialists that the opening up of Eastern Europe would divert West German investment to countries in this area, in due course followed by companies from other North European countries. As one of Spain's leading bankers stated: 'The danger is that regions in the South of Europe that have been gaining ground at the expense of the developed regions in the North may now begin to lose this to the East' (quoted in *Financial Times*, 1 December 1989). When asked during an interview with *The Financial Times* how Spain could deny membership to countries in Eastern Europe while having been helped by EC membership itself, Felipe González refused to accept this comparison as a fair one.

Spain went through a very deep economic crisis between 1975 and 1985. We got a great deal of moral support, but we never received a single peseta in assistance. We should not pull the wool over our own eyes. I don't think Lech Walesa realises that Western Europe is not going to foot the bill for 40 years of Communism. Just like it didn't pay for 40 years of Franquismo. No one feels obliged to pay this bill.

(*Financial Times*, 9 May 1991)

Returning to the three aforementioned debates, Socialist-led Spain takes a clear stand on one side of the dividing line between the twelve member states, supporting a future course of European integration which is the exact opposite of that supported, for instance, by the United Kingdom. Spain defends a Europeanist orientation aimed at gradually loosening the Atlantic ties with the United States; it favours some kind of supra-national institutionalism; and it stresses the need to deepen the process of European integration first. Essential for understanding this 'full steam ahead' strategy is the continual plea for financial solidarity and additional cohesion funding accompanying it. Both before and after the Maastricht summit, Spain threatened to veto any progress in deepening the process of European integration and in extending the geographical scope of the EC to the countries of the EFTA (European Free Trade Association). The treaty establishing a European Economic Space could only be signed after the EFTA members had committed themselves to creating a cohesion fund in support of the less wealthy EC members. Spain entered the 'multidimensional' negotiations in Maastricht with an inflexible 'without cohesion no treaty' attitude. As the State Secretary for European Affairs, Carlos Westendorp, stated on the eve of the summit, 'being competitive depends on the efforts of the economic agents and on the economic policy of the government. The cohesion serves to contribute to this objective, and that is the only thing we want' (quoted in *El País*, 8 December 1991).

It is along these lines that a future hegemony (in the Gramscian sense, see Chapters 1 and 2) of German social and political forces is acceptable to the Spanish Socialists. Such a German-centred transnational hegemony in Europe would be based on monetary union in exchange for economic convergence, 'cohesion funding' in exchange for open and deregulated markets, economic and political openness to the outside world in exchange for a 'controlled deepening' of regional integration, and stronger coordination of foreign policies and, eventually, the construction of a European armed force aimed at intervening in extra-European affairs (and particularly in regional conflicts in the so-called Third World). When asked for his opinion on the large German influence in European decision-making, Felipe González replied:

it is very difficult to tell the best student that we find his position at the top of the class intolerable.... What do we want? Do we want Germany to be unsuccessful? This does not seem sensible to me, because if Germany fails we will all fail as well.

(quoted in *El País*, 23 February 1992)

However, Spain has no historical reasons to fear a strong Germany. It is the largest beneficiary of the Community cohesion funds (with Germany as largest net contributor), and it depends heavily on German direct investments in its economy. As long as rising foreign direct investment and an increase in Community resources to be transferred to the less wealthy member states continue to compensate for the short-term deterioration in economic performance, especially with respect to trade, and, in short, manage to bring about 'a better balance of rich and poor' (González in *Financial Times*, 9 May 1991), the Spanish Socialists will continue to defend their foreign policy orientation based on enhanced European unification. In this sense, financial solidarity, economic convergence and social cohesion are conditionally related to all the other issues of European co-operation and integration. To quote State Secretary of European Affairs Westendorp once more: 'Our country [participates] with the clear intention of impelling European construction in all fields, but it has one problem: cohesion' (*El País*, 8 December 1991).

EPILOGUE: PROGRAMME 2000 AND THE RHETORIC OF EURO-SOCIALISM

After mentioning González' hobby – collecting and cultivating Japanese bonsai trees – reporters of *The Financial Times* concluded that 'the symbolism is clear: the political project is no longer a grand system, but a myriad of small growths' (*Financial Times*, 17 December 1990). They obviously referred to the growing contradiction, and discrepancy between the ruling party's Socialist ideology, on the one hand, and the conservative drift of government economic policy and, more generally, the shift towards 'pragmatism', on the other. In the next chapter we will elaborate on the content of this policy, its macro-economic priorities, and the growing contradiction between externally induced austerity and domestic social cohesion.

In the present chapter an attempt has been made to illustrate the progressive subordination of the ideological (social–democratic) elements in the party programme to the all-embracing objectives of European integration and economic convergence by analysing the Socialist foreign policy orientation in general, and the change of priorities in the course of the Socialist decade in particular. During the first term of office of the González government, efforts were directed at a rapid and successful conclusion of the accession negotiations with the EC, and at convincing the Spanish electorate of the necessity of Spain's continued membership of NATO. After full EC membership was realized, and the NATO referendum effectively manipulated, active participation in the construction of a united Europe went hand in hand with the subordination of Spain's foreign policy objectives and the nation's domestic policy to 'the cardinal and transcendent thought' of making Spain one of the leading countries in the New Europe. On numerous occasions members of the government and party leaders explicitly expressed the importance of this medium-term strategic goal. 'With ten more years of Socialist government,' Alfonso Guerra, for instance, stated in 1989, 'Spain will be able to position itself at the head of Europe' (*El País*, 23 September 1989). It would be equally wrong to trivialize such statements as mere electoral rhetoric, or to uncritically accept them without further ado as the expression of the Socialists' primary motive force.

In recalling the intra-party confrontations between Guerristas and neo-liberals (see Chapter 3), the growing contradiction between the party's ideological stance and the externally induced macro-economic programme of market reforms was initially resolved by compensating the short-term impossibility of Socialist or social–democratic policies at the national level by projecting the ideological objectives in time to the year 2000 and beyond, and in space to a united Europe. The foreign policy elements in Programme 2000 were a case in point. This 'platform for renewed encounter of the left in the medium and long-term' was presented by its coordinator Manuel Escudero as the answer by the Spanish Socialists to an international challenge:

> a large part of the most decisive changes are nowadays taking place at the international level. The answer cannot be a rhetorical one because we are faced with a huge concentration of international economic power which requires a growing control at the international level too.
> (quoted in *El País*, 3 January 1990)

In the introduction of Programme 2000, it is stated that

> today Europe is the scene where the game is played between the neo-conservative model of society and the democratic socialist project, and our country is now in a crucial position with respect to both the battle of ideas and the task of the construction of Europe. Therefore the power configuration in a united Europe will partly depend on the orientation of Spain ...
> (*Manifiesto del Programa 2000*, 1991: 30)

Such a democratic Socialist transnational counterforce should be based on a common ideology, a common political platform and political action, and a single Socialist organization in the Community. To this end a genuine federal party of European Socialists should come into existence (ibid.: 107–108). Once Socialism becomes the 'hegemonic political force in the Community' (ibid.: 104) it will give direction to the process of deepening European integration and must reformulate the external relations and foreign policy objectives of the Community according to the principles of democratic socialism and international solidarity. Finally, a politically united, economically prosperous, and socially integrated European Community can become the political motor that impels a New International Order based on common development, shared by the North and the South, and the East and the West, and that can promote the creation of an International Ecological Order (ibid.: 111–112). This strategy of Euro-Socialism (aiming at the creation at the European level of 'a new society in the horizon of the year 2000') was explicitly intended to ideologically compensate for the short-term conservative drift of government economic policy.

But things changed rapidly after Programme 2000 was approved during the 32nd party congress of 1990. Subsequent developments at three different levels came to play a decisive role in the final subordination of ideological objectives to the 'pragmatism' of macro-economic adjustment. First, intra-party conflicts between Guerristas and neo-liberals were temporarily resolved by the strengthening of the latter as a result of the March 1991 reshuffle of the Cabinet (see Chapter 3). Second, the 'extended relaunching' of European integration, and particularly the Maastricht agreement on monetary unification, increased the need for macro-economic adjustment in order to meet the convergence criteria. Finally, post-Maastricht developments, and particularly the economic stagnation and monetary crisis in the course of 1992, effectively showed the enormous discrepancy between the Spanish Socialists' ambitions and the politico-economic reality of being one of the less developed member states.

In terms of international power relations, this last point reaffirmed another reality: that the role of Spain as a force in international and European relations is a limited one, both with respect to the structural power of transnational mobile capital and with respect to the social and political forces that give momentum to the process of European integration. As a small power, its role is certainly not one of taking the lead in this process. Spanish interests are best served if the government and the Spanish diplomatic staff carefully try to seek compromises between the three most important member states in order to avoid a final breakdown of the whole enterprise altogether. In addition to this, the Socialist government's continual stress on additional cohesion funding, and its willingness to block all further negotiations if this demand is not satisfactorily met, are a case of defending narrowly defined national interests rather than attempting to construct a transnational counterforce based on the principles of Euro-Socialism.

More generally, these three developments have forced government policy further into the direction of short-term crisis management and economic convergence, resulting in one of the most important paradoxes of Socialist rule in Spain: in order to become one of the leading nations of Europe, and in order to eventually give impetus to the European project of democratic Socialism, Spain has first to catch up with the most developed member states; but the restructuring needed to obtain economic convergence tends to strengthen all those social and political forces which are less concerned with ideology and more with instituting market reforms. In the next two chapters, we will first elaborate on the general outline of the Socialists' economic policy, relating its 'technocratization' to external constraints, and then proceed with an analysis of the social forces that support this policy. It will be argued that the apparent objectivity and inevitability of economic adjustment actually serve specific interests related to the most dynamic sectors of Spanish capitalism.

5 Socialist economic policy and European integration
The internationalization of domestic politics

INTRODUCTION

Having dealt with the progressive subordination of Spain's traditional foreign policy objectives to the Socialists' comprehensive European project in general, and to the exigencies of economic integration in particular, we can now turn to the structural imbalances of the Spanish economy, and the Socialist government's attempt to correct them in a context of global interdependence. As indicated in the previous chapter, the 'extended relaunch' of European integration provided both the institutional framework and external legitimization for the implemented austerity policy, or rather for its continuation after the 1986 general elections, because austerity and macro-economic adjustment had been the central policy objectives ever since the Socialists took office in October 1982. Fighting the structural causes and short-term consequences of the economic crisis were then the primary motives.

The impact of the world economic crisis of the 1970s and early 1980s on the Spanish economy had been particularly severe. The well-known economist (and until February 1978 Minister of Economic Affairs during the first post-Franquist, democratic government) Enrique Fuentes Quintana even speaks of a 'differential crisis', inasmuch as all the defining characteristics of the international crisis had their maximal impact in the Spanish case (Fuentes Quintana 1988: 32; see also Donges 1990: 560). Indeed, in terms of economic stagnation, inflation, unemployment, and external deficits, Spain was clearly among the worst performers within the OECD area (see Rojo 1987).

This relatively strong impact of the global crisis on the Spanish economy was related to three mutually reinforcing factors. First, it was the result of the gradual coming into line of the economic evolution of Spain with that of the other European OECD states during the 1960s and 1970s. This articulation of national and international cycles took place alongside the growing importance of foreign trade to the Spanish economy (see Rodríguez López 1989: 119). In particular the growing import dependence on raw materials and investment goods, together with a tendential downward pressure on the national currency, made the Spanish economy highly vulnerable to external price shocks and international stagnation. Second, the Spanish industrial structure was characterized by a relatively high participation by the so-called critical sectors which were most affected by economic stagnation (see Segura *et al.* 1989; Vázquez 1990). Consequently, the Spanish economy experienced a process of de-industrialization, in relative terms, during the second half of the 1970s and early 1980s.[1] Finally, the economic crisis coincided in Spain with the process of democratic transition which, for obvious reasons, postponed a true adjustment policy. Macro-economic policy was initially subordinated to the general political goal of consolidating democracy. In a sense, the primary concern of the UCD government was not so much the correction of macro-economic imbalances, but the maintenance of social peace. The so-called '*Pactos de Moncloa*' were perhaps the most essential achievement in this respect (see section on p. 162), but these agreements were insufficient to reduce the structural imbalances of the Spanish economy (see Fuentes Quintana 1990; Linde 1990; Rodríguez López 1989; Nieto de Alba 1984).

The rise to power of the PSOE in 1982 coincided with the consolidation of Spanish democracy (see Chapter 3). In fact, the centre-right UCD had initiated the first, political transition; now the PSOE should start the second, economic transition. This implied in the first place the implementation of a policy of adjustment, and second a policy of industrial reconversion. Macro-economic adjustment, and the short-term subordination of labour interests inherent to it, were seen as a necessary precondition for (and as such part and parcel of) a more comprehensive, internationalist strategy, aimed at preparing the Spanish economy and its agents for free competition, Spain's future position and role within the Common Market being the ultimate stake.

This becomes particularly clear if we summarize the three central objectives of Socialist economic policy (see de la Dehesa 1990). In the first place, the correction of Spain's macro-economic imbalances (inflation, trade deficit, etc.) constituted the basic point of departure. Second, a policy of 'structural reforms to correct the weaknesses and inefficiencies in the factor and products markets' (ibid.: 8) was aimed at restructuring the production process and improving the competitiveness of Spanish industry in the light of progressive trade liberalization. Third, negotiations with the European Community were accelerated in order to conclude the Treaty of Accession as soon as possible. It was this sequence of macro-economic adjustment and industrial reconversion – full membership of the EC – and reindustrialization and sustained economic growth that the newly elected government had in mind. Managing the 'supply side crisis' was not an end in itself, but a necessary step in the process of economic modernization, on the one hand, and a logical consequence of the European vocation of Spain, on the other.

This macro-economic policy, which is part and parcel of the 'internationalization of domestic politics' inherent to 'Felipism', has become subject, both inside and outside Spain, to contradictory interpretations as regards its ideological and strategic underpinnings and the socio-economic interests it represents. In the first place, there is disagreement as to whether the hegemonic project of the PSOE may be labelled neo-liberal, even though very few still hold the view that this plan is a genuinely Socialist one. For some – the major trade unions UGT and CCOO being a case in point – reasoning along the lines of 'if not Socialist, then neo-liberal' has become highly opportune. For others, not even the Socialist government's economic policy can be compared with, for instance, Thatcherism. The welfare state, it is argued, could not be dismantled, simply because no such phenomenon ever existed in Spain (see, for instance, the editorial in *El País*, 13 December 1988).

In this chapter it will be argued that no simple solution can be offered to this problem of contradictory interpretations. It may even be asked whether the problem has been rightly formulated at all. For it is not the 'art of labelling' that is at stake, but the detection of alternative policies, their content and impact, and, particularly, the socio-economic and political interests behind them. To this end, the next section contains a comprehensive survey of the Spanish economy during the 1980s, together with a provisional evaluation of the effectiveness of the government's economic policy. In the section on p. 136 the latter point is elaborated in a more abstract way, inasmuch as both the austerity policy implemented by the Socialists and their strategic aims are linked with the changing position of Spain within the transnational (European) division of labour. In the section on p. 147, two interrelated topics will be dealt with: the impact of EC membership on the Spanish economy after 1 January 1986, and the government's industrial policy in reaction to these new challenges. In the final section, the deteriorating relationship between the government and the trade unions, and the subsequent more general erosion of social consensus as regards the Socialists' European project, are analysed. It will be argued that the increasing social unrest during the second half of the 1980s, culminating in the general strike of December 1988, and the growing opposition of important sections of the Spanish business community, particularly after 1990, have their origins in the following features: the unwillingness of the Socialist government to redistribute a greater share of the national welfare generated by the economic boom in the second half of the 1980s; the changing role of the state in economic planning in general and in industrial restructuring in particular, a process in which the state tends to withdraw into mere macro-economic adjustment, using deregulation, privatization and external liberalization as the principal tools of its industrial policy; and the growing contradiction between the all-embracing objective of the government to converge with the most advanced member states of the EC in the fields of macro-economic performance and industrial production, and the rapidly deteriorating economic situation after 1990, reflected in declining industrial profits and rising unemployment. This situation reinforces the impression that by the end of its third period in office the hegemonic project of the Socialist government as directed by the neo-liberals gathered round the Minister of Economy and Finance, Carlos Solchaga, had been exhausted and had lost a substantial part of its legitimation in Spanish society. The increase in assertiveness of these technocrats and their growing influence on the government's decision-making in economic matters, especially after the 1989 elections (see the previous chapters), may therefore be well interpreted as a Pyrrhic victory.

STRUCTURAL IMBALANCES AND SOCIALIST MACRO-ECONOMIC POLICY

Initially, until the economic boom in the second half of the 1980s, one of the mainstays of Socialist socio-economic policy was the so-called social dialogue or coordination with the trade unions (*la concertación social*), and particularly with the Socialist Unión General de Trabajadores (UGT). In order to reverse the process of de-industrialization during the years 1977–1982 wage restraint became the motto. A moderately restrictive fiscal and budgetary policy (that is, a policy expansive enough to improve infrastructure and further extend the social security system) was combined with a tight, restrictive monetary policy (to curb inflation), and an industrial policy directed at reorganizing and reconverting the companies belonging to the public holding, the Instituto Nacional de Industria (INI).

The results of this policy were not altogether favourable. Among the 'positive outcomes'[2] were, *inter alia*:

1 A decrease of the rate of inflation from 14.4 per cent in 1982 to the decade's lowest point of 4.8 per cent in 1988 (Economic and Social Committee 1989: table 5). In the following years, however, annual inflation rates increased again to more than 6 per cent (OECD 1993: 115).
2 An increase in the Gross Domestic Product (GDP) at constant market prices from an average annual increase of 1.2 per cent during the period 1977–1985 to an average annual increase of 4.6 per cent during the period 1985–1988 (ibid.). GDP further increased by 5 per cent in 1989, but growth slackened thereafter to 3.6 per cent in 1990, 2.4 per cent in 1991 and went down again to a rate under 2 per cent in 1992 (see Banco de España 1990: 51; Alcaide Inchausti 1990: 8; OECD 1993:13).
3 A doubling of the profitability (i.e. profit + gross interest charges/total assets) of private companies during the first two terms of office of the PSOE. During the same period the interest/gross profit ratio declined by more than half, and the proportion of internally financed investment rose as the retained profit/investment ratio increased from 86.3 per cent in 1983 to 110.4 per cent in 1987 (see Economic and Social Committee 1989: 6 and table 4). This considerable improvement in private business performance was due to an increase in productivity, wage restraint and, particularly, persistent labour shedding, resulting in a sharp decline in real unit labour costs. An international comparison of the development of real unit labour costs (in industry) shows that these costs fell further in Spain during the first half of the 1980s than in any other of the selected OECD countries (see Table 3).

Table 3 Real unit labour costs in industry in selected OECD countries, 1975–85 (1975 = 100)

	1975	1979	1980	1982	1984	1985
United Kingdom	100	98.6	100.4	96.1	91.0	91.4
Belgium	100	96.0	99.5	97.5	92.6	92.6
Denmark	100	103.0	99.6	97.0	84.5	85.9
France	100	97.9	97.8	96.4	92.0	87.2
Germany, Fed.	100	100.4	105.0	104.3	98.6	97.4
Republic of Italy	100	89.3	86.0	90.5	86.8	84.7
Netherlands	100	99.8	101.1	98.8	88.6	86.3
Spain	100	125.2	122.4	114.9	104.9	102.2

Source: López-Claros 1988: 24

The Economic and Social Committee of the European Communities attributes this decline in real unit labour costs primarily to wage restraint, though redundancies and a rise in productivity are mentioned as additional factors (ibid.: 14). Augusto López-Claros, member of the European Department of the International Monetary Fund, points to the evolution of employment in the Spanish industrial sector, which declined by 20 per cent between 1979 and 1985, as the most important explanatory factor (López-Claros 1988: 24), in spite of the fact that he affirmatively quotes an OECD economic survey which states that the development of wages in Spain is strongly correlated to that of prices and quite insensitive to the rate of unemployment. In fact, this 'points to the existence of a wage–price spiral, the unwinding of which has been extremely slow' during the 1980s (ibid.: 24, n. 32). If we take 1988 as our reference year, the average annual increase over the previous five years amounts to 9.3 per cent with respect to wages and 7.8 per cent with respect to consumer prices (OECD 1991: basic statistics). The decline in real unit labour costs, then, seems primarily the result of redundancies and rising productivity, factors that offset a rise (albeit decelerated) in real labour costs. It is this combination of rising wages and unemployment (to some extent paralleled by the simultaneous mix of a restrictive monetary policy and a moderately expansive fiscal policy) and declining real unit labour costs that laid the foundations of the economic boom in the second half of the 1980s.

4 An eventual nett increase in employment which resulted in a decline of the rate of unemployment from the decade's highest point of 21.5 per cent in 1985 to 17.3 per cent in 1989 (OECD 1991: 96). Actually, this feature can also be included under the heading of policy failures. One of the appealing promises of the PSOE during the 1982 electoral campaign was the creation of 800,000 new jobs, once in power. For several years this unfulfilled promise had been the millstone around the party's and government's necks. It was only in 1986 that total employment started to rise again, a rise exclusively due to higher dependent employment. By far the largest share of this post-1985 rise was the result of an increase in the number of wage and salary earners in the non-agricultural private sector.[3]

Apart from being caused by declining employment in agriculture, an increase in the size of the labour force (explaining the high percentage of unemployed who are less than twenty-five years old, on the one hand, and the continuous rise of female unemployment, on the other), and other factors of minor importance, the rise in the rate of unemployment during the late 1970s and early 1980s was strongly related to the belated reaction of the Spanish industrial sector to the global economic crisis of restructuring. Rafael Myro has specified this phenomenon by differentiating between industrial sectors characterized by strong demand (such as aerospace equipment, office machinery, pharmaceuticals, chemicals, electrical machinery), by average demand (motor vehicles, rubber goods, railway equipment, etc.), and weak demand (steel industry, shipbuilding, textile industry, etc.). Correlating these three sectors with the general decline in industrial employment, Myro points to different motivations: whereas in the average and strong demand sectors competitive and cost factors (i.e. supply side factors) were the primary motive force in reducing the labour force, in the weak demand sectors the reduction of productive capacities and the subsequent redundancies were inextricably bound up with the contraction of the domestic market (i.e. demand side factors) (Myro 1988a: 226ff.). Conversely, this implies that the post-1985 rise in industrial employment was almost completely due to the expansion of the strong and average demand sectors, a picture which is confirmed by the continuous decline of employment in public enterprises operating in traditional, weak demand growth sectors.

In the second half of the 1980s, the Socialist government was confronted with a new problem: the so-called overheating of the Spanish economy. As a result of the restrictive monetary policy of the government, the interest rate had been dramatically increased during the previous years, which in turn generated a huge influx of short-term, speculative capital ('hot money') from abroad. This influx of short-term capital finally led to a substantial appreciation of the peseta.

In addition, the accelerated growth of the Spanish economy led to increasing foreign sector imbalances. The foreign trade sector certainly showed the most problematic imbalance of the Spanish economy. In the course of the 1980s the structural trade deficit decreased from 9,258 million dollars in 1982 to 4,190 million dollars in 1985, and then sharply rose to a deficit of 24,556 million dollars in 1989 (Table 4). By and large there are two main factors explaining this spectacular increase: first, the entry of Spain into the Common Market;[4] and, second, the domestic demand-led boom in the second half of the 1980s. This explains why the deterioration of the trade balance was due to rapidly increasing imports (and not so much caused by stagnating exports, which more than doubled during the 1980s).[5]

Booming demand in part resulted in a change in the spending pattern of the average Spaniard, showing a greater inclination to buy durable consumer goods from abroad. One had only to look around in the major urban centres of

Table 4 Balance of payments (transactions basis) in million dollars

	1982	1983	1984	1985	1986	1987	1988	1989
Imports (fob)	30,579	27,463	26,939	27,740	33,164	46,234	57,573	67,777
Exports (fob)	21,321	19,874	22,660	23,550	26,714	33,399	39,570	43,221
Trade Balance	−9,258	−7,589	−4,279	−4,190	−6,450	−12,835	−18,003	−24,556
Services, net	3,430	3,883	5,228	5,834	9,245	10,150	9,805	9,013
of which:								
Tourism	6,153	6,003	6,922	7,087	10,442	12,827	14,233	13,172
Investment income	−2,328	−2,463	−2,395	−1,806	−1,997	−2,753	−3,522	−2,970
Transfers, net	1,585	1,163	1,089	1,099	1,126	2,615	4,508	4,607
Current balance	−4,242	−2,542	2,035	2,744	3,922	−70	−3,690	−10,935
Private long-term capital	788	2,217	2,678	−1,274	489	9,301	10,324	16,451
Official long-term capital	992	994	469	−36	−2,131	−101	−875	−503
Total long-term capital	1,780	3,211	3,147	−1,310	−1,642	9,200	9,449	16,954
Basic balance	−2,462	669	5,182	1,434	2,280	9,130	5,759	6,019
Short-term capital	743	356	515	107	134	1,855	456	−900
Monetary movements (increase in assets =)	3,672	899	−3,076	1,305	−1,245	−12,430	−7,226	−3,905
Changes in reserves (increase in reserves =)	3,274	48	−4,795	2,213	−2,261	−12,888	−8,247	−4,868
Errors and omissions	−1,218	−1,557	−2,091	−1,875	63	−1,294	−2,355	−2,609

Source: OECD 1991: 99

the country to note that expensive foreign cars, VCRs, and other durables were in vogue. Rising imports, on the other hand, were related to the large-scale modernization of Spanish business. The substantial increase in the rate of self-financing, together with the progressive trade liberalization with the other EC member states, had led part of the Spanish business community to invest in new, more efficient machinery. These capital goods had to be largely imported from abroad, which accounts for a considerable share of rising imports during the boom years 1987–1988 (see Table 5).

Table 5 Merchandise trade: imports (c.i.f.)

	Volume, percentage changes			
	1985	1986	1987	1988
Total	7.0	16.6	22.2	13.9
Non-energy	10.0	23.5	26.8	20.2
Food	5.3	17.6	24.3	25.1
Raw materials	6.6	2.7	11.7	−4.0
Manufactures	11.9	30.0	30.2	23.5
of which:				
Intermediate goods	9.1	37.2	14.7	14.8
Capital goods	13.6	18.1	39.3	29.1
Consumer goods	14.1	36.9	41.3	27.2

Source: OECD 1989: 27

Imports of machinery and equipment went up by 26 per cent in volume and transport equipment by as much as 44 per cent. Both items contributed two-thirds to the nominal increase in merchandise imports (OECD 1989: 27).

In 1989 the Secretariat of State for Commerce (part of the Ministry of Economy and Finance) drew up three scenarios with respect to the future trade performance. The so-called 'optimistic scenario' foresaw a current account deficit of 18,000 million dollars in 1992 (3.8 per cent of GNP), if exports were to increase at a nominal rate of 12 per cent and imports at a nominal rate of 15 per cent. The 'realistic scenario', which remained close to the official forecasts, predicted a current account deficit of 39,000 million dollars (or 8.2 per cent of GNP) in 1992. Finally, the 'pessimistic scenario', which was an extrapolation of the first five months of 1989, described the following spectre (see *El País*, 11 July 1989), see Table 6. Though the government did launch a National Plan of Export Promotion (the impact of which was necessarily limited because of restrictive EC legislation), it gave no priority to this macro-economic imbalance. According to Carlos Solchaga, the main focus was on curtailing inflation. Through supply side government intervention, the macro-economic environment for private restructuring would be improved. In order to succeed, however, rising productivity should not be neutralized by rising wages. Gaining competitive force on the base of wage restraint was thus viewed as the only viable option for the Spanish economy, because 'the integration of the peseta into the EMS impedes the use of devaluations for competitive purposes' (*El País*, 9 December 1989).

Table 6 'Pessimistic Scenario' (current account deficit, 1989–1992)

Increase in exports of goods and services		8.7%
Increase in imports of goods and services		25.5%

Current Account Deficit year	million dollars	percentage of GNP
1989	15,000	4.4%
1990	30,000	7.8%
1991	50,000	11.7%
1992	76,000	16.2%

We can now draw some interim conclusions from the analysis of the performance of the Spanish economy during the 1980s. If we recall one of the basic objectives of the Socialists' macro-economic policy, viz. the reduction of the macro-economic imbalances (see the introduction to this chapter), it must be concluded that the government's priority was curtailing inflation rather than promoting employment.[6] In realizing this goal, however, the Socialists were to a considerable extent depending on external factors. In fact, it was a combination of falling oil prices, worldwide disinflation and an appreciation of the peseta which made the government's restrictive monetary policy work (see OECD 1991: 20). This particular feature indicates another important conclusion with respect to the Socialist adjustment policy: the 'transition to a full market economy' through domestic and external liberalization has only accentuated (and forms in part a reaction to) a more fundamental process, i.e., the so-called internationalizing of the state, which, according to Robert Cox, is 'the global process whereby national policies and practices have been adjusted to the exigencies of the world economy of international production' (Cox 1987: 253ff.). For the sake of clarity, this world economy of international production includes Spain, that is, is not external to the Spanish economy, and, indeed, is basically transnational in character (see Chapter 1). In this global economy of transnational production characterized by a progressive liberalization of movements of goods and capital, the trade performance of a national economy becomes a less important factor in macro-economic decision-making. That is, macro-economic policy is no longer primarily aimed at protecting and stimulating domestic markets and opening up foreign markets, i.e. oriented from the demand side, but increasingly oriented from the supply side. Trade policy (i.e. exchange rate policy, direct and indirect trade barriers, export

Economic policy and European integration 135

subsidies, etc.) has lost ground to (restrictive) monetary and fiscal policies; the optimization of investment conditions and the realization of economies of scale through concentration and transnationalization of production have become the principal means of attracting capital and increasing market shares. In the global economy of transnational production, national governments are no longer exclusively concerned with obtaining or maintaining structural national trade surpluses, since the dichotomy of national and foreign markets as inherent to the 'international economy of classical trade' has been superseded by the growing importance of transnationally mobile capital. The growth of intra-company trade (in terms of its share in world trade), being the result of a fast developing, cross-national, intra-concern division of labour, forms another indication of both the declining role of state-led trade policies and the trend towards 'uni- (instead of 'multi-') nationalization' of transnational companies.[7]

This may help one to understand the apparent contradiction between the liberalizing and deregulating effort of the Socialist government, on the one hand, and the rapidly increasing trade deficit, on the other. The primacy of supply side adjustment over demand-led growth is one thing. The promotion of an outward-looking mentality of Spanish business is another component of its macro-economic policy, and this is to be realized through a strategy of sink or swim. 'Swimming' means increasing productivity and profitability, investment in strong demand sectors, investment abroad, co-operation with foreign capital. 'Sinking' means being swallowed up by foreign capital at best, or breakdown at worst. It is this fundamentally anti-protectionist attitude, together with an offensive, internationalist (or rather, Europeanist) strategy of selective sectoral expansion, that characterize the government's guidelines for the private sector. As Solchaga argued in clear reference to the less competitive sections of Spanish business that are more inclined to some kind of selective protection,

> After all, what is continuing to preoccupy employers most is the profit level they will reach next year, or the measures we have to take in order to protect them from abroad. This idea of economic nationalism still continues to weigh heavily, and there is scarcely laid stress on the co-operative aspect inherent in the creation of this great single market of 370 millions of consumers. They have to start looking at German or French businessmen, not only as competitors, but as people with whom they are doing good business. After 1993, a German employer will be for a Spaniard what a Basque employer is right now for a Catalan one.
> (Carlos Solchaga, quoted in Díaz-Varela and Guindal 1990: 318)

In order to understand the Socialist macro-economic paradoxes, we have to go into more detail of the causes of the general policy direction. In the following section the external environment will be treated, the so-called external restraints imposed on a country by the 'international economy of classical trade'. Special emphasis will be given to the correlation between the position of the capital goods sector in a country's industrial structure, on the one hand, and the country's external, macro-economic vulnerability, on the other. This analysis offers a partial answer to the question of why the Spanish Socialist government started an austerity policy from the very beginning of its political mandate. It is only a partial answer, because the strategic interests behind this policy, and its actual content, have to be explained from the domestic power configuration in the 1980s. It is not enough to analyse external constraints, which appear as structural constraints, without taking note of the various alternative strategic options still left to the policy-makers. Indeed, it is the process in which the Spanish policy-makers become part and parcel of these 'external structures', i.e. the process of transnationalization, that is of relevance to the central argument of both this and the following chapter. In other words, it is the dependent incorporation of Spain into the international economy of classical trade that formed the vehicle for the incorporation of its dominant social and political forces into a 'denationalized' transnational ruling class, cemented around a common comprehensive strategy as to the contents and course of the process of European integration.

EXTERNAL RESTRAINTS AND SOCIALIST ECONOMIC POLICY

Though the leadership of the PSOE was composed of young and, in general, inexperienced members who came to learn political craftsmanship and to realize political reality mainly after the victory in the 1982 elections, the major planks in the party's political platform had undergone some fundamental changes during the preceding years. In aspiring to political power, the leadership had carefully modified one 'truly Socialist' objective after another (see Chapter 3). This gradual deradicalization and shift towards a social-democratic position in the political spectrum finally resulted in what the party strategists of the PSOE had first and foremost in mind: gaining a sufficient percentage of total votes in order to be able to govern. Once in power, the Spanish Socialist party was confronted with no political margins whatsoever to fulfil what was left of its initial objectives. Especially in the field of economics the newly elected government was forced to pursue moderate and even restrictive policies. It would be oversimplistic to explain this development merely from the middle-class background of a large part of the electorate and the consequent adjustment of the objectives held by the PSOE before its accession to power (see also Chapter 3). Indeed, one must also consider the international economic dependence of the Spanish economy and the resulting constraints on its Socialist government to pursue an alternative, more or less independent economic policy (e.g., a policy of stimulation within an international context characterized by the 'internationalization' of the so-called austerity policy). This is particularly so when the linkage of a national economy with international movements of circulating and productive capital results in the progressive articulation of national and international economic cycles, as was the case for Spain since the early 1960s.

In a famous essay of 1943, Kalecki introduced the term 'political business cycle' for the relationship between state economic policy and the development of the economic cycle. According to Kalecki's theory, in a slump a situation of full employment can, in principle, be established through a Keynesian economic policy, which increases effective demand by 'deficit spending'. However, in the consequent boom such a policy will conflict with the interests of business, as the disciplinary effect of unemployment gradually falls off and the power of the labour movement accordingly increases. Subsequent wage increases will put profits under pressure and business will react by raising prices and/or reducing production. Politically, a powerful bloc is likely to be formed between big business and the *rentier* interests, which will put the government under pressure to provoke a 'cleaning up' crisis by means of a restrictive policy, which must bring the 'disturbed relations' (excessive wage and price levels) into renewed equilibrium with productive capacity.

> The pressure of all these forces, and in particular of big business would most probably induce the Government to return to the orthodox policy of cutting down the budget deficit. A slump would follow in which Government spending policy would come again into its own.
> (Kalecki 1971: 144)

Such an approach errs by failing to consider the conflict of interest between different factions of the bourgeoisie with regard to economic policy. It is outdated by assuming that macro-economic decision-making is autonomous relative to structural external constraints, since the contents of a government's economic policy are strongly determined by the political pressure of national interest groups and can decisively influence the national economic cycle. If this continued to be the case in the 1980s, then it would be interesting to raise the question as to the domestic forces behind the adjustment policy implemented by the Socialist government after 1982.

Or to put it another way: what domestic balance of social powers restrained the Socialists from stimulating the Spanish economy? And how is one to explain, for example, that the Socialist government decided to introduce the peseta into the Exchange Rate Mechanism of the EMS in June 1989, after previous appreciations and despite accelerating deficits in foreign trade? Could such an entry not have been postponed until a more favourable currency rate had given domestic companies the benefits of cheaper exports and more expensive imports? Why was Spanish big business not in a position, then, to induce the government to adopt a policy of flexible (downward moving) exchange rates? In answering these questions, we first have to deal with the external constraints on a national government's ability to carry out an expansionist economic policy in an international setting of austerity.

In recent decades, international trade flows have become less sensitive to changing exchange rates. Four reasons can be mentioned (Holman and Poot 1983: 59) as follows.

1 An increasing product specialization within the international division of labour, in the course of which many products are no longer (or not yet) produced in a growing number of countries.
2 A fast developing intra-concern division of labour within transnational companies, which directly or indirectly control an ever greater share of world trade.
3 The central role of the import of raw materials, in the 1970s particularly oil, which cannot be substituted by national products.
4 The extension of so-called commodity forward transactions, as a result of which changes in price level influence actually payable prices only with a delay.

As a consequence, a renewal of the debate over fixed versus flexible exchange rates in the late 1970s has put the emphasis on the influence of exchange rate adjustments – particularly downward ones – on national rates of inflation (see Artus and Young 1979). Nominal prices in goods markets are usually downwardly inflexible, so that at least initially the increase in the domestic prices of goods tends to be larger in depreciating countries than the decrease in these prices in appreciating countries. Representatives of the so-called cost–push school have pointed out that a government that tries to meet a current account deficit by external adjustment stands in danger of pushing the country into a vicious circle of depreciation and inflation. For if workers are prepared to defend their real living standards from all forms of attack, they will simply respond to this depreciation-induced rise in the cost of living by lodging compensatory wage claims. In this way a situation can arise in which a spiral of depreciation – increasing inflation – depreciation will accelerate and ultimately result in hyperinflation (see Trevithick 1980). Add to this that an appreciation of a currency with respect to other currencies produces the same effect as a depreciation of these currencies with respect to the appreciating currency, and we see that depreciations of deficit countries generate not only inflationary spirals, but also appreciations of surplus countries. Moreover, expansionary monetary policies following incipient domestic cost and price increases can aggravate this situation (Cezanne and Möller 1979: 61).

The consequences for the international competitiveness of national industry, which are inseparable from the influence of changing exchange rates on inflation, play an important role in a government's choice between a flexible or fixed exchange rate system. The experiences of the economically weaker countries with the influence of depreciation on international competitiveness have led to a strong scepticism about this means of improving their competitive position. The purported positive effects of a depreciation are in practice totally or almost totally undone by a national inflationary spiral. That is why the governments of these countries are opting a system of fixed exchange rates. This in turn makes a restrictive economic policy extremely urgent.

We have already mentioned the increasing specialization of national economies within the international division of labour, and the consequent need of most countries to import products that they cannot or no longer produce. For instance, with regard to the second expansion of the Common Market to include Spain, Portugal and Greece, some argued that these countries would enter into a complementary division of labour with the highly industrialized countries of the EEC (see Deubner 1982: 13). The effect this would have on these countries' ability to adopt an independent economic policy has become dramatically visible in the moderate policies the new 'Socialist' governments were in fact pursuing from the very moment of their installation (with the exception of the Greek case, see below). In order to explain this in more detail, we must consider the central role of the capital goods industry in the postwar process of international specialization.

The expansion of world trade after World War II was characterized by an increase in trade between industrial nations and a subsequent decrease of the share of trade between these and the underdeveloped countries in world trade. As a consequence, this trade pattern was linked with a relative increase in trade of industrial products, particularly capital goods. This created a new kind of dependence within the highly industrialized part of

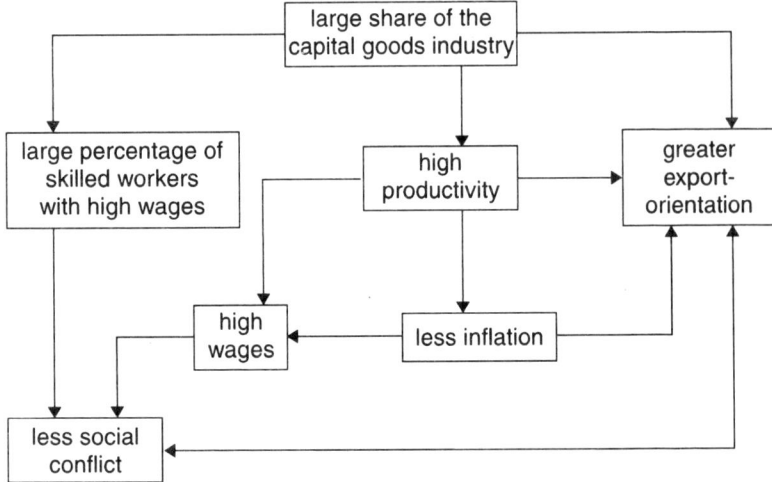

Figure 1 Implications of a large share of the capital goods industry in the national economy[8]

the world, involving countries with a large share of the capital goods industry in their national economies and countries without such a strong capital goods industry. Along these lines a new intercapitalist hierarchy has come into existence (see Schlupp 1980: 53–54). According to Frieder Schlupp, the main elements determining the place of a country in this hierarchy are the national specialization in industrial production (and trade) in general, and capital goods in particular; the 'outward' trade orientation towards the world market in general, and the most 'central', more developed foreign markets in particular; and the level of inclusion of the labour movement into the national, 'bourgeois–capitalist' economic and political system. These elements tend to reinforce or weaken each other (see Figure 1).

Spain shows some remarkable differences from the countries at the top of this intercapitalist hierarchy. In the first place, the Spanish economy is characterized by a relatively low share of the capital goods industry (Alonso *et al.* 1982; Buesa and Molero 1988). This means that to a certain extent it depends on other countries for the import of capital goods. This in turn means that the lower the absolute and relative national specialization in modern industries and technologies (especially in capital goods production) is, the lower the structural coherence of the national production apparatus, and also the lower the relative homogeneity of economic modernization and productivity in all sectors and industries.

Such a national specialization pattern of modern industries and capital goods production tends to favour, by multiple spin-off effects, a relatively 'autocentered' socio-economic national development. A contrasting specialization in traditional industries and production-chains in turn tends to result in a much less auto-centered, even structurally dependent national development pattern, because of absolutely or relatively incoherent, incomplete, and heterogeneous inter- and intra-sectoral linkages within the framework of the national economy.

(Schlupp 1980: 53)

In the case of Spain, the relatively low share of the capital goods industry generates, at least partially, a lower degree of productivity, higher inflation rates, a lower general wage level, a relatively small percentage of skilled workers, and potentially more social conflict.

In the second place, as a result of the first situation, the Spanish economy is characterized by a relatively low export orientation in industrial goods. Exports of goods as a percentage of GDP in 1988 amounted to 11.8 per cent, compared with a percentage of 25.9 for the EC as a whole (OECD 1991, and author's own calculations).

We can now return to the central question of this section: why has the Socialist government in Spain not been able to stimulate its national economy? It is a fact that after 1975 a real internationalization of austerity took place. In almost every OECD country a relatively successful stabilization policy became dominant. This internationalization of austerity was by no means the result of a coincidental synchronization. In fact, the austerity policy was 'exported' from the countries at the top of the intercapitalist hierarchy to the less developed countries. This can be clearly illustrated by the example of Spain, whose economic and social problems were aggravated by relatively successful stabilization policies in the highly developed countries. This process eventually made it necessary for Spain to pursue a stabilization policy, or, what comes to the same thing, limit the margins within which a stimulation policy could be pursued. The experiences of the French Socialist government in 1981 made it clear that a unilateral stimulation policy would not go 'unpunished'. Instead of an impetus to national industry with positive effects on employment, this expansionist policy produced an increase in imports and an enlargement of the trade deficit. In anticipation of a devaluation of the French franc, there was massive speculation and capital flight, which produced further downward pressure on the franc. This eventually led to a nominal devaluation in June 1982 and a second one in March 1983. Subsequently, the French government was forced to abandon its stimulation policy.

Another case in point is Greece. During the same period the Greek Socialists had similar experiences as the French. After coming to power in 1981, PASOK initially took some measures to stimulate demand, as a result of which investments were expected to increase and unemployment to decrease. Thus, for example, minimum wages and pensions were substantially raised and loans for public housing were increased (Axt 1984: 197–198). However, in 1982, under the influence of a general deterioration of the economic situation in Greece, this policy was changed. Fighting inflation and controlling wage increases became the central objectives during 1983. After the elections of 1985, in which PASOK again obtained an absolute majority in parliament, an even more restrictive adjustment policy was put forward. The austerity measures that were announced in October 1985 meant a 'dramatic U-turn in policy-making' for some (*Financial Times*, 3 February 1986). This interpretation is, however, an exaggerated one, for the actual adjustment was introduced more gradually, beginning in 1982–1983 when the reduction of inflation became the highest priority. In any case, and in contrast to the PSOE (and the Socialist party of Portugal), PASOK did try to stimulate the Greek economy in the first years of its first term of office. Still, as the Greek and French examples clearly show (and has also been the case in Spain and Portugal), the government of a country with a tendentially depreciating currency is inclined to stabilize the national exchange rate, because of the inflationary effects of a depreciation. To do so, the Socialist governments had at least to abstain from stimulating their economies.

Why did the Socialist government in Spain not make the same error as those in France and Greece in 1981? Why did it initially not try to pursue a stimulation policy? This can be explained partly by the fact that this government anticipated the effects of such a policy. But could the austerity policy also be the result of internal power structures on the basis of which this Socialist government secured political legitimacy? To answer this question we have to look more closely at the impact of the process of internationalization and Europeanization on political and social relations in Spain. The remainder of this chapter will proceed by focusing on the strategic objectives inherent in Socialist European policy with respect to adjusting Spanish social and economic relations to the exigencies of the world economy of transnational production. Structural deficiencies of Spanish industry (notably its relatively incoherent and heterogeneous sectoral linkages and the low share of the capital goods industry in the general framework) made the government opt for a leap forward: instead of choosing an ambiguous policy of supporting weak sectors and half-heartedly innovating more viable ones, it decided to rely on the market forces, on foreign capital and on developing a couple of 'national champions' that could eventually form the backbone of a genuine transnational implantation of Spanish capital. In the following chapter we shall focus on changing power configurations within the Spanish bourgeoisie (the other side of the coin of Spain's enhanced incorporation into the European heartland) with the main purpose of specifying those factions most akin to this policy.

In Chapters 3 and 4 we dealt with the constituent elements of the Socialist hegemonic policy and the progressive subordination of Spain's foreign policy objectives to the European ambitions of the ruling party's leadership. It was argued that the 'cardinal and transcendent thought' of making Spain one of the leading countries in the New Europe depended on the country's capacity to adjust its industrial structure and to converge with the most developed member states. We focused on the intra-party conflicts, notably between the party apparatus and the neo-liberals in government, without paying full attention to the social power configuration underlying this dominant, strategic orientation. In abstracting again from the role of private social forces for the time being, it is first necessary to elaborate in more detail on the general framework of European integration, and its 'extended relaunch' in the course of the 1980s.

In a recent essay on the European Community as an 'emergent and novel form of political domination', Philippe Schmitter convincingly criticizes the 'state-centric' approaches to mainstream integration theory. In elaborating on the notion of 'Post-Hobbesian' order in which the 'relevance of territoriality' and the 'necessity for sovereignty' are declining and in which the functional difference between the state and the civil society becomes blurred, he speaks of the EC as a paradigmatic case of 'Post-Hobbesianism'. However, though the emergence of 'non-state systems of authority which find a variety of institutional forms' is 'distinctive, virtually unique, to the European Community', his more ambitious claim is 'that *the contemporary context systematically favors the transformation of states into either confederatii, condominii or federatii in a variety of settings*' (Schmitter 1991: 15). Neither the return of the nation–state nor the emergence of a supra-national state will be the likely outcome of the present process of institutional restructuring in a global setting of transnational production. Nor will this process be confined to the EC. In other words, when speaking of competing strategies in terms of political regionalization versus economic globalization, we should focus on the development of transnationally effective concepts of control unifying factions of the ruling class into different coalitions at the European and global level (and the eventual elaboration of a uniform conception that can 'articulate different visions of the world in such a way that their potential antagonism is neutralised'; see also Chapter 1). Let me explain this point by sketching the competing, and ideal–typical, comprehensive concepts of control that stand at the heart of present-day political and economic decision-making in Europe and, more particularly, the Spanish position in the rearrangement of forces in the course of the 1980s.[9]

In dealing with different comprehensive strategies with respect to European integration, we must first distinguish four ideal-typical groups of economic actors:[10]

1 Import-competing producers of tradeable goods for the domestic market.
2 Import-competing producers of tradeable goods for the European market.
3 Export-competing producers of tradeable goods for the world market.
4 Globally operating financial institutions.

If we attempt to relate these groupings to individual member states, it can be stated that the first group of national producers has a dominant position in the national capitals of countries like Greece, Portugal, and to a lesser extent Spain. In all three countries, however, the position of foreign (and especially German) companies producing for the European market has been considerably strengthened over the last decades. In the case of Spain, for instance, the evolution followed by foreign direct investment not only shows a spectacular rise during the 1982–1988 period, but also a sharp decline in the position of the USA in exchange for a leading role of EC countries (see Table 7).

Table 7 Authorized investment in Spain by country of origin (% of total)

	1960–75	*1976–81*	*1982–88*
EC	35.16	42.40	48.14
West Germany	10.54	11.33	10.09
France	5.42	10.47	7.73
United Kingdom	10.13	8.54	8.53
Netherlands	4.37	6.11	14.10
USA	40.61	25.32	9.21
total (billions current psts)	142.77	343.24	2869.60

Source: Molero 1992: 163

This foreign penetration indicates that a form of dependent accumulation has come to characterize the Spanish economy, coinciding with a virtual amalgamation of interests between national and foreign bourgeoisie.[11]

The second category, 'European business', is particularly strong and influential in a country like France, its electronics and car industries being cases in point. The third category of globally operating enterprises has obtained an increasingly dominant position in Germany since World War II (van der Pijl 1991), while the last group, global finance, forms the stronghold of British capitalism (Overbeek 1990). In relating these ideal–typical categories of socio-economic actors to their primacy in individual states we must emphasize, however, that, with the exception of the first group, all these actors transcend national frontiers, operate at a transnational level and find allies within other countries. That is, all categories are to a greater or lesser degree represented in every member state.

If we now return to the three interrelated debates referred to in the section on p. 114 of the previous chapter, the Atlanticist option, favouring intergovernmentalism and opting for widening rather than deepening the European Community, seems paradigmatically related to globally mobile financial capital, whose comprehensive concept of control is best described with the orientation of liberal internationalism.

The Europeanist orientation, supporting some kind of supra-national institutionalism, and stressing the need to deepen the process of European integration first, is effectively represented by the category of import-competing producers of tradeable goods for the European market. It is to this ideal–typical group of economic actors that the Socialist macroeconomic and industrial policy is addressed. As a working hypothesis for the subsequent sections and the following chapter, it can be stated that the Spanish ruling party's European policy (which resembles all the integrating elements of the second orientation, as we saw in Chapter 4) is congruent with its dual policy objective of attracting foreign 'import-competing producers of tradeable goods for the European market', on the one hand, and promoting the transnationalization (which in the short and medium-term primarily means Europeanization) of the most viable, spearhead sections of Spanish big business, on the other. In this sense, the Spanish position is best summarized as aiming at political regionalization rather than economic globalization.

We can now identify five major reasons for the moderate impact of the PSOE on socio-economic policy in Spain. One is the middle-class character of part of the electorate. This explains the deradicalization of the party's political platform before the 1982 elections. Another is the increasing international economic dependence of Spain, which decisively limited its field of operations in economic policy. The factor linking these two explanations is the general process of internationalization and subsequent, accelerated industrialization of the Spanish economy in the 1960s and 1970s. Without this process, no substantial and politically emancipated middle class would have come into existence, and no full integration into the world market, resulting in increased external dependence, would have taken place. Finally, it was these middle classes that benefited most from the domestic demand-induced economic boom in the second half of the 1980s. A rise in real wages and a depreciation of the peseta affected them most in terms of, *inter alia*, rising purchasing power and greater access to foreign durable consumer goods. A third reason is the pressure from foreign governments and foreign owners of private financial and productive capital on domestic decision-making. It is difficult to document the extent to which direct influence was exercised on the Spanish government, but we have been able to demonstrate that the so-called internationalization of austerity from the late 1970s onwards clearly constrained the range of alternative policy measures. If we recall the distinction between structural and behavioural power of transnational capital (as elaborated in Chapter 1), it is the former phenomenon in particular that must be emphasized. Supply side government intervention during the 1980s tried to provide an appropriate social and economic infrastructure, aimed at attracting large flows of direct foreign investment, short-term capital and long-term portfolio investment. Next to this, market liberalization and European integration, in combination with the restrictive monetary policy of the Socialists, provided foreign companies with a large consumer market characterized by relatively high growth rates.

Two other reasons have been pointed out, but they deserve more detailed attention in the following pages. One is the comprehensive Europeanist project itself. In directing its efforts first and foremost at full market integration, the macro-economic policy of the Socialist government was further constrained by the 'extended relaunch' of European unification. In the following section we will pay particular attention to the impact of the completion of the Single European Market and the agreements on a European Monetary Union. The other is the domestic power configuration supporting the comprehensive policy. The industrial policy of the PSOE, aiming at the reconversion and internationalization (and partial privatization) of the most viable companies belonging to the public sector, will be dealt with in the section on p. 156. In the following chapter, the government's intervention in the merger process of private banking is analysed from the perspective of the fractionalization of Spanish business.

It will be concluded that the ruling party's project was mainly supported by, and to the benefit of, part of private bank capital and the most competitive, outward-looking sections of public enterprise (and the party affiliates at the top of these public firms), a domestic power configuration moulded in close co-operation with foreign transnational capital.

THE IMPACT OF FULL EC MEMBERSHIP ON MACRO-ECONOMIC POLICY-MAKING AND INDUSTRIAL RESTRUCTURING

As stated in the introduction to this chapter, the PSOE concentrated its efforts on three interrelated objectives: the correction of macro-economic imbalances through a policy of austerity, with the emphasis on curtailing inflation; the restructuring of Spanish private and public industry by way of progressively deregulating and liberalizing the Spanish labour, commodity and capital markets in order to obtain major strength and efficiency, and to recover company profits; and, finally, an accelerated integration into the Common Market which, in 1982, implied a relaunch of the negotiations between Spain and the EC. The realization of this final objective in 1986 gave added force to the other two priorities, while a new, synthesizing objective came to the fore. That is, the coming into force of the Single European Act in mid-1987 and the subsequent developments towards a European Monetary Union make macro-economic convergence with the stronger economies a precondition for participation – and participation seems the prime concern of the Socialist leadership and government. To join is to be accepted as equals, and the very prerequisite for future leadership.

The reason for recalling these objectives is to stress once more the European ambitions of the Spanish Socialists. It is this attitude that to a large extent explains the policy shift in the course of the 1980s. A shift from a policy mix characterized by a restrictive monetary policy, a moderately restrictive fiscal policy, and a policy of industrial conversion, to a situation in which adjustment and austerity seem to become goals in themselves; in which all initiatives are left to the private (or privatized) sector; and the state progressively withdraws from the economic scene, even renouncing its economic involvement in the process of reindustrialization. If this description is true, then it may be concluded that the neo-liberal wing of the PSOE has substantially strengthened its position within the government. This in turn raises the question of how and to what extent the opposition within the government and the party apparatus, and in Spanish civil society, has been (perhaps temporarily) defeated.

Before answering these questions, we have to emphasize a fundamental discontinuity in the 'extended decade of the 1980s': the years 1985–1986 mark a clear breaking-point. As we saw in the section on p. 128, the great majority of macro-economic indicators show a different, if not reverse, trend from 1986 onwards. Decreasing unemployment and inflation rates are accompanied by increasing GNP growth rates and foreign trade deficits. Three important features are not only essential in understanding this breaking-point but are also helpful in answering one of the underlying questions of this chapter, i.e., whether the macro-economic policy of the Spanish Socialists is to be labelled neo-liberal or not. First, formal accession to the European Community was realized, and the first economic effects were soon felt. Second, a new phase in the government's industrial policy was initiated in this biennium, after the period of industrial reconversion had come to an end. Third, the 1985–1986 biennium heralded a new era in the relationship between the Socialist government and the trade unions, a situation which worsened in the course of the economic boom during the second half of the 1980s. It can be argued that the rupture between the government and the trade unions, and the subsequent isolation of the party apparatus from the most relevant decision-making circles (personified in the departure of Alfonso Guerra, see Chapter 3) left the political vacuum to be filled by the neoliberals who aptly made use of the Europeanist argument (i.e. the irreversible and ineluctable involvement of Spain in the process of European – economic – unification) to strengthen their position in the macro-economic decision-making process. The dramatic deterioration of the Spanish economy in the course of 1992, then, renewed debates both within and outside the ruling party, and created a climate of social conflict over the general premises of the Socialist European policy.

The impact of EC membership on the Spanish economy

The consequences of the entry of Spain into the Common Market may be subdivided into its economic impact, i.e. the effects that free competition (including the completion of the Single European Market) have, for example, on Spain's foreign trade and industrial structure; and its policy impact, i.e. the effects of the acceleration of the process of European integration on macro-economic decision-making in Spain. Potentially, these two major impacts increasingly contradict each other at the level of government. A medium-term policy of reindustrializing the Spanish economy through active state participation, implying flexible fiscal and budgetary policies, contradicts the short-term necessity of macro-economic convergence in the light of the creation of a European Monetary Union. After briefly reviewing some studies dealing with the effects of full membership and the completion of the internal market on the Spanish industrial structure, the policy measures of the Socialist government necessary to meet the EMU convergence criteria will be examined. The question will be tackled of whether this so-called convergence policy conflicts with another fundamental objective, that of industrial regeneration.

The impact of the internal market on the Spanish economy

The entry of Spain into the Common Market concluded a twenty-five year period of seeking rapprochement with Western Europe. The first, unsuccessful, application for membership in 1962, the signing of a preferential trade agreement in 1970, the second application in 1977, and the subsequent accession negotiations, were all steps in a long-term process that eventually resulted in the signing of the Accession Treaty in June 1985. Since a transition period of seven years for the bulk of industrial and agricultural goods was agreed upon during the negotiations, full participation by Spain in the European Customs Union would coincide with the completion of the Single Market on 1 January 1993. Hence we can group together those studies stressing the impact of full membership on the Spanish economy with those analysing the impact of the completion of the Single Market.

In the period prior to the successful completion of the accession negotiations between Spain and the EC, a large number of studies were made of the impact of future membership on the Spanish economy in general and on the Spanish industrial structure in particular.[12] A common characteristic of these studies was that they started from an analysis of existing productive structures in the late 1970s and early 1980s and then forecast the problems and prospects of each sector in a situation of full competition, in order to conclude, in some cases, with a number of recommendations on government industrial policy and the future behaviour of private economic agents. The impact of these studies was limited, however, due to their strictly academic significance. In a situation in which a large part of the Spanish business community was fully occupied with dealing with the short-term consequences of the international economic crisis (see Segura *et al.* 1989), i.e. still under conditions of selective protectionism, no comprehensive long-term strategy directed at innovating and modernizing the Spanish productive structure in the light of future integration was to be expected. In fact, a 1981 study by the Spanish employers' organization on the impact of EC membership on Spanish industry did not offer a blueprint of anticipatory restructuring and specialization, but aimed primarily at influencing the accession negotiations in a defensive way. An extended period of transition, during which export restrictions for Spanish industrial products would be progressively reduced while import barriers would continue to exist in a substantial way, it was argued, formed the only guarantee for a smooth adaptation of the Spanish industrial structure to new circumstances (see Confederación Española de Organizaciones Empresariales 1981). It was only after the first effects of membership became apparent after 1986 that a more comprehensive political discussion of the benefits of integration *per se* and its implications for domestic industrial policy was sparked off.

In addition to the Cecchini Report, which set out to analyse the macroeconomic effects of the internal market, the European Commission's departments collaborated with national experts to carry out a study on its impact by industrial sector. After selecting forty industrial sectors most affected by 'Europe 1992' out of 120 sectors considered,[13] some general conclusions were drawn for each member state. In the case of Spain (and Portugal) it was more difficult to draw such comparative conclusions since tariff and quantitative trade barriers were still quite significant during the period of research, thus raising questions about the appropriateness of the forty preselected sensitive sectors (Martín 1990: 205). Nevertheless, in general terms the outcome of the study for Spain was quite congruous with the results and forecasts of a couple of national studies on the impact of EC membership *per se* (ibid.: 209–215):

> since accession, Spain's manufacturing imports as a whole, and particularly those of the most sensitive sectors, have experienced a sharp increase. That increase is higher in the case of imports from the EC. On the contrary, manufacturing exports have suffered a deceleration in the EC market and a dramatic drop in the whole of the other third countries. In consequence, . . . since EC membership a substantial worsening in manufactured products trade balances . . . has taken place. (pp. 209/210)

> industries in which Spanish trade performance is relatively good (12 out of 40) are less important in terms of value added and employment than those where Spanish firms perform moderately or badly. (p. 212)

> if the distribution of trade strength and weakness is related to demand growth for each industry's products in the Community, the major part of the activities where the Spanish firms suffer a clear disadvantage are average or strong demand sectors. . . . By contrast, the nucleus of Spanish comparative advantages mainly consists of industrial activities for which there is weak growth in demand . . . (p. 212)

> the bulk of industries where public purchases (telecommunications equipment, office equipment, railway equipment, etc.) are concentrated is within the group in which Spanish firms' competitiveness is relatively poor. Thus, the opening up of public purchasing to EC-wide competition could lead to a substantial increase in import penetration. (p. 212)
>
> finally, the weak trade performance of Spanish firms seems most noticeable in the industries which, in general, are characterized by relatively high capital/labour ratios, high R&D content, and high potential for economies of scale. In contrast, Spanish firms seem to perform relatively more strongly in products which are characterized overall by the opposite features. (p. 215)

These conclusions are quite similar to those drawn from other recent research both inside and outside Spain. All the relevant studies in this respect point in the same direction: in comparative terms Spanish industry is characterized by a high labour/capital ratio and a low competitive power *vis-à-vis* its counterparts in the highly developed member states; a concentration of manufacturing activities in low growth industries; an import dependence on investment goods and foreign technology; and a progressive export orientation on labour intensive products and natural resources.[14] Seen from the present competitive position of Spanish business, it seems appropriate to conclude that the main beneficiaries of the Spanish integration into the Single European Market are foreign companies which are active in the export of high tech products and/or will profit more than local producers from the opening up of public procurement, and those foreign companies looking for low-cost production locations. Hence the need for a profound industrial reconversion of both the public and private sector has become particularly urgent in recent years (see Velarde Fuertes 1992: 191). Since this chapter is primarily concerned with the economic policy of the Socialist government in the 1980s, and less so with private business strategies at the company or sectoral level (we will deal with these in the next chapter, where the strategies of the Spanish banking sector in anticipation of the completion of the Single European Market are analysed), we must continue our analysis by posing the question whether the Socialists have developed an active industrial policy directed at public involvement in the process of industrial restructuring. Before doing so, however, we must first enter into another major consequence of full membership, that of the 'externally' induced constraints on domestic economic policy as a result of the so-called extended relaunch of European integration in the late 1980s and early 1990s.

152 *The Socialist decade (1982–1992)*

As indicated on several occasions in the previous chapters, the impact of EC membership was not only felt in private and public industries (or, indeed, in other economic sectors). In so far as the project of completing the Single Market was accompanied by supportive policy measures at supranational level (in the fields of, for instance, social, regional and technology policies) and, eventually, extended by agreements on monetary and political union, the process of European integration increasingly came to have an impact on national decision-making in a formal and institutional sense. Most importantly, *de facto* dependence on international movements of capital, and particularly their disciplinary effect on national policies, was formally reinforced by the monetary union-induced pressure to converge these member states' economic policies, as we shall see in the next section.

Monetary unification and economic convergence

As mentioned in the previous chapter, the Maastricht summit had to decide upon a range of interconnected issues affecting not only the member states' sovereignty in the field of economic and monetary policies, but also, and far more delicately, in foreign policy and defence matters. Let us confine ourselves here to the results of Maastricht with respect to the European Monetary Union.

Decision-making in this field was certainly the least difficult part. Before the actual summit was held, the Dutch presidency reached total agreement among the EC 12 on the main points of monetary unification. Part of this agreement was the clause allowing Britain to opt out of the third and final phase of the EMU. In a separate protocol attached to the EMU treaty Britain is given the right not to join the single currency.

The Community's decision-making on the passage to this final stage of the EMU will begin in 1996. If at least seven countries meet so-called 'convergence criteria', a summit will decide when EMU should start. If not, a single currency will be adopted automatically in January 1999 by those member states that are ready, for the time being leaving outside those that are not. Decision-making will take place by qualified majority, and will be guided by the following five criteria. First, the criterion on price stability implies that a successful candidate shall have a rate of inflation (observed over a period of one year before the examination in 1996) 'that does not exceed that of the at most three best performing Member States ... by more than 1.5 percentage points'.

Second and third, under the so-called 'excessive deficit procedure', compliance with two criteria will be examined: the ratio of the planned or actual government deficit to gross domestic product and the ratio of

Table 8 European Community convergence indicators (1991)

	Inflation	Long-term interest rate	Govt balance as % GDP	Debt as % GDP
Belgium	3.1	9.3	−6.4	129.4
Denmark	1.9	10.1	−1.7	66.7
Germany	4.3	8.6	−3.2	46.2
Greece	20.0	20.8	−17.9	96.4
Spain	6.6	12.4	−3.9	45.6
France	3.1	9.0	−1.5	47.2
Ireland	2.1	9.2	−4.1	102.8
Italy	7.2	12.9	−9.9	101.2
Luxembourg	3.7	8.2	+1.9	6.9
Netherlands	3.6	8.9	−4.4	78.4
Portugal	14.6	17.1	−5.4	64.7
United Kingdom	6.5	9.9	−1.9	43.8
Eur. Community	5.5	10.4	−4.3	61.8

Source: European Commission 1991[15]

government debt to gross domestic product. The reference values are respectively 3 per cent and 60 per cent.

Fourth, the criterion on participation in the Exchange Rate Mechanism of the European Monetary System (EMS) means that a member state's currency 'shall have respected the normal fluctuation margins provided for by the Exchange Rate Mechanism of the European Monetary System without severe tensions for at least the last two years before its examination'. In this period, a national currency must not have been devalued. The 'normal fluctuation margin' of the ERM is 2.25 per cent.

Fifth, the criterion on the convergence of interest rates means that a member state 'shall have a nominal long-term interest rate that does not exceed that of the at most three best performing Member States ... by more than 2 percentage points' (Treaty on European Union 1992) in the last year before the examination.

European monetary integration has always resulted in a two-tier Europe, leaving low-income countries on a second plane. This was the case with the so-called 'Snake', its successor the EMS, and it will be the result of the conditions set for being allowed into the third phase of EMU. In particular, the criteria with respect to 'a high degree of price stability' on the one hand,

Table 9 Criteria satisfied (in December 1991)

	Inflation	Long-term interest rate	Govt balance as % GDP	Debt as % GDP	Currency
Greece	no	no	no	no	no
Portugal	no	no	no	no	no
Spain	no	no	no	yes	no
Italy	no	no	no	no	yes
Netherlands	yes	yes	no	no	yes
Ireland	yes	yes	no	no	yes
Belgium	yes	yes	no	no	yes
Germany	no	yes	no	yes	yes
Britain	no	yes	yes	yes	no
Denmark	yes	yes	yes	no	yes
Luxembourg	yes	yes	yes	yes	yes
France	yes	yes	yes	yes	yes

Source: European Commission 1991[16]

and 'a sustainable government financial position' on the other, probably will have two (perhaps not completely unintentional) side-effects: the period prior to the examination of the member states' suitability for EMU will show an austerity race between governments, but, in spite of this, and ironically, will culminate in the exclusion of some member states from the third stage because of their inability to meet the five convergence criteria.

If we look at the convergence indicators at the time of the Maastricht summit, we can conclude that ten member states did not satisfy the conditions for EMU (see Tables 8 and 9). In fact, some member states will have extreme difficulties in catching up with the 'top of the class' countries. Italy is widely seen as a case in point. Spain, Portugal, and Greece are other candidates for dropping out. This forecast is partly based on the already visible consequences of the economic liberalization inherent in EC membership and the completion of the Single Market for the economies of these three countries. The deterioration in economic performance, especially with respect to trade, a deterioration that is only partially compensated by reverse capital flows in the context of the EC's various 'cohesion' activities, can only be met by extreme austerity measures. These externally induced neo-liberal economic policies are only to be aggravated in the near future in order not to be excluded from EMU. John Grahl and

Paul Teague rightly foresaw these developments when they stated that 'the market integration programme carries a major threat of monetary *disintegration*, which can only be avoided by an acceptance of much tighter constraints on domestic policy and thus a narrowing of the scope for growth-oriented class compromise' (Grahl and Teague 1989: 45). This tendency is quite similar to what Danièle Leborgne and Alain Lipietz have labelled 'competitive austerity' (Lipietz and Leborgne 1990: 194). Indeed, one example of the different national policy reactions after Maastricht was what the 'convergence race' may boil down to in individual member states. The Spanish government immediately took action after the summit to launch a so-called *plan de convergencia* for the period 1992–1996. The main contours of this convergence plan were: control of public expenditure through a tight fiscal policy; reduction of inflation and interest rates; deregulation and flexibilization of capital and labour markets; control of nominal wage increases; and an accelerated (partial) privatization of public enterprises (*El País*, 4–5 March 1992, and 3–4 April 1992). In concrete macro-economic terms the plan (which was approved by the Spanish parliament in May 1992 and by the EC Council of Finance Ministers in June) projected, *inter alia*, the following (see Table 10):

Table 10 Convergence plan 1992–1996: macro-economic projection (% annual change)

	1992	1993	1994	1995	1996
GDP	3.0	3.3	3.6	3.6	3.5
Inflation	6.0	4.7	3.8	3.3	3.1
Unit labour costs	4.1	3.6	2.7	2.3	2.3
Unemployment*	16.3	15.8	15.1	14.3	13.5
Current balance (% of GDP)	–2.9	–2.8	–2.5	–2.4	–2.3
Public deficit (% of GDP)	–4.0	–3.5	–2.7	–1.8	–1.0

Source: *El País*, 6 September 1992
*Percentage of active population

Leaving aside for a moment its deregulatory underpinning (which clearly reflected a political decision in line with the neo-liberal restructuring in other EC member states), the macro-economic component of the Convergence Plan was presented as the sole realistic alternative for two reasons:

first, it was intended to change the previously implemented policy mix of a moderately expansive fiscal policy and a restrictive monetary policy into its opposite, i.e. a tight fiscal policy in combination with a less restrictive monetary policy, in order to meet the dual objective of reducing public deficit and stimulating the Spanish economy through lowering the interest rate. This policy mix was regarded as superior to the alternatives of growth stimulation, i.e. an expansive fiscal policy, on the one hand and a devaluation of the peseta, on the other (see de la Dehesa 1992).

Second, meeting the objective of nominal convergence with the other member states was seen as a necessary condition to realize real convergence later on, i.e. the approximation of macro-economic variables like productive structure, GDP per capita, and level of employment (Alcaide 1992). In this respect the government's industrial policy, and particularly its approach to the role of public enterprise in economic restructuring, were determined by the instruments of rationalization and privatization.

Industrial policy and the Instituto Nacional de Industria

In the previous section we discussed the two most important consequences of full membership (under conditions laid down by the extended relaunch of European integration): first, the exposure of an unbalanced, uncompetitive, and, hence, highly sensitive industrial structure to free competition; second, the constraints on domestic macro-economic policy-making as a result of the EMU convergence criteria. The former impact called for an active participation of the Spanish state in industrial restructuring, either directly through the promotion of public companies, or indirectly through developing an adequate productive environment. The latter implied drastic cuts in public spending (see also Fuentes Quintana 1992). This contradiction between the need for an active industrial policy, on the one hand and the exigencies of monetary union, on the other, was solved in the course of 1992 in favour of the latter policy goals. It is inaccurate, however, to see this policy shift as merely the result of the Maastricht agreements. In fact, already in the second half of the 1980s, and in conjunction with the strengthening of the neo-liberals in the Socialist government (see the previous chapters), a start was made with the reduction of government involvement in industrial production and with the application of free market rules to the public sector in general. A short account of the government's policy towards the public holding Instituto Nacional de Industria (INI) can illustrate this point.

We first have to return to the beginning of the PSOE's political leadership, and to one of its initial objectives, i.e. the accelerated modernization of

Spanish industry. In general terms, the newly elected government opted for a double politico-economic strategy (Etxezarreta 1991: 51): first, it emphasized the vanguard function of private capital as the primary motor of economic recovery. This implied, *inter alia*, the creation of an optimal macro-economic environment for the free movement of market forces, and the progressive reduction of the active and direct involvement of the public sector in demand management and industrial production; second, it embarked on a forced restructuring of the productive structure through the enhanced internationalization of the Spanish economy. The improvement of productivity and profit levels in the private sector, a prerequisite for a successful start to this externally induced modernization, was supported by the above-mentioned macro-economic policy of adjustment.

Next to the macro-economic sustainment of private economic restructuring, an industrial policy was implemented characterized by the deregulation, reconversion, privatization and 'multinationalization' of the public companies belonging to the state holding INI (see García Fernández 1990: 236–237). More concretely, industrial policy during the Socialist decade went through different phases.

During the first phase, from 1982 to 1985/86, the main objective of the Socialist government was to restore profitability. As a result of this, private enterprises in crisis were no longer incorporated in the public sector (as had been the practice in the 1960s and 1970s) and no new public companies were created (Myro 1988b: 490). As to the existing industries within the INI, the initial reconversion strategy of the government aimed at reducing the 'surplus of staff' by 70,000 workers (its destructive component), and at restructuring industrial activity towards more technologically advanced production methods (its constructive impact). However, the substantial reduction of employment in the public sector, affecting 54,000 workers up to December 1985, fulfilled the objective initially laid down in the government's reconversion plans by 78 per cent, whereas at the same date only 30 per cent of the projected investments had been realized. It can be concluded, then, that the first phase showed a primacy of destruction of productive capacity over innovation and modernization (see Buesa and Molero 1988: 247).

During the second phase, from 1986 to 1990, a more active policy can be discerned. In this period public investment plans related to the policy of reconversion were finally realized. This led some commentators to argue that the Socialist government had successfully reversed the downward trend of de-industrialization through the productive and financial reorganization of traditional low demand sectors in decline, the promotion of more dynamic activities in medium and strong demand sectors, and the improvement of the competitive position of Spanish industry *vis-à-vis* its European competitors (see Vázquez 1990: 108; and Fernández Marugan 1992: 155ff.). This conclusion seems too optimistic, since more than 70 per cent of total investments went to two traditional 'sectors in reconversion', i.e. the steel and textile industries (Vázquez 1990: 105). In any case, the general reorganization of productive capacity in the public sector in conjunction with the accelerated economic growth after 1985–1986 did result in 1988 (for the first time in many years) in a profit of 31 billion pesetas for the INI as a whole, a result which increased by almost 165 per cent to 82 billion in the following year (*Actualidad Económica*, 20 March 1989; *El País*, 10 March 1990).

Another feature of this second phase was the policy of privatization and 'multinationalization'. Having started in 1984, it was during the 1985–1990 period that a substantial number of companies belonging to the public sector were privatized (see *El País*, 25 November 1990; and Gómez Uranga 1991: 479). Some of the most important of these companies were sold to foreign capital (for example, SEAT to Volkswagen and ENASA to Fiat). For some commentators critical of the industrial policy pursued by the Socialist government, this indicates more pragmatic, neo-liberal motives. For Julio García Fernández it confirms a more general tendency to nationalize companies in crisis (the so-called socialization of private losses), to liquidate some of them and to reorganize the most viable ones and restore their profitability, in order to sell them subsequently to a foreign company. 'It is, then, a rescue operation while waiting for a multinational partner' (García Fernández 1990: 238). He goes so far as to predict that

> within ten years, the majority of the large Spanish companies will either have obtained a strong position in Europe, which is unlikely when starting from a country with a limited technological capacity, or will have been taken over by multinationally operating firms.
>
> (ibid.: 240)

For Josep González i Calvet, finally, this particular feature of the Socialists' industrial policy clearly illustrates the more general neo-liberal outlook of their economic policy. They have failed to formulate a comprehensive strategy or even concrete objectives for the public industrial sector, except for that of profitability, which is part and parcel of the macro-economic goal of extending and strengthening the private market forces. 'The public sector adopts a position of strict subsidiarity *vis-à-vis* the private sector, absorbing and handing down to the taxpayer the costs of the crisis and the restructuring of capital, in order to privatize the profits afterwards' (González i Calvet 1991: 228).

Both interpretations of the course followed during the second phase seem partially incorrect inasmuch as they stress either the overall innovating and modernizing impact of the Socialists' industrial policy or its general, neo-liberal emphasis on privatization (and 'multinationalization') and market liberalization. In particular, developments during the third phase indicate the elaboration of a dual strategy aimed at reducing capacity, extended rationalization and (partial) privatization of the less competitive sectors within INI, on the one hand, and at strengthening productive capacity, innovation and accelerated internationalization of the most viable sectors, on the other (see below). This assessment is congruent with some of the conclusions on the Spanish industrial structure as a whole drawn in the study by the European Commission on the impact of the completion of the Single Market on industrial sectors. In distinguishing two alternative adjustment scenarios for the less developed countries of the Community, the inter-industry and intra-industry scenarios,[17] a tendency to move investments from inter- to intra-industrial specialization is observed, a tendency which is also reflected in changing trade patterns (Commission of the European Communities 1990: 6), but an important conclusion is added to this adjustment path. In the years between 1985 and 1989 the volume of manufacturing investment in Spain increased by 79 per cent, while the growth of industrial production amounted to 17 per cent. During the same period, however, 35 per cent of manufacturing investment was accounted for by foreign-owned companies and tended to be centred on high demand growth sectors (computers, electronics, pharmaceuticals). Between 1986 and 1989, 88 per cent of the investment in these sectors originated from foreign capital. Finally, foreign-owned companies accounted for only 11 per cent of investment in low demand growth sectors. 'In Spain, foreign direct investment should therefore aid the progression of activities with a higher technology content in the framework of an intra-industry development scenario' (ibid.: 7). In this respect the policy of (partially) privatizing and 'multinationalizing' public enterprises must be understood as part and parcel of a more general process of modernization of enterprises and the promotion of R&D activities in order to enhance their productivity and international competitiveness (see Martín 1990: 218).

During the third phase, from 1990 to 1993, the institutional and financial rearrangement of the INI drew the restructuring of the Spanish public sector to its ultimate conclusion, i.e., formed the climax of a dual strategy, in tune with the general policy lines set out in the previous phases. Four, to some extent interrelated, factors contributed to this rearrangement: first, after the boom of 1985/86–1989, the Spanish economy re-entered a period of stagnation in the course of 1990, a recession which was further deepened in the following years; second, the state holding INI saw its profits reduced to 9 billion pesetas in 1990, and made a deficit of more than 60 billion pesetas in 1991 (see *El País*, 23 March 1991, and 28 March 1992); third, as a result of the European Council of Maastricht in December 1992, and particularly the convergence criteria agreed upon, the Socialist government committed itself to further reduce public deficit in the years to come; finally, the new balance of power between the party apparatus and the neo-liberals in government to the detriment of the former (see Chapters 3 and 4) pushed the general macro-economic policy of the Socialists further in the direction of deregulation and forced transnationalization.

In this context of slackening economic growth and externally induced pressure on enhanced industrial restructuring and public expenditure control, the Socialist government decided in 1991 to split the state holding INI into two subdivisions, the INISA (INI company limited) and INISE (INI state company). The former subdivision would regroup the profit-making and viable companies like the electricity company ENDESA, the investment goods firm Babcock & Wilcox, aluminium and uranium industries (INESPAL and ENUSA), the insurance company Musini, etc. Funding through the state budget would be stopped in 1993, so that INISA would have to operate on the same basis as a private holding group. If necessary, the issue of shares on the Stock Exchange or the acceptance of outside, private participation were projected options to augment the capital base of the INISA companies. On the other hand, the new subholding could take shares in private companies or exchange shares with other groups, and could enter into all kinds of R&D collaboration agreements. In short, INISA would be characterized by managerial and financial self-determination. Its principal objective would be the strengthening of the productive structure of the group within the European context, which implied an active role in the internationalization of Spanish business (see OECD 1992: 52; and *El País*, 25 September 1991).

INISE would regroup the companies running at a structural loss in, *inter alia*, the mining (HUNOSA), steel (ENSIDESA), shipbuilding (AESA, BAZAN) and defence (SANTA BARBARA) industries. These were the companies that would remain in the subholding; they would be subjected to extensive restructuring and would continue to receive public subsidies, though at a diminishing rate. Other INISE companies which ran at a loss would be either sold to the private sector or simply liquidated (ibid.).

We can now summarize the most important constituent elements in the comprehensive strategy of the Socialist government with respect to its dual objective of meeting the Maastricht convergence criteria and reconverting public industry as follows:

1 A policy directed at improving the macro-economic environment, i.e. the so-called supply side intervention, characterized by anti-inflationary measures and measures to reduce public deficit.
2 A policy directed at full integration into the Single Market, characterized by the complete abolition of all kinds of barriers to the free movement of goods and capital.
3 A policy directed at firmly maintaining the peseta in the Exchange Rate Mechanism at a tendentially over-appreciated currency rate, which supports the implemented stabilization policy, reduces the costs of industrial restructuring (import of investment goods and technology), encourages the internationalization of Spanish business, and deprives national companies of a quasi-protectionist means to improve international competitiveness (through a devaluation of the peseta).
4 A policy directed at intra-industry specialization, characterized by the retrenchment of direct financial government involvement in public firms (either through eliminating all links with the state budget or through privatization), the reorganization of the state holding INI into a spearhead group of profit-making and viable firms oriented at innovation, economies of scale and progressive internationalization, on the one hand, and the extensive restructuring, privatization or liquidation (at high social costs) of the remaining companies belonging to the INI, on the other.
5 A policy directed at the enhanced transnationalization of Spanish business, by attracting foreign investment and through the Europeanization of (public) industry (in the fields of both trade and investment) 'as a prior step to the full globalization of our industrial activities' (see the illuminating article by the Spanish Secretary of State for Industry, Alvaro Espina, under the title 'Public Enterprise and Internationalization' in *El País*, 18 September 1991).

This raises the question as to the beneficiaries of these comprehensive macro-economic and industrial policy priorities. It must first be established that the Socialist government deliberately chose to incorporate Spain fully into the Single European Market and the Exchange Rate Mechanism, and to accept the conditions for entering the EMU in full. As a result of this enhanced integration into the European heartland of free trade, free movements of capital and monetary discipline, domestic macro-economic policy became subject to external constraints, which in turn served as a domestic legitimation for the adjustment measures taken. This process, referred to in Chapter 3 as the 'internationalization of domestic politics', served first and foremost the interests of transnationally mobile capital inasmuch as it implied the opening up of a previously protected area, the optimization of the macro-economic environment through supply side government intervention, and the privatization and 'multinationalization' of public (and private) companies under favourable buyer's conditions. Second, it served the interests of those sections of Spanish national capital that were best prepared to meet the challenge of free foreign competition and strong enough to enter themselves (albeit reluctantly and on an inferior scale in comparison to their counterparts in the most developed member states) into transnational activities. This includes the most profitable and viable segments of public capital and part of private bank and industrial capital. Among Spanish social scientists and economists, Miren Etxezarreta is one of the few who have raised some important research questions from the global political economy perspective adopted in this book.

> Are we confronted with decisions taken under the impulse of powerful external, economic and political forces, who are more concerned with other interests than with the welfare of the Spanish population? What is the articulation between these forces and the dominant groups within the state? How are these relations moulded in order to obtain legitimation and acceptance in a parliamentary democracy?
>
> (Etxezarreta 1991: 67)

These questions confront us, again, with the issue of hegemony. In the following chapter we will attempt to isolate those domestic social forces that were the principal beneficiaries of the European policy of the Spanish Socialists. We will argue that it was particularly the most dynamic faction of private bank capital and public industrial capital that supported the government's macro-economic policy. First, however, the final section of this chapter will deal briefly with the deteriorating relationship between the Socialist government and the trade unions and the more recent questioning of the convergence course followed – and, indeed, of the entire European project – by more and more segments of Spanish civil society.

INTERNATIONAL PRIORITIES AND DOMESTIC PROTEST

In Spain, the social dialogue started in October 1977 with the so-called *Pactos de Moncloa*. More accurately, it started as a political dialogue between the principal political parties, mainly because the workers' and employers' organizations were only embryonic at the time of the Moncloa Pacts. The major trade unions UGT and CCOO were well represented during the negotiations because of their intimate connections with the PSOE and PCE respectively, and in general agreed with the outcome. The

Economic policy and European integration 163

employers' organization CEOE had not yet been founded, but business interests were represented by both the Alianza Popular and the businessmen in the Suárez government (see Martínez-Alier and Roca 1987–88: 75). The most important measures agreed upon included a devaluation of the peseta, a deceleration of public consumption, a restricted growth of the money supply, a wage rise equivalent to the expected inflation rate, a substantial rise in public investment, an extension of the social security system, a tax reform increasing progressive direct taxation, and some other reforms in the fields of education, housing, etc. (Rodríguez López 1989: 134). These Moncloa Pacts were explicitly intended to create a social and political consensus with respect to the general direction of macro-economic policymaking. This implied the postponement of stabilization and adjustment policies, and the subordination of crisis management to the exigencies of democratic transition.

During the first mandate of the Socialist government, the social dialogue continued to be the backbone of the macro-economic policy. It has been frequently said that Felipe González himself was one of the staunchest supporters of the continuation of this societal corporatist system of interest mediation. In any case, it was the Socialist trade union UGT which became one of the instruments of the ruling party in implementing its policy of austerity and industrial reconversion without too much social conflict. The UGT strategy of moderation and reconciliation produced a rupture of the concerted action with the Communist CCOO, thereby weakening the strength of the labour movement to a considerable extent (see Albarracin 1991: 413ff.). One of the clear examples of this development was the tripartite agreement between the Socialist government, UGT and CEOE, the 1984 Economic and Social Agreement, which was designed to apply for the period 1985–1986 (see Ministerio de Trabajo y Seguridad Social 1985).

In the course of the second half of the 1980s, the previous close co-operation between the social partners (tendentially excluding the CCOO) and the Socialist government came to an end.[18] In the words of the Economic and Social Committee of the EC, '(the) cooperation system which had been so valuable during the recession lost steam as expansion began in 1986 and greater social demands began to emerge' (ESC 1989: 22). After years of collective wage bargaining, the trade unions now also wanted a greater say in policy issues (such as labour market regulation, industrial and technology policies, policies related to social protection, public services, etc.), which until then had been the exclusive competence of the government. In short, a *giro social* was demanded, a U-turn in the government's social policy. The trade unions no longer accepted the official argument that sustained economic growth was necessary over a long period of time before a redistribution of the nation's welfare could take place. The dictum of González that Socialism did not stand for a redistribution of poverty (see *NRC Handelsblad*, 26 November 1986), was no longer accepted. Neither was it taken for granted any longer that the present policy was the only viable one for the Spanish economy. Two other factors contributed to the deteriorating relationship between the Socialist government and UGT. First, the union election results of 1986 (as part of an institutionalized representation system according to which employees can vote for representatives in the so-called works' committees (*comités de empresa*) at company level), resulted in a victory for the CCOO to the detriment of the UGT. This forced the latter to reassess its co-operative strategy and moderate position *vis-à-vis* the PSOE and its policy of austerity (see Paramio 1992: 534; and Albarracin 1991: 417ff.). In reaction to this, the party apparatus of the PSOE started a campaign aimed at disciplining the leadership of the UGT, while at the same time the neo-liberals in government remained totally insensitive to the growing social demands. As personal confrontations and conflicts over the government's macro-economic policy increased in the course of 1988, and after the re-establishment of the concerted action between the major trade unions, the general strike of December 1988 (which was the first of its kind since the formal end of the Franquist dictatorship) announced the final break between the PSOE and the UGT, and started a period of continuous hostility.[19]

In the following years, and particularly after the third victory of the PSOE in the 1989 elections, the government's macro-economic policy became even more restrictive than in the preceding years. In September 1990 the government approved the most restrictive budget since 1983 (which implied that for the first time the rise of public spending would be below the general growth of the Spanish economy including inflation; see *El País*, 29 September 1990). The convergence plan of early 1992, then, reaffirmed this restrictive course. In mid-1992, finally, the assumptions underlying this plan had already been superseded by more recent evidence on the general performance of the Spanish economy. All macro-economic indicators pointed to an accelerated deterioration (see *El País*, 2 July 1992), a situation which came openly to the fore during the monetary crisis in the second half of 1992. Once again, the Socialist government stuck to its course of enhanced austerity and forced economic convergence (for a more detailed account of the post-June 1992 period, see Chapter 7). As a result of these developments, the open opposition to the general course of the government's macro-economic policy and, more saliently, to its European orientation, extended to other social and political forces, notably the main party in opposition, Partido Popular, and the employers' organization, CEOE. For the first time during the 'Socialist decade', the general consensus on the foreign policy orientation of the Socialists came seriously under pressure. For the first time, the common, generally accepted view on the future role of Spain in a united Europe showed signs of wear and tear. In the following chapter, however, it will be argued that these discrepancies in the ranks of the Spanish bourgeoisie already existed long before the exhaustion of the Socialist project in the early 1990s, but were effectively neutralized as long as the benefits of economic growth could offset the sectorally perceived disadvantages of economic and monetary integration.

Ironically, the strategic objectives of the Socialist government seem to have been bypassed by yet another development. Its Europeanist orientation, supporting some kind of supra-national institutionalism and stressing the need to deepen the process of European integration first, and its inclination to strive for political regionalization rather than economic globalization, seem to have become part of a minority view in the post-Maastricht context. Both the leading sectors of pan-European business (as embodied, for instance, in the European Roundtable of Industrialists) and the governments of the major European powers are moving at present to a more offensive, globalist approach to European integration (see Holman 1992). Indeed, they seem to be seriously allowing for the emergence of a two-tier Europe. In such a scenario, the hegemonic project of the Socialists (and their European ambitions, for that matter) will be deprived of their very essence, not only as a result of the declining domestic consensus, but also by virtue of changing external realities.

6 Merging into Europe
Private bank capital and the Socialist government

INTRODUCTION

In the previous chapter we analysed the Socialist economic policy, among other things, from the perspective of the government's European project. One of the constituent parts of this policy was the creation of a sound macro-economic environment through government supply side intervention, aimed at improving the competitive position of Spanish business *vis-à-vis* its foreign (and notably European) competitors. Part of this strategy of promoting strong companies and sectors that could stand on their own in a European setting of free competition was the accelerated internationalization of its most viable components. The Spanish public sector was a case in point, and particularly the government-led concentration of the public oil companies in the state holding Instituto Nacional de Hidrocarburos (INH), and the internationalization (and partial privatization) of its most prominent company Repsol, were examples of both the Socialist government's approach towards strategic economic sectors and its attempt to create a transnational business structure of Spanish origin (see Correljé 1990).

In this chapter we will go more in detail into the government's policy with respect to what is regarded as another strategic sector, i.e. Spanish banking. The Socialist policy is best described as a continuous effort to concentrate activities in this sector, in order to protect the sector as a whole from foreign takeovers, and to improve its international competitiveness. Faced with a profound liberalization of financial markets, it was argued, Spanish private and public banks could no longer ignore economies of scale as a precondition for survival.

An underlying motive for government intervention in Spanish banking was to increase its control over a sector known for its all-embracing presence in the Spanish economy and notorious for its capacity to bend political decision-makers to its will. For some, Spanish bank capital became the exclusive game preserve of the PSOE in the course of the concentration process (see for instance *Cambio 16*, 14 March 1988). For others, it was the 'socialist bankers' favourable to the hegemonic project of the new ruling party who took an active role in the private banking mergers during the second half of the 1980s (see, for example, Rivases 1988). In this chapter the development of Spanish banking will be analysed from the latter perspective.

In the next section the history of Spanish banking will be dealt with. After a short introduction on early forms of private finance in Spain, the development of Spanish bank capital as a whole and its close links with the different phases in Spain's social and political modernization during the twentieth century will be analysed. In the section on p. 175, some general observations on the foundation and subsequent development of the seven largest private banks, the so-called '*siete grandes*',[1] will introduce the subsequent analysis of the present-day banking configuration, the different views within private bank capital as to economic and foreign policy in general and the Socialist project in particular, and the particular relations between the Socialist government and individual private banks in the light of the 'managerial revolution' and the concentration process in the second half of the 1980s. In the section on p. 179 the most important centres of social and political power during the Socialist decade will be pinpointed, with a special emphasis on the differences between the two Basque private banks Banco de Bilbao and Banco de Vizcaya, on the one hand, and Banesto, on the other, as far as their relationships with the Socialist government are concerned (the former two being closely linked to the Socialist project, the latter rather hostile to it). It will be argued that these differences can only be understood completely if one takes the historical development of these banks into account. In the section on p. 192, the main results of the government-led concentration process of Spanish banking will be discussed.

PRIVATE BANK CAPITAL AND THE MAKING OF A NATIONAL BOURGEOISIE

A descriptive account of the history of Spanish finance could start with the so-called '*Taulas di Canvi*' of Barcelona (founded in 1401) and Valencia (founded in 1407), semi-official credit institutions which came into existence in an attempt to curtail financial malpractices (e.g. usury) carried out by Jewish and Italian *cambists* and money-lenders (see Canosa 1945: 13–24; and Ruiz Martín 1970: 8–12).

Such an account could also start with the activities of 'cosmopolitan' bankers like the Fuggers, Höchstetters, Frescobaldis and Gualterottis, who from the early sixteenth century onwards came to Spain in search of the new wealth, i.e. the gold and silver bullion from the Americas. In order to gain possession of these precious metals, they made full use of the perfect opportunity: the continuous budgetary crises during the reigns of the '*Reyes Católicos*' (1474–1517), Carlos V (1517–1556) and Felipe II (1556–1598) as a consequence of the indebted expansion of the Spanish Crown (see Carande 1965). The resulting dependence on foreign credit has been linked with the eventual collapse of the Spanish empire, the 'inversion' of the economic role of Spain within the world economy, and the decline of an incipient domestic bourgeoisie to the benefit of pre-capitalist forces like the combine of wool producers, the *Mesta* (see Braudel 1986: 476–517; Wallerstein 1974: 191–196; Elliott 1990: pp. 181–211; 1989: ch. I and X).

Finally, an account of Spanish banking could start with the establishment of the Banco de San Carlos in 1782, which in 1856 was converted into the Banco de España and, in 1874, became the national Bank of Spain, from that moment onwards holding the monopoly of the issue of banknotes. Although privately owned, the Banco de San Carlos (and its 1829 successor, the Banco Español de San Fernando) was characterized by its strong ties with the Spanish Crown and the Royal Treasury. Its very establishment and troublesome existence were closely related to the chronic public debt of Spain, the wars against England and France, the paralysis of the colonial trade with the Americas as a result of the British blockade of the Atlantic Ocean, and the long-term downward swing of the Spanish economy during the eighteenth and nineteenth centuries.

Though these early examples of Spanish banking are of some historical interest, illustrating among other things the decline of empire from the early sixteenth century onwards, for the purpose of this study a history of Spanish finance must start with the establishment of those private banks which continue to play a predominant role in the Spanish economy. That is, it is not the history and chronology of Spanish banking as such which are of interest here. Only those elements in the history of Spanish banking which can offer us a better understanding of the present situation must be selected. It is the correct definition of the problem, and the posing of the right historical questions, which are of primary importance. According to the Annales principle of '*histoire problème*', history is construction, in the sense of a problem-oriented and analytical activity (Split 1982). This is why the following sections will present well-known historical data while selecting and analysing these data in a relatively original way on the basis of two related questions: what is the historical background of the dominant position of private banking in the Spanish economy? And what is the historical origin of the fragmentation of Spanish bank capital, exemplified in the different positions of individual banks with respect to the hegemonic project of the Socialist government in the 1980s?

From agrarian to industrial society: the role of private banking (1885–1975)

The dominant position of private banks in the Spanish economy is historically the result of a series of legislative measures which had explicitly the intention, or the more or less intended effect, of encouraging the promotion of industrial projects by a progressively concentrated and centralized bank capital.

One of the first important regulations regarding private banking was the Commercial Law of 1885, through which so-called credit companies were allowed to operate, *inter alia*, in both industrial and merchant, and commercial activities. According to Juan Muñoz, this Commercial Law introduced the legal framework within which the later development of genuine mixed banks could take place (Muñoz 1970: 37–38).[2] In the subsequent two decades a period was concluded in which all the major private banks of today (with the sole exception of the Banco Popular) were formed as mixed banks.

In the period between 1915 and 1926, Spanish bank capital experienced its first phase of expansion due to, first, the boom years of the Spanish economy during World War I (see Roldán *et al.* 1973, II: 163–269), and, second, the *Ley de Ordenación Bancaria* of 1921 (see Muñoz 1978; Banco de Bilbao 1982: 95ff.; and Tortella Casares 1970: 303ff.). The legal framework provided by this Bank Regulation Act made it virtually impossible for foreign-owned banks operating in Spain to expand. As a result, these foreign banks withdrew their capital from Spain in the early 1920s. Second, a clear-cut legal division was introduced between the Central Bank and private banks. Finally, this newly established 'Banker's bank' provided the private national banks with all kind of monetary concessions with the explicit intention, as the Finance Minister of the time, Francisco de Asís Cambó, stated, 'to create a Spanish banking aristocracy' (quoted in Muñoz 1970: 53). In the following years, Spanish mixed bank capital consolidated itself through extending its industrial involvement, on the one hand, and through the policy of opening branch offices, on the other. As to the latter, a first tendency of financial concentration can be discerned (see Muñoz 1978: 106).

A second, and far more important period in the formation of Spanish banking as we know it today, is the so-called period of *status quo* between 1936 and 1962. Unlike the expansion phase of the 1920s, it was the method of absorptions that characterized these years. In August 1936, the nationalist government prohibited the establishment of new banks and branch offices, a measure which was officially reaffirmed in 1940 (i.e. after the Civil War) and only slightly modified in the following years. This *status quo* was especially to the benefit of the largest private banks, which were perfectly capable of continuing their expansion and their network of branch offices through the take-over of minor, regional banks. Between 1940 and 1960 a total number of sixty-nine banks were absorbed by the five largest private banks (Bilbao, Vizcaya, Banesto, Hispano Americano, Central; see Muñoz 1970: 65). 'The "status quo" solidified the existing banking situation of 1936,' Juan Muñoz rightly argues, 'strongly intensifying the tendency of concentration and monopolization of the sector' (ibid.: 63). In 1962, the 250 banks in 1940 had been reduced to only 103 banks. During this period the five largest private banks multiplied their profits by a factor of 7 in the 1940s and by a factor of 4.3 in the 1950s. In addition, a spectacular increase of paid-up capital and accumulated reserves made these banks the principal protagonists of Spain's industrialization during the autarkic phase (ibid.: 64–69).

In the 1960s and early 1970s the Spanish banking system underwent some important changes, due to a couple of legal reforms, the renewed entry of foreign capital (both industrial and bank capital), and the subsequent symbiosis of the latter with domestic bank capital. During the same period the *siete grandes* strengthened their position in the economy even more, and came to form what some have labelled a 'financial oligarchy' (see below). From the late 1960s onwards, and as the Franquist regime entered its final stage, the 'tentacles of all-pervasive involvement' (Graham 1984) of private bank capital created a sense of identity, and a common interest in anticipating and directing the political changes to come. In the 1970s both the democratic transition and the outbreak of the international economic crisis determined the domestic and international context in which the degree of consensus and co-operation among the *siete grandes* reached its temporary climax.

In the wake of the 1959 economic liberalization and the subsequent period of accelerated industrialization, a new Credit and Banking Regulation Act (the *Ley de Bases de Ordenación del Crédito y de la Banca* of April 1962) officially attempted to control the ongoing banking concentration and to introduce a greater degree of specialization. In the preamble to the Law, it was stated that the mixed character of Spanish finance could endanger its liquidity and hence could threaten the safety of savings entrusted to individual private banks. Moreover, the practice of mixed banking generated an excessive influence of private banks on economic activity in general, and had a discriminatory impact on the granting of loans, to the benefit of industrial companies within the orbit of private banks (see Tamames 1978, II: 985). In order to prevent a further concentration of activities and economic power, as it was formally presented, all existing entities had to decide whether they should continue either as commercial or as industrial banks. The decreed incompatibility of activities put an end to the phenomenon of mixed banking, but, as it soon turned out, only in legal terms. The largest banks all opted for commercial banking, meanwhile creating their own industrial banks, which in the following years came to function as subsidiaries, albeit on a formally independent basis.[3]

Another feature of the 1962 Act was the opening up of the Spanish financial system to foreign capital. It was first and foremost the large American Banks (Bank of America, Chase Manhattan Bank, Manufacturers Hanover Trust Co.) which opened representative offices in Spain. More importantly, foreign banks were allowed to participate in the capital of newly created industrial banks up to a limit of 50 per cent (see de Usera 1974: 203). In at least two cases, Banesto's Bandesco and Vizcaya's Induban, a consortium of foreign banks, composed of both American and European banks, took a share of respectively 50 per cent and 40 per cent.[4] In one case, Santander's Banco Intercontinental, the 50 per cent share was wholly taken by one single bank (Bank of America). The predominance of American banks during the 1960s had an important bearing on the primacy of American industrial investment in total foreign direct investment in the same period. Between 1960 and 1974 the United States accounted for about 35 per cent of foreign investment, Switzerland for 19 per cent and West Germany for 12 per cent. Swiss foreign investment came in a large part from US companies. According to a Common Market study of 1969, 200 of the world's 400 largest companies were North American; 92 of these US companies had 101 affiliates in Spain, whereas only 50 of the remaining non-American companies had 63 Spanish affiliates (see Harrison 1978: 165–166).[5]

The entrance of foreign bank and industrial capital in the 1960s did not fundamentally weaken the dominant position of the *siete grandes* in the Spanish economy. As we have indicated in previous chapters (particularly Chapters 1 and 2), the economic liberalization of 1959 was a necessary precondition for the subsequent period of rapid growth and profound modernization, and it was the co-operation between foreign capital and Spanish bank capital, cemented by complementary interests, that came to play a decisive role in this economic take-off. On the basis of an impressive study of the economic power of Spanish private banks, Juan Muñoz in 1970 concluded that the reappearance of foreign investment has entailed the break-down of the monopoly of private banking on industrial financing and the start of a capitalism in which bank capital and the big international consortia form a new, more powerful and dynamic, front.

(Muñoz 1970: 70)

And: 'The Spanish oligarchy and the big foreign corporations have formed a common . . . front, which has turned out to be in their mutual interest' (ibid.: 317). A first glance at the links between foreign and national capital in the 300 largest industrial companies (1971), manifested *inter alia* through the interlocking directorates between the main economic actors, can show the impact of this new 'powerful and dynamic front' in the period prior to the death of Franco. Both foreign capital and private banks were present in as much as 40 per cent of these 300 largest firms. Foreign capital directly controlled a total of fifty-nine firms and participated in another sixty-one companies; private banks directly controlled fifty-two and participated in another sixty-one firms. Moreover, the firms which were in some way or another related to private banking absorbed 55 per cent of total sales and as much as 66 per cent of total profits (Muñoz *et al.* 1978: 280–281). This last phenomenon can be explained by looking at the presence of private banks in the 100 largest industrial firms. In this case they directly controlled 54 per cent and participated in no less than 83 per cent (absorbing 83.55 per cent of total profits), whereas foreign capital participated in only 28 per cent of these 100 largest firms (ibid.: 272).

However, the power of the *siete grandes* went beyond their participation in the 300 or 100 largest industrial companies. Both Juan Muñoz, in his study of the economic power of private banks (1970) and in his analysis of the internationalization of capital in Spain (together with Santiago Roldán and Angel Serrano 1978), and Ramón Tamames, whose early study of the monopolies in Spain (1966) and his later work on the financial oligarchy in Spain (1977) are of great importance in this respect, have amply documented the wide range of additional mechanisms through which private banking maintained its control over the Spanish economy. Apart from the different forms of control over industry, exercised either through equity participation, cross board membership between the banks and the firms, or through credit (a control which, according to a conservative estimate of the former *Financial Times* correspondent Robert Graham, amounted in 1975 to about 40 per cent of total industry, Graham 1984: 94), the *siete grandes* consolidated their position as the bastion of Spanish capitalism in the period prior to 1975 along the following lines: a further concentration (through absorptions and the extension of the network of branch offices) resulting in a certain degree of monopolization in which the seven largest banks controlled some 70 per cent of total banking activities; an increasing amount of interlocking directorates, directly between banks and indirectly through common participations in industrial firms, giving the *siete grandes* at least the appearance of a cohesive and solidly integrated power bloc; links between the largest banks through family relations, 'which gives the banking community its oligarchic character' (Muñoz 1970: 187); and, finally, the exercise of its power through the *Consejo Superior Bancario*. This banking council officially functioned as a consultative committee to the Ministry of Finance, but in practice it was the body *par excellence* through which the *siete grandes* came to influence government economic and monetary policies and the very vehicle of the forming of a sense of class consciousness, i.e., the forming of 'a corporate consciousness of a disciplinary nature' (Velarde Fuertes 1969: 82). Of the twenty-six members of this council, twenty were representatives of private banks; since the largest banks had a majority, and simple majority voting determined the decision-making process, and since, finally, the recommendations of the council were almost always adopted by the Franquist regime, it is no exaggeration to conclude that the council was the politico-economic extension of the social power of the *siete grandes* (Muñoz 1970: 169–175; Tamames 1977: 183–184).

The 'Club de los Siete' and the transition to democracy

A final remark has to be made on another, more informal platform of political action of the largest private banks, the so-called *'Club de los Siete'*, founded in 1971 on the initiative of the president of Banesto, José María Aguirre Gonzalo. The presidents of the seven largest private banks started to meet each other on a regular basis during lunch-time. Without doubt, the primary motive of these meetings was the uncertain political future of Spain with the prospect of the imminent death of Franco. The *Club de los Siete* became one of the forums of Spanish banking in which future developments were anticipated and a common strategy for the post-Franquist period was elaborated. It is important to note that the Spanish business community in general and private bank capital in particular were not hostile to a smooth and controlled transition to democracy. In the early 1970s, the economic elites of Spain were faced with two choices: a further economic liberalization eventually leading to entry into the Common Market, a prospect inevitably conditioned by a prior political democratization; or a 'progressive nationalist involution' which would result in severe social and political conflict. A decision in favour of one of these options, however, was no longer a matter entirely in the hands of the Franquist ruling elites; the formerly politically marginalized social classes had now become part and parcel of such a decision (Moya 1984: 146). In this sense, the accommodation of the *siete grandes* with the process of democratization can be explained from the fact that this process was controlled and directed from above, under the banner of the constitutional monarchy. The political 'revolution from above', as propagated by the ideologists of the early twentieth century, finally came about, made possible by almost forty years of social and economic modernization.

During the period of democratic transition, the *Club de los Siete* continued to function as one of the most important manifestations of social cohesion within the Spanish banking community, though the first fissures in the bastion of Spanish capitalism emerged with respect to, for example, the question of whether they should finance the Communist and Socialist parties during the first democratic elections (see González Ledesma *et al.* 1977: 249ff.; and Rivases 1988: 27ff.). By and large, however, its vigilance regarding political changes and its control over the economic policy of the transition governments continued to be decisive, first through informal interventions at government level and, second, through overlapping directorates of the government executive and the largest private banks. The first four cabinets after the death of Franco (one headed by Carlos Arias Navarro, and three under the presidency of Adolfo Suárez) included a total of twenty-six ministers directly linked to private bank capital and twenty-four indirectly connected through family ties (see Lancaster 1989: 146–147; see also Muñoz *et al.* 1978: 417ff.).

Despite this relatively privileged position in the principal power centres of the new democratic regime, things had fundamentally changed for Spanish big business. It succeeded in controlling the transition in such a way that changes in the political system left the economic system, and the underlying social property relations, largely intact. However, other, sometimes conflicting interests, institutionalized *inter alia* through labour organizations and oppositional political parties, had entered the political scene and could no longer be excluded completely from the decision-making centres by authoritarian practices. In fact, it was the fragile democracy, in conjunction with the impact of the international economic crisis, that made the post-Franquist governments of the centre-right prone to demands from the previously marginalized classes. This in turn had a double effect on the intrinsic relation between social power and the governmental Executive: first, unaccustomed as they were to sharing their influence on the general course of government economic policy, the most traditional and reactionary elements in the Spanish business community progressively withdrew their support for the UCD government, and for Prime Minister Adolfo Suárez in particular, viewing the right-wing Alianza Popular (headed at the time by the former Franquist minister Manuel Fraga) as the only viable democratic alternative;[6] second, and more importantly, as the process of democratization became irreversible in the course of events, new and more sophisticated modes of political domination had to be introduced. It is the distinction between institutionalization, as related to the notion of hegemony, and the use of force which is at stake here. Hegemony refers to the capacity of a class or class section to take into account the interests of other classes or class sections in the formulation of its specific interests as the general interest. 'Institutions may become the anchor for such a hegemonic strategy since they lend themselves both to the representations of diverse interests and to the universalization of policy' (Cox 1986: 219; see also Chapter 2). In the short term, then, the cohesion among the *siete grandes* was based on the common interest of controlling the smooth transition 'from above' towards parliamentary democracy; at the same time, however, the different ways in which particular factions of the Spanish bourgeoisie accommodated themselves to the new democratic institutions, inextricably linked to their respective comprehensive views on the political and socio-economic future of Spain in an increasingly transnational (European) setting, heralded their intrinsic relationship with the Socialist project in the 1980s. In order to fully understand this point, we first have to look more closely at the individual private banks, and their different origin and subsequent development, since it is only from these historical differences that we can discern the emergence of alternative comprehensive concepts of control in the course of the Socialist decade.

LOS SIETE GRANDES

The founding history of the largest private banks in Spain can be divided into several sub-periods: the late 1850s, with the establishment of a Basque and a Cantabrian bank, the Banco de Bilbao (1857) and the Banco de Santander (1857), as a result of the incipient industrial, commercial and mining activities in these Northern regions; the years 1900–1902, in which the Banco Hispano Americano (1900), the Banco de Vizcaya (1901) and the Banco Español de Crédito (1902) were founded, partly as a result of the repatriation of capital after the loss of the last colonies in Latin America (Cuba and Puerto Rico) and the Philippines; the years 1918–1919, characterized by the economic boom induced by World War I, in which, among others, both the Banco Urquijo (1918) and the Banco Central (1919) were established. Finally, the last member of the so-called *siete grandes*, the

Banco Popular Español, was founded in 1926, an event which does not correspond to a more general pattern.

On the basis of these founding phases no clear-cut conclusions can be drawn with regard to the present-day division of Spanish bank capital. The main differences between the largest private banks in the 1980s and early 1990s as regards their relationship with the Socialist government, their interest articulation with respect to the Europeanist course of the Socialist project, and their stand in the process of concentration of private bank capital, rather depend on other factors: different regional origin, involvement in different industrial sectors, etc. On the basis of a more extensive study (see Holman 1993b; 1995), we can distinguish the following criteria and characteristics as to the main historical differences between the *siete grandes*.

First, it is important to emphasize the regional origin of the five major individual banks (Bilbao, Vizcaya, Banesto, Central, and Hispano Americano). Given the peculiar centre–periphery division between Madrid (political and geographical centre) and the Basque Provinces (political and geographical periphery but centre of an incipient industrial capitalism) at the turn of the century, it is not surprising that there has always been some ambiguity in the relationship between the Basque bourgeoisie and those social forces supporting the process of nation-building 'from above'. More specifically, the private banks of Basque origin were traditionally less inclined to see the creation of a 'great nation' as a goal in itself; they relied on state intervention and even co-operated with the central oligarchy inasmuch as this could serve their own particular interests. The Madrid banks, on the other hand, were much more fully integrated with the traditional oligarchy of the Restoration regime, manifested *inter alia* in the close links between Banesto and the Banco Central, on the one hand, and the Spanish aristocracy and monarchy, on the other. An indication of this difference is the timing and speed with which the two groups of private banks expanded their operations to the whole of Spain.

Closely related to the regional context is the origin of the founding capital of individual banks. The Basque banks (Bilbao and Vizcaya) were founded in the wake of the incipient industrialization of the region in the second half of the nineteenth century. In the case of the Banco Hispano Americano, it was commercial capital repatriated from the Americas which constituted its founding capital, and the two other Madrid banks were created on the basis of a heterogeneous composition of commercial and agricultural capital, stemming from different regions. Apart from the common tendency at the turn of the century to support protectionist state legislation (a common interest which united both agricultural and industrial capital, as we have seen in Chapter 2), the very nature of the individual banks' activities made them dependent to a greater or lesser extent on active state intervention in the economy. Generally speaking, Basque heavy industry did benefit from the state-led development and the general tendency of economic nationalism in the early decades of the present century (and, indeed, during the first phase of Franquism), while commercial and particularly agricultural capital were inclined to oppose state monopolistic regulation, and in the latter case even industrialization as such.

Closely connected with the preceding is the relationship between individual banks and the Franquist regime. Although private bank capital as a whole was the single actor that most benefited from Franquism, in general terms it can be stated that the Basque banks were more closely related to the regime during the autarkic phase, while Banesto and the Banco Central only improved their relationship after the economic liberalization of 1959. In both cases this was illustrated by the switch of individuals from the bank's board of directors to the government and vice versa. In more economic terms, this difference seems to be explained by the different phases of development during the Franquist period, the first mainly directed at strengthening basic industries, and the second more oriented towards developing a domestic consumer goods industry. Whereas the Basque banks were particularly involved in this first phase of industrialization, the Madrid banks experienced their major industrial expansion in the 1960s.

Another criterion is the reliance of individual banks on state intervention and their views on the role of public enterprise in economic development. Due to the very nature of their business activities, the two Basque banks supported direct state interference more than their Madrid counterparts. This came dramatically to the fore in the 1960s when the Spanish state had to fund, and eventually had to participate in those companies running at a loss that had traditionally been in the orbit of the Basque bourgeoisie. The two major Madrid banks (Banesto and Banco Central) were known for their staunch free marketeer stand, and their aversion to state interference and the draining of public funds through the state holding INI. It must be emphasized, however, that this economic liberalism did not necessarily include a liberal internationalist defence of the free movement of capital and goods across national borders. Being strong enough on the home market to fiercely oppose interventionist state regulation did not mean that the same free market principles were propagated in their relationship with foreign competitors; one is inclined to argue the contrary, given the relatively underdeveloped character of the Spanish economy in the 1960s and 1970s. In fact, it was the peculiar combination of free market capitalism at home and selective protectionism with respect to international trade and finance that was so characteristic of these banks, and, indeed, still played an important role in the discussions on the viability of the Socialist government's European project in the 1980s and early 1990s.

A final criterion is the way in which the *siete grandes* and their management anticipated the revolutionary changes in Spanish finance and the industrial crisis of the 1970s and early 1980s. In the case of the Basque banks, and due to the specific circumstances of the 1960s, at a relatively early stage (i.e. in the early 1970s) a start was made with the rejuvenation and professionalization of management, the diversification of activities, and the progressive reduction of the stake in traditional industries. In the case of Banesto and the Banco Central, the managerial apparatus remained largely intact, and as a result of a general lack of innovation, both banks experienced decreasing rates of profitability and came under increasing pressure from the Socialist government and the Banco de España to change direction. The Banco Hispano Americano, finally, occupied an intermediate position inasmuch as its crisis dated from the 1960s, a crisis which, once it had deepened in the 1970s, inspired the Banco de España to take immediate action, eventually resulting in the appointment of several managers closely connected with the Socialist government.

Despite all differences, we have to remember, however, that the development of the Spanish economy during the period of Franquist dictatorship, the general politico-economic and legislative framework supportive to the development and concentration of private bank capital, and the progressive modernization of Spanish society under state corporatist practices, did create a national bourgeoisie with a common identity and a common, general interest. Particularism, based on individual interest mediation, gradually made way for a more sophisticated mode of class domination through the vehicle of economic and socio-political modernization and, indeed, vertebration. And it was only on the basis of this 'bourgeois evolution' that a posterior fragmentation of the Spanish bourgeoisie could take place, based on alternative concepts of control, i.e. different long-term strategies and visions of the world, and no longer primarily characterized by the narrow, particularistic defence of short-term interests. As we saw in Chapter 2, alongside this development, the state came to play a dramatically different role in the course of events, moving away from repressively protecting capitalist interests from the dominated classes to a post-authoritarian, hegemonic articulation of interests in a rapidly changing international (European) context. Whereas Franquism created the space in which a self-sustaining cohesion between and within social classes could emerge, the period of democratic transition paved the way for a genuine fragmentation of the Spanish bourgeoisie, coming openly to the fore during the subsequent period of consolidation.

THE SOCIALIST GOVERNMENT AND PRIVATE BANK CAPITAL: CO-OPERATION AND CONFRONTATION

From 1975 onwards, four developments were of paramount importance with respect to the elaboration of alternative comprehensive concepts of control in the highest echelons of Spanish bank capital on the one hand, and the relationship of individual banks with the Socialist government on the other:

1 The application for EC membership in 1977, and the subsequent discussion on whether Spain should liberalize its foreign economic relations and, in particular, deregulate and open up its financial sector. After decades of protection, foreign commercial banks were allowed to enter the Spanish market in June 1978, although they were subjected *inter alia* to the following limitations: the sum of 750 million pesetas in initial capital was established for branch offices and 1500 million for subsidiaries; peseta deposits were not allowed to exceed 40 per cent of a foreign bank's total assets; and foreign banks could not open more than three offices in Spain (Tamames 1986: 204; see also Andréu 1983: 36ff.). In March 1982 the Spanish government and the European Commission reached agreement on the period of transition for the Spanish banking sector. In the seven years following formal entry, the above mentioned limitations on foreign banks should be progressively abolished (see Roldán Jiménez 1985: 55–56; and Rodríguez Antón 1990: 51ff.). From its very start, Banesto in particular fiercely opposed this (albeit limited) opening of the Spanish financial market, an opposition which 'was motivated almost exclusively by a primitive fear of competition' (Graham 1984: 100).

2 The banking crisis of the late 1970s and early 1980s, and the question whether political and monetary authorities could interfere in the management of particular banks. Consensus existed on the concerted action of the largest private banks and the monetary authorities in preventing the banking system from total collapse. Through the Bank Deposit Guarantee Fund (the so-called 'bank hospital') a total of fifty-one smaller commercial banks were rescued (on the banking crisis, see Ontiveros and Valero 1988: 378ff.). It was only during the 1980s when government interference was also felt in some of the largest private banks, particularly in Hispano Americano and, to a lesser extent, in Banesto and the Banco Central. The latter two banks fiercely resisted the public intervention, with varying degrees of success.

180 *The Socialist decade (1982–1992)*

3 The completion of the Single European Market in January 1993, and the related question of whether Spanish bank capital should opt for an economies of scale approach in challenging full competition in an integrated and deregulated financial market (see Casilda Béjar 1992: 423ff.). In the years following the agreement on the Commission's White Paper and the Single European Act in 1985–1986 (which included the harmonization of national legislation in the field of finance and the free movement of capital) the characteristics of the *siete grandes* with respect to their European adversaries were the following: first, in terms of size, prior to the mergers in the years 1988–1990, Spanish commercial banks were small by world and European banking standards (see Rodríguez Antón 1990: 59ff.; and Torrero 1989: 137ff.); only one bank, the Banco Central, was listed among the 100 major banks in 1987 (see Table 11). As a result of the mergers this situation considerably improved, though the newly created 'super banks' still did not occupy a position among the truly greatest. The Banco Bilbao Vizcaya, for instance, was only the thirtieth bank (in terms of assets) of Europe in 1987 (Rodríguez Antón 1990: 66). On the other hand, in terms of absolute profits Spanish private banks performed a good deal better, with six of the *siete grandes* ranking among the twenty-five most profitable European banks (see Table 12).

In terms of relative profits (ratio between net profits and total assets) the same picture emerges, though the ranking among the Spanish banks is a different one, since the Banco Popular Español is the number one bank in Spain and the fourth in the EC. This phenomenon was confirmed by a 1990 survey by *Euromoney*, which for the first time did not rank the biggest banks ('it is increasingly clear that, in banking, size has little relevance any longer. The biggest banks are now the sluggards') but the world's best banks.[7] Surprisingly, the Banco Popular Español ranked as the 'best' in the world, while two other Spanish banks (Santander and Bilbao Vizcaya) were among the world's ten best banks (*Euromoney*, December 1990; see also *Actualidad Económica*, 16 July 1990; and Berges *et al.* 1990: 169ff.).

4 The full incorporation of Spain in the Lockeian heartland of transnational production and the related question of whether emerging global structures of transnationally mobile capital should be accompanied at the regional, European level by some degree of supra-national regulation. In essence we are dealing here with the symbiosis of the long-term strategy of a particular section of Spanish bank capital with the Socialist European project as elaborated in Chapter 3. Before discussing the mergers of private (and public) banks as an illustration of how the levels of material forces, state institutions and ideas were integrated into one single and comprehensive

project aimed at neutralizing the adverse (and to some extent pre-hegemonic) elements in the Spanish bourgeoisie, on the one hand, and at promoting the transnationalization of the stronghold of Spanish capitalism, on the other, we first have to distinguish the most important social and political actors in the unfolding of the Socialist project during the 1980s.

Table 11 Spanish private banks among the 500 largest banking entities of the world (assets)

	1983		1987	
Central	19,171	99	46,071	84
Banesto	20,034	95	30,797	119
Hispano Am.	12,632	134	30,866	110
Bilbao	14,206	122	*	
Santander	12,928	131	26,870	137
Vizcaya	15,078	117	*	
Popular	8,251	188	16,617	214

Source: Rodríguez Antón 1990: 64

Notes: data in millions of dollars and ranking position
*Although the merger between Bilbao and Vizcaya was only effectuated in 1988, data for the year 1987 already group the total assets of both banks together: 56.884 million dollars, which situates the Banco Bilbao Vizcaya at position 71 in the ranking.

Table 12 Spanish private banks among the 100 most profitable banks of the world in terms of net profits before taxes (1987)

	Net profits	Position in the world	Position in the EC
Bilbao Vizcaya*	898	12	4
Central	609	35	12
Banesto	372	57	21
Santander	367	58	22
Popular	349	60	23

Source: Rodríguez Antón 1990: 108

Note: data in millions of dollars and ranking position
*Net profits of Bilbao Vizcaya are the sum of the results of Bilbao and Vizcaya in 1987, i.e., prior to the merger.

182 *The Socialist decade (1982–1992)*

Centres of social and political power during the Socialist decade

In anticipation of an eventual victory in the 1982 elections, the leadership of the PSOE not only moderated the party's political platform (see Chapter 3), but also tried to convince the leading sections of the Spanish business community that a future Socialist government would not basically harm their interests. It has been reported, for instance, that Felipe González as early as 1977 participated in one of the lunch meetings of the *Club de los Siete* in order to present his ideas before an audience of reticent, not to say hostile, bankers (Rivases 1988: 26–27; Díaz Herrera and Tijeras 1991: 640–641). Conversely, some of the more enlightened presidents of the largest private banks, and particularly Bilbao's president José Angel Sánchez Asiaín (see below), were on friendly terms with the Socialist leadership prior to October 1982. It has been frequently stated that the strong relationship between the Socialist government and part of bank capital during the 1980s was the result of personal friendships stemming from common professional backgrounds and reflecting an alternation of generations both in politics and in the Spanish banking world. This individualistic perception of power relations tends to neglect the common strategic objectives that underpin this post-1982 coalition of social and political forces. Before illustrating this point in more detail in the next section, we first have to distinguish the most important, and partially overlapping, groupings of social and political power during the Socialist decade. The following groupings will be discussed: the so-called 'beautiful people'; the members of the *siete grandes* most closely linked to the Socialist party; the group of public companies which are organized in the *Club de Empresarios*; foreign capital; and the most important oppositional grouping composed of Partido Popular, the employers' organization CEOE, and two of the *siete grandes* most openly opposed to the Socialist project, i.e. Banesto and, to a lesser extent, the Banco Central.[8]

The 'beautiful people'

The so-called group of 'beautiful people of the PSOE' was composed of some personal friends who occupied leading posts in the administration and the private (financial) sector. Its most prominent members at the political level were Miguel Boyer, the superminister of Finance and Economics in the first Socialist government, and from 1985 onwards continuously involved, through various leading positions in Spanish finance, in the spectacular battle between the Socialist government, on the one hand, and the Banco Central and Banesto, on the other; his successor in the Socialist government, Carlos Solchaga; and the governor of the Bank of Spain, Mariano Rubio. Other important members of this group included Claudio Boada, who, after occupying several leading functions in private and public companies, became president of the Banco Hispano Americano, mainly as a result of the intervention of both Mariano Rubio and Miguel Boyer in the bank's management in the early 1980s; and José María López de Letona, a former Minister of Industry under Franco, former governor of the Bank of Spain, and close friend of both Mariano Rubio and Claudio Boada. These men, and some other more peripheral members of the 'beautiful people', had known each other for quite a long time (in the case of Boada and López de Letona dating back to the early 1950s) and had collaborated with each other in different public functions (see Cacho 1988: 165ff.; and *Cambio* 16, 25 January 1988). In fact, it is of interest to note that every member of the group of 'beautiful people' had a professional career with a public industrial background, either in the state holdings INI and INH or the Ministry of Industry. It was this common background which made them, together with the members of the next two groupings, the very representatives of the new aggressive business strategy of the Socialist government (see Chapter 5). The forced restructuring and modernization of traditional economic sectors, and the redirection of public and private capital towards, and the promotion of, innovative activities in viable strong demand growth sectors, both through direct or indirect state intervention, were intended to create highly concentrated and competitive, transnationally operating firms, composed of either national, public and private, or foreign capital, or a combination, in which public participation would be gradually reduced to a minimum.

In the period 1986–1990 this group exerted its greatest influence on the government's economic policy and played a leading, though not always successful, role in the process of concentration of Spanish bank capital. It was the period of rapid growth, together with the changing power configuration within the Socialist ruling party, that considerably strengthened the position of Solchaga and Rubio; next to this, other members of the 'beautiful people' either came to control a particular bank (Boada) or played an important role in the attempt to bring the two most traditional private banks, Banesto and Central, into the orbit of the Socialist government (López de Letona and Boyer). Finally, it was the extended relaunching of the process of European integration (from the agreement of the Europe '92 project to the preparatory phase of the Maastricht Treaty) that gave the 'beautiful people' external legitimacy both with respect to the general course of the implemented macroeconomic policy and the creation of 'European champions' of Spanish origin capable of facing the challenge of full competition.

Banco Hispano Americano, Banco de Bilbao and Banco de Vizcaya

Besides the links between the Socialist government and the Banco Hispano Americano through the group of 'beautiful people', the two Basque banks, Bilbao and Vizcaya, were most intimately related to the new rulers. José Angel Sánchez Asiaín and Pedro Toledo were known to have close personal relationships with Felipe González and Carlos Solchaga respectively. They were even sometimes called the 'Socialist' bankers, not so much for their genuine Socialist ideas, as for their ideological and strategic proximity to the hegemonic project of the PSOE.

In the case of Sánchez Asiaín his contacts with the leadership of the PSOE date back to the transition years, during which he became one of the mentors of Felipe González. He himself confirmed this on several occasions. After being asked about the themes he discussed with the future prime minister, he replied in 1988: 'We talked about the country, about the future. Felipe González has always been worried about the great economic challenges of this country. A prime minister of any country needs contacts, and Felipe has propitiated them as no one else' 'interview in *El País Semanal*, 19 June 1988). Identified as an authentic organic intellectual[9] of Spanish banking (see the editorial of *El País*, 21 January 1990), Sánchez Asiaín introduced the concept of banking mergers into the Spanish business world as the only way to prevent Spain from becoming completely dependent on the big European banking consortia in a Single Market characterized by the free movement of capital (see Sánchez Asiaín 1987; 1992).[10] In fact, he was the one who convinced González of the need to create strong and big private banks capable of competing with the European giants (Rivases 1988: 117–118).

This man of middle-class origin, who had been a senior official in the Ministry of Industry during the Franquist dictatorship, became general manager of the Banco de Bilbao in 1968 and the first president from outside the traditional family clans in 1974. In the subsequent years he directed the modernization of the bank's activities to such an extent that 'the profitability of Bilbao as a Group is substantially higher than that of Bilbao as a Bank – a notable difference from the situation in other financial groups' (Sánchez Asiaín, quoted in *Euromoney*, Supplement on Spain, January 1985). Though an outsider with respect to the families who had governed the bank for more than 100 years, Sánchez Asiaín fitted perfectly well into the bank's culture and into its tradition of political links. Ever since its foundation in the late 1850s, the Banco de Bilbao had depended on the modernizing impact of economic state intervention. This came particularly into the open in the 1960s, when state intervention in heavy industry conditioned its survival and subsequent restructuring. During the Socialist decade, it was the accelerated modernization of the Spanish economy through the progressive integration of Spain into the Single European Market that came closest to Bilbao's corporate strategy and the views of its president. The present structural transformation of the world economy characterized by globalization, deregulation and innovation, Sánchez Asiaín argued, could not be challenged any longer by means of 'conservative and protectionist' practices at the national level. Imbalances resulting from the working of global market forces should be met, however, by the supra-national coordination of macro-economic and monetary policies and 'supranational regulation' at the European level. In fact, Europe should recover its 'global protagonism . . . through the possible leadership of the ECU in the concert of standard currencies' (Sánchez Asiaín 1987: 70, 95, 103; 1992: 134–135). The similarity of these ideas to the European policy of the Socialist government seems quite obvious, inasmuch as in both views deregulation and liberalization at home should be paralleled by the strengthening of supra-national institutions at the European level.

Whereas Sánchez Asiaín was more closely related to the statesman González, Pedro Toledo had been friends with Carlos Solchaga ever since the latter had been working under the former's direction in the Banco de Vizcaya (see Díaz Herrera and Tijeras 1991: 211ff.; and Rivases 1988: 137–138). Three other former executives of the Banco de Vizcaya obtained important positions during the Socialist decade: Claudio Aranzadi was first appointed as president of INI and then became Minister of Industry; José Luis Leal succeeded Rafael Termes (a member of Opus Dei and known for his extreme defence of the principles of economic liberalism; see for example Termes 1992) as president of the Spanish Association of Private Banking (AEB) – the institutional arm of the *Club de los Siete* (see *El País*, 17 May 1990); and Francisco Luzón was appointed as president of the Corporación Bancaria de España (Argentaria), the holding which came into existence as a result of the merger between six public banks in 1991 (*El País*, 4 May 1991). These close personal interrelationships between the Banco de Vizcaya and the 'neo-liberals' in the Socialist government generated a clear favouritism, manifested *inter alia* in the absorption of the Banca Catalana by Vizcaya in 1984 and the extremely profitable mediation of the then Banco Bilbao Vizcaya in the partial privatization of the public oil company Repsol in 1989, converting the bank into the largest private shareholder with a 4.2 per cent stake in this 'strategic firm' (see Amigot 1990: 36–41; and Díaz Herrera and Tijeras 1991: ch. IX).

Public companies and the 'Club de Empresarios'

In addition to its close links with important sections of private bank capital, the PSOE increased its involvement in the Spanish economy through the public industrial sector. In the course of the Socialist decade, a large part of public enterprise came to be controlled by affiliates or sympathizers of the Socialist party, organized in the so-called '*Club de Empresarios*'. This employers' club, headed by a former executive of the Socialist trade union UGT (Jesús Prieto), was founded after the PSOE came to power in 1982 in an attempt to break the monopoly of business representation of the CEOE. Among its members were the presidents and managing directors of all the major public companies belonging to the state holdings INI and INH, such as Iberia and the oil company Repsol, and other public companies like Telefónica and the rail company RENFE (see *El Independiente*, 2 December 1988).[11] The *Club de Empresarios* favoured a conception of (public or private) industry as an element of modern society whose traditional objective of generating profits should be conditioned, as regards the methods used, by the 'consolidation of the values of modern democracy within the institutional channels' (ibid.). The 'progressive development' of existing business relations should be based on a social dialogue with the trade unions. Furthermore, the Club aimed to function as a platform for Spanish business in the strengthening of its ties with foreign governments and capital. In short, the Club became one of the anchors of the Socialist strategy to restructure and modernize Spanish big industry and to promote its subsequent internationalization (see the previous chapter).

Foreign capital

The interrelationship of the Spanish Socialists and foreign capital can be subdivided according to the distinction between the structural and behavioural power of transnationally mobile capital (see Chapter 1). The structural power of capital is related to the geographically and economically extended operation of the market mechanisms as a result of, *inter alia*, the integration of Spain into the Common Market. In general, the increasing importance of transnationally mobile capital has forced national governments to adjust their policies and practices to the exigencies of the global economy; the resulting 'austerity race' is reflected in national attempts to optimize the macro-economic environment through supply side government intervention. As indicated in the previous chapter, in the Spanish case both the balancing of the structural trade deficits and the government's strategy directed at intra-industry specialization were premised upon the continuous influx of foreign capital and technology, which in turn depended on the general macro-economic environment. Part and parcel of this strategy, which included the privatization and 'multinationalization' of Spanish industry, was the sale of public companies to foreign, primarily European, companies (such as the sale of SEAT to Volkswagen in 1986) under favourable buyer's conditions. The Spanish banking sector was deliberately excluded from foreign takeovers because of its strategic importance. In fact, the Socialist government actively defended Spanish private banks from 'foreign sharks', as a senior official of the Bank of Spain commented in 1988, 'in exchange for which private banking must strengthen itself and define its strategies in view of the imminent completion of the Single European Market, within which protectionism will not be possible any longer' (*Cambio 16*, 8 February 1988). From the perspective of the Socialist government, the principal mechanism of defence against future takeovers was the concentration of private bank capital. It is interesting to note that in one case the Spanish authorities took a rather flexible stand: already in 1986 the Deutsche Bank had acquired a 39 per cent stake in the medium-sized Catalan Banco Comercial Transatlántico, a percentage which was extended to 72 per cent in early 1990 (see *El Independiente*, 31 March 1989; and *El País*, 28 February 1990). In another case, however, the government and the Bank of Spain directly intervened in defence of two of the largest private banks. As soon as it became known that the Kuwait Investment Office (KIO) had taken a considerable stake in the Banco de Vizcaya (i.e. prior to the merger with the Banco de Bilbao) and the Banco Central it was forced to sell its participation to the bank in the first case and agree upon a 'renationalization' in the latter case by taking '*los Albertos*' (the nickname of two private financiers) into partnership (see *Cambio 16*, 8 February 1988; *El País*, 31 January 1993; and García-Abadillo and Fidalgo 1989).

Finally, the Socialist ruling party was related to foreign capital through all kinds of transactions, links which were established either directly between members of the party apparatus and individual companies or indirectly through the mediation of the Socialist International. It was the acquisition of lucrative public contracts in exchange for huge payments to the PSOE in the form of commissions that characterized these links. Unfortunately, we have to rely on rather sketchy evidence to illustrate this phenomenon. An example which only recently emerged was the financing of the PSOE by the German company Siemens during the period 1989–1992. In exchange for the company's participation in the construction of networks of high-speed trains in Spain, it funded the party's 1989 electoral campaign and continued to pay commissions in the following years (see *El*

País, 26 and 31 January 1993; and 21 February 1993). From the German side the SPD, the German government and the former German ambassador in Spain Guido Brunner (at present a member of the board of directors of Siemens) successfully pressurized the Socialist government to concede a considerable part of the public contracts to Siemens (ibid. 21 February 1993; and Díaz Herrera and Tijeras 1991: 295ff.). Another example is offered by the 'Italian connection' in the Spanish arms trade. The Italian Socialist Party (PSI) took part in the financing of the PSOE during the period of democratic transition, and several of its most important leaders established close personal relationships with the top level of the PSOE. One of them, the former president of the Banca Nazionale di Lavoro, Nerio Nesi, used his personal contacts with Felipe González, Alfonso Guerra and the 'Socialist' banker José Angel Sánchez Asiaín to mediate between the Socialist government and the Italian public company Contraves, resulting in the purchase of the Italian Skyguard-Aspide missiles (see Díaz Herrera and Tijeras 1991: 32ff.; and *El Independiente*, 16 and 17 September 1989).

The opposition: Partido Popular, CEOE, and Banesto

In the wake of its October 1982 electoral victory, the PSOE thus succeeded in configuring a new balance of social and political power, uniting the most outward-looking social forces and the central state institutions around a single, hegemonic project. It was this project, centred on the key elements of political consolidation, economic modernization and European unification, which was meant to articulate different visions of the world in such a way that their potential antagonism was neutralized. And so it did, at least until the early 1990s. A closer look at the conservative opposition to the Socialist government (from both the traditional political establishment and sections of the business community) can clearly illustrate this point.

From the very start of the political transition in 1976, by far the greatest part of Spanish private bank and industrial capital supported either the right-wing Alianza Popular (AP) of the former Franquist minister Manuel Fraga or the centre-right UCD of Adolfo Suárez. Though, as indicated above, it was in the common interest of the Spanish bourgeoisie to ensure that the political transition would leave social property relations intact, differences existed with respect to the question of which of these two political parties could best serve this interest. Banks like the Hispano Americano and Bilbao were more inclined to support the UCD while Banesto and Central turned to the AP. The same differences also came to the fore within the Spanish employers' organization, CEOE: its first president, the Catalan Carlos Ferrer Salat, who was a distinguished member of the organization of the liberal Catalan bourgeoisie *Círculo de Economía* and known for his strong Europeanist views (see *El País*, 3 July 1983), initially supported the UCD; Ferrer's successor, José María Cuevas, a prototype of the small Castilian rural bourgeoisie, openly supported the AP (Díaz-Varela and Guindal 1990).

After the Socialists had obtained their first absolute majority, and particularly after their renewed victory in the 1986 elections, both the AP and the CEOE entered a profound crisis, even leading to a public confrontation between both organizations (see, for instance, *Cambio 16*, 23 May 1988). The reason for this was threefold: first, both organizations experienced serious identity problems. In the case of the AP, the 1986 elections had resulted in a slight decrease of the number of seats in parliament, and subsequently in an internal struggle over the party's leadership and future direction. As one of the leaders of the AP commented on the eve of the 1989 elections: 'we don't want to be the party of the [economic right], our project is above all a populist one'. And: 'private banking is very important, but in Spain there are only seven big bankers and thousands of taxi drivers' (quoted in *El Independiente*, 17 February 1989). It was only after the present leader José María Aznar took over the 'refounded' Partido Popular (PP) in 1990, that the party could gradually abandon its Franquist image and try to become a political alternative to the PSOE. In the case of the CEOE, the emergence of various alternative forums of Spanish business (such as the above mentioned *Club de Empresarios*) and the inclination of certain affiliated companies and sectors to enter separately into negotiations with the trade unions eroded its strength to a considerable extent (see, for example, *Actualidad Económica*, 11 June 1990; and *El País*, 22 May 1990).

Second, the hegemonic project of the PSOE, and particularly its macroeconomic and foreign policy components, did not leave much room for an alternative strategy. Economic austerity and industrial reconversion, on the one hand, and the opening towards the Common Market, on the other, could not be seriously counterattacked during the greatest part of the Socialist decade. A clear case in point was the attitude of both the AP and the CEOE during the NATO referendum of 1986. Incapable of formulating an alternative to Socialist foreign policy, in an act of mere political obstruction both Cuevas and Fraga advised the Spanish electorate to abstain from voting, and tried to convince the *Club de los Siete* to do the same (an attempt which was aborted as a result of the pressure of the presidents of the Banco de Bilbao and Vizcaya) (see Chapter 4; and Díaz-Varela and Guindal 1990: 253ff.).

Third, the 1985–1990 economic boom not only strengthened the coalition of forces headed by the 'beautiful people', but it also proved, at least for the time being, the viability of the general course of the macroeconomic policy pursued, that is, seen from the perspective of the Spanish business community. As long as booming economic growth and rising corporate profits continued to satisfy the largest part of Spanish business, and as long as the full impact of EC membership on Spanish industry was yet to come, there would be no political space to the right of the PSOE for an alternative policy. It left CEOE's president, Cuevas, no other choice than to state that 'what we are doing through the rise of imports is to give work to and help to create employment in other countries' (quoted in *Cambio 16*, 12 January 1987).

Cuevas' statement points at the existence of a very important, though until recently rather dormant, current of thought within the leadership of the CEOE, whose representatives defend a peculiar combination of three basic concepts: economic liberalism on the domestic market, which implies the progressive withdrawal of the state to the benefit of private enterprise; selective protectionism, which implies the maintenance of certain mechanisms (including the freedom to adjust the exchange rate downward) to control imports and promote exports; and economic nationalism, which implies at present a plea for the defence of a genuine Spanish capitalism against the massive infiltration of foreign capital (the so-called 'colonization' of the Spanish economy). It was a banker, the president of Banesto, Mario Conde, who publicly defended this line of thought years before the PP and CEOE started to do the same in the course of 1992.

Conde had made a fortune in the pharmaceutical industry by selling his stake in Antibióticos Españoles to the Italian company Montedison in early 1987. He then invested heavily in Banesto stock, which made him the largest shareholder of the bank, and one of the most important examples of a new species of bankers: those who had enriched themselves by realizing windfall profits in all kinds of speculative activities in order to subsequently buy themselves into one of the largest private banks. Through his share in Banesto's stock he obtained a seat on the bank's board of directors. Only a couple of months later, in December 1987, he became the bank's president and in his new function he headed Banesto's successful effort to fight off the hostile takeover by the Banco de Bilbao (see the next section). In the following years Conde became one of the public figures in Spain who, not only because of his appearance as 'a snappy dresser with an engaging manner'[12] but particularly because of his continuous political statements and attacks on the Socialist government, was suspected of harbouring political ambitions, aspiring to become the future leader of the Partido Popular (see for example *Tiempo*, 18 April 1988). He always denied these ambitions, identifying himself as 'a man who has decided to work and succeed in the bosom of civil society by doing business' (quoted in *Actualidad Económica*, August 1990).[13]

More importantly, in his public statements after 1987 he not only came to criticize the European project of the Socialist government, but also elaborated his own alternative ideas. One of the recurring themes in his speeches was his plea for a strengthening of civil society *vis-à-vis* the state in which businessmen would assume a protagonistic role in creating wealth. Historically, he stated, the Spanish state could only play such a dominant role in the process of industrialization because of the absence of a strong and innovative entrepreneurship. 'When a weak business class exists, and when not enough independent initiatives are taken in the bosom of society, a culture medium is generated prone to the emergence of interventionist philosophies on the part of the state' (Conde 1990: 16). Conversely, the existence of strong private enterprise should be accompanied by a withdrawal of the state, leaving the creation of social cohesion to the institutions of a strong civil society (Banesto 1991: 22–23). With respect to the integration of Spain into the EC, it was evident that Spanish industry was still lagging behind and that it would take a long time to consolidate 'an enterprising business class which looks beyond our frontiers, and is able to divert resources to the creation of profitable projects' in the framework of international competition (ibid.: 25). Instead of concentrating too much on what Conde called the 'institutional debate' (i.e. the discussions on the necessity of a European Central Bank and a single European currency, or on the future legal and political structure of the EC), one should look at the micro-economic consequences of the Single European Market (Conde 1991: 1). Though Spanish industry needed to improve its competitiveness through innovation and concentration, one should also be aware of the high costs that go with a policy of an overvalued peseta (Conde 1990: 23). More specifically, directly addressing the Socialist government (and its policy of keeping the peseta within the Exchange Rate Mechanism of the European Monetary System), Conde argued again and again in favour of the instrument of devaluation to improve the international competitiveness of Spanish business and to promote exports; he criticized the 'premature' entry of the peseta in the EMS and its maintenance within the ERM at an unrealistically high rate; and he criticized the rash decision of the Socialists to agree to the Treaty of Maastricht, *inter alia* because of the strong interventionist tendency inherent in this treaty (see the interview with Mario Conde in *El País*, 29 November 1992; see also *El País*, 7 June 1992). Finally, in commenting on the role of private bank capital in the Spanish economy, Conde emphasized the industrial vocation of Banesto. 'Given the narrowness of the Spanish capital market, the presence of private banking in industry is a valid instrument to keep a part of our industrial fabric in the hands of national entities'. And in criticizing the Socialist economic policy for its major preoccupation with macro-economic instead of micro-economic aspects, and its lack of sensitivity to specific business problems, he even came to conclude that the Socialists were convinced that 'Spain had no alternative than to convert itself into the service sector of the European Community' (Banesto 1991: 4). For Conde, effective defence of Spanish industry through the involvement of private bank capital would not necessarily imply that private banks should merge. Moreover, in clear reference to the intervention of political and monetary authorities in the concentration of Spanish bank capital, the decision whether or not Banesto should merge with another bank belonged to the exclusive competence of the bank. 'Banesto is a private entity . . . and we are responsible for our own future. We will take the decisions that we think most appropriate to guarantee this future' (ibid.: 15).

Operation Europe: the government-led concentration of Spanish banking

In December 1987 the merger process in Spanish banking started with the 'assault' on Banesto by the Banco de Bilbao. This dealt a final blow to the already rather cosmetic cohesion between the members of the *Club de los Siete*. Until May 1991 various abortive and other successful attempts to merge were carried through. A first glance at the newspaper reports during this relatively short period, and a closer look at the books that were published immediately after the first attempt by the Banco de Bilbao, may easily give the impression of a rather contingent course of events in which a great number of individuals (both politicians and businessmen) entered into alliances, only to break them shortly afterwards, with the sole purpose of personal enrichment and/or maintaining or obtaining more power. However, this prevailing picture of a hopelessly divided banking sector, exemplified in takeover attempts of a hostile nature, on the one hand, and an ever more powerful and controlling government, illustrated by the Socialists' role in the concentration process, on the other, fails to take into account a very important feature of Spain today: the unification of the Spanish bourgeoisie into a single operating force, necessary for domestic reasons, has tended to mask underlying structural differences and conflictive, historically determined strategies between parts (or factions) of this bourgeoisie, differences which only re-emerged after the assumption of power by the Socialist party in 1982. It is this very reality, and more particularly the internationalist (or Europeanist) implications of this reality, which divided Spanish bank capital. The coming into existence of an apparently united Spanish business community as a result of domestic, social (the Spanish Civil War and its aftermath) and political (the period of democratic transition) developments gave way to a new stage in the modernization of the Spanish bourgeoisie, i.e. its fractionation, as a result of international developments. It is not the integration into the Common Market as such which divided bank capital, but rather the way in which to confront this new challenge, and the strategic projections of the PSOE in this respect. In a sense, it was the old debate between '*europeizar*' versus '*españolizar*' (see Chapter 2) which divided the Spanish bank community, though under completely different socio-economic and political, domestic and international conditions.

The banks (and their presidents) which most paradigmatically came to represent these two positions during the Socialist decade were the Banco de Bilbao and the Banco de Vizcaya, on the one hand, and Banesto, on the other. As to the former, as early as the 1970s both Basque banks had redefined their corporate strategies, had reduced their stake in traditional, crisis-prone industries, and had centred their activities on diversification, innovation and internationalization. Banesto, on the other hand, had experienced its greatest expansion during the 1960s and had become involved in those industrial sectors that were primarily directed at the domestic market. In the 1980s it was these low demand growth sectors which were threatened most by the accelerated opening up of the Spanish economy, particularly after Spain's entry into the EC and the subsequent completion of the Single Market. The speed at which the Socialist government adjusted its policy to the exigencies of transnationally mobile capital and the exchange rate policy pursued (see Chapter 5) were the two elements most to the detriment of these sectors. Therefore, it was not so much the merger process as such that divided private bank capital, but the underlying Socialist strategy of enhanced transnationalization in particular. In the final analysis, it was the collision of different accumulation strategies, and the subsequent inclination among private banks to either support or reject the Socialist project, that gave the merger process in the second half of the 1980s its transcendent importance.

The way in which the concentration of bank capital was strategically planned, legitimized and executed, and the list of authorities and bankers involved in the process, point to five interrelated aspects: first, that the primary reason for the Socialist government's support and active participation in the mergers was its at times rather blind ambition to create a couple of 'national champions' which could enter into competition with their European competitors on equal terms and could give the transnationalization of Spanish business a strong impetus; second, that an additional objective was the modernization of the management of the largest private banks, if possible through the replacement of representatives of the traditional families by persons who favoured the Socialist project; third, that a recurrent theme in the respective mergers was the confrontation between Mario Conde and the Socialist government; fourth, that the group of 'beautiful people' was in one way or another always involved in the various mergers, with the sole exception of the merger involving Catalan savings banks in 1991; and, finally, that the fractionation of private bank capital, separating the two Basque banks from Banesto and the Banco Central on historical and strategic grounds, on the basis of their different adjustment to the economic crisis of the 1970s and early 1980s, and as a result of their different relationships with the Socialist government, was by and large reconfirmed during the process of concentration.

The following resumé of the main events between December 1987 and May 1991 confirms these assertions:

1 On the last day of November 1987 the Banco de Bilbao made a hostile takeover bid for the majority of the shares in Banesto after previous negotiations over a friendly merger had been deadlocked. From the start, Sánchez Asiaín had concerted his action with González, Solchaga and Rubio, who gave him full support. Within the executive of the bank he was supported by López de Letona, who had been appointed as vice-president in 1986 as a result of the intervention of the Bank of Spain in Banesto's management. On the same day that Bilbao's hostile bid was announced, Banesto's board of directors, still dominated by the traditional families, appointed Mario Conde as the bank's new president in an effort to fight off the takeover. A salient detail is that this appointment was suggested, or at least supported, by the Guerristas (see Chapter 3) in an attempt to obstruct the ambitions of Solchaga (Amigot 1990: 59).[14] Conde, supported among others by the president of CEOE, José María Cuevas, took immediate action by using the Petromed oil company, controlled by Banesto, to make a counterbid for the bank's shares. As a result of this and other events, Sánchez Asiaín had to cancel his hostile takeover bid one week after he had started the operation (nicknamed 'Operation Europe').

2 In January 1988 the Banco de Bilbao and the Banco de Vizcaya agreed on a merger as a second-best solution. Prior to this agreement, Vizcaya had attempted to merge with the Banco Central without any success. In

short, the two private banks closest to the Socialist government came to realize the first banking merger as a last resort: both the presidents of the two Basque banks and the Socialist government would have preferred the twin takeover Bilbao–Banesto and Vizcaya–Central in order to kill two birds with one stone, i.e. concentration of and control over the most conservative private banks.

3   In May 1988, then, Banco Central and Banesto announced their merger. For Mario Conde this project offered a great opportunity to become Spain's most important banker, since part of the merger agreement was that, after a short period during which Central's president Escámez and Conde would both be co-president, he would become president of the country's largest bank (also outstripping the Banco Bilbao Vizcaya). For Escámez the merger with Banesto formed the only defence against the growing pressure of 'the Albertos' to hand over the control of the Banco Central. The two cousins had obtained a 12 per cent share in the Banco Central through their investment company Cartera Central (in which KIO had a 40 per cent share), a share which was to be reduced considerably after Central's merger with Banesto. In an attempt to counteract this development, Cartera Central tried to increase its stake in the Banco Central and to obtain a stake in Banesto, and appointed Miguel Boyer as its president. With the support of the 'beautiful people', and with the leadership of what would be Spain's largest bank by far at stake, a 'duel of the century' (*International Management*, March 1989) was fought between Boyer and Conde – that is, until one of the Albertos, Alberto Cortina, spoilt the whole operation by starting an extramarital relation. Since his wife, Alicia Koplovitz, and her sister, Esther Koplovitz, who happened to be the wife of the other Alberto (Alcocer), had inherited the capital with which the 'Albertos' had started their investments, the Cortina matrimonial crisis came to jeopardize the very success of the 'assault'. The withdrawal of KIO from Cartera Central dealt the whole enterprise its final blow. Continuous obstruction on the part of the Bank of Spain and the Socialist government in the ensuing period, and a struggle between the two boards of directors on the future distribution of power, eventually also resulted in the rupture between the Banco Central and Banesto in May 1989.

4   After the merger of Catalan savings banks in June 1990 (a process in which the Socialist government only participated indirectly as a consequence of the links between the public oil company Repsol and the newly-founded savings bank through their joint control of a Catalan gas company) it took another year before the Socialist government renewed

its efforts to concentrate bank capital. In May 1991 six public banks, including the Banco Exterior and Caja Postal, were grouped together in the Corporación Bancaria de España (CBE). A former executive of the Banco de Vizcaya, Francisco Luzón, became the public bank's president (see *El País*, 12 May 1991).

5 A couple of days after the establishment of the CBE, the Banco Hispano Americano and the Banco Central announced their merger to form the Banco Central Hispanoamericano (BCH). Part of the agreement was that Escámez would function as the BCH's president until his retirement in December 1992. The president of Hispano Americano, José María Amusátegui (who had taken over the bank from Claudio Boada in January 1991) would then succeed him. It was with great satisfaction that the Socialist government received this merger: first, because it was the first concentration of private bank capital since the merger between Bilbao and Vizcaya more than three years before; second, because the merger agreement guaranteed the foreseeable removal of the last patriarch from the Spanish banking scene. His successor Amusátegui, finally, former vice-president of the public holding INH and a close friend of Boada, had entered the group of 'beautiful people' in the 1980s and was known for his good relationship with the Socialist government (see *Futuro*, June 1991: 7–11). This last merger resulted in a situation in which four of the five largest private banks had entered into the orbit of the Socialist government, leaving one bank for the time being without a partner and outside the most important centres of decision-making.

Again, and despite the recurrent theme of the struggle for power between the protagonists in the merger process, it was the project that was more important than the individuals. More specifically, it was the Socialist project of integrating Spain into the Lockeian heartland of transnational production, centred on the most viable and competitive sections of Spanish business, that cemented the cohesion between the neo-liberals in the Socialist government, the top echelons of the most outward-looking private banks, executives of the large-scale public companies, and the repre- sentatives of foreign (basically European) capital. Moreover, it was the projected 'transnationalization of Spain' that inspired the Socialist government to push for a further concentration of private banks. The creation of a couple of large private banks – large, that is, in European terms – could not only protect this vital sector against foreign competition and hostile take- over bids (i.e. as part of a defensive strategy), but could also give the transnationalization of domestic capital a strong impetus. From the latter perspective, the transnationalization of Spain was a strategy and not a reality. If we look at some recent data as regards the outward expansion of Spanish private banks (see Appendix), we can come to the following conclusions.

Even after the various mergers between private and public banks during the period 1987–1991, Spanish banks still occupy at best an intermediate position in the group of 200 greatest banks of the world, though in terms of net income and real profitability the picture is more favourable (see Table 15, Appendix). In terms of real profitability almost all the Spanish banks rank at a higher position (Banco Santander even at rank 12), with the sole exception – strikingly – of Banesto, which is at rank 94 with respect to assets and at rank 108 as to real profitability (*Business Week*, 5 July 1993).

In comparison to other EC member states, the degree of internationalization of Spanish banking in terms of deposit banks' foreign assets is still very low (see Table 14, Appendix). Especially when compared with the leading economies of the EC this difference is striking, even though an above average increase in foreign assets can be noticed between 1987 and 1992. In absolute terms, only deposit banks in Denmark, Greece, Ireland and Portugal are at present less internationalized than the Spanish ones.

A similar conclusion can be drawn if we look at Spanish banks' foreign assets as a percentage of total assets (Table 13, Appendix). With claims on non-residents only amounting to 5.72 per cent of total assets in 1991 (the same percentage as in 1987, despite the substantial increase in foreign assets), the Spanish banking community as a whole is positioned at the lowest rank, even below Portugal.

However, if we look at individual banks, this last conclusion must be altered in a fundamental way. Building upon a July 1991 listing of the world's largest banks by Tier One capital (see *The Banker*, July 1991), *The Banker* surveyed the 'true global players among the banking majors', ranking the banks by percentage of business conducted overseas. It turned out that three Spanish banks, the Banco Santander, the Banco Bilbao Vizcaya and the Banco Hispano Americano (before the merger with the Banco Central) were listed among the sixty-eight banks with the highest percentages of assets domiciled overseas. Topping the list of the global players were the two British banks, HSBC Holdings and Standard Chartered, with 78 per cent and 64 per cent respectively of group business outside the UK. For the three Spanish banks the figures were respectively 29.1 per cent, 21.3 per cent and 11.3 per cent of total assets. Income generated overseas (as a percentage of total income) amounted to respectively 29.1 per cent, 14.6 per cent and 9.0 per cent (see *The Banker*, February 1992; see also *El País*, 1 March 1992). On the basis of these percentages and the figures in the Appendix, we can conclude that these three banks account for approximately 50 per cent of Spain's deposit banks' total foreign assets. This in turn seems to confirm our previous conclusion that the private banks which were most supportive of the Socialist project and were most active in the merger process – i.e. the Banco de Bilbao, the Banco de Vizcaya and the Banco Hispano Americano – also are among the most outward-looking Spanish entities.

In short, on the basis of these figures two features of present-day Spanish banking can be distinguished: only three private banks show a degree of internationalization that is comparable to the group of 'global players' in relative terms; in absolute terms, however, the Spanish banking community as a whole is still lagging behind, in terms of both total assets and total foreign assets. Viewed separately, none of the Spanish banking majors can even come close to the size of the leading European banks, let alone to the size of their Japanese competitors. At the end of Chapter 5 we argued that the European policy of the Spanish Socialists, and particularly its emphasis on supra-national integration, seems to have become part of a minority view in the post-Maastricht context. The same can be said of the Socialist government's strategy to create European champions in the field of banking. Globalization rather than regionalization of banking and finance seems the dominant tendency at present. In this context, the top echelons of global business and decision-making are still far beyond the reach of the Spanish ruling elites.

APPENDIX: SPANISH BANKING IN INTERNATIONAL COMPARISON

Table 13 Claims on non-residents as a % of year-end balance sheet total of commercial banks in selected European countries (1987 and 1991)

	Foreign assets as % of total assets, 1987	Foreign assets as % of total assets, 1991
Belgium	51.11	49.42
Denmark	24.04	32.62*
France	30.30	31.80
Germany	13.69	16.35
Italy	9.02	8.17
Netherlands	33.03	27.55
Portugal	5.47	6.39
Spain	5.71	5.72[15]

Source: OECD 1993b

*1990

Table 14 Deposit banks' foreign assets by EC member state (billions of dollars)

	Foreign assets 1987	Foreign assets 1992
Belgium	149.13	188.52
Denmark	24.15	45.63
France	290.10	542.43
Germany	232.61	386.80
Greece	1.88	4.36
Ireland	5.90	18.61
Italy	68.81	96.00
Luxembourg	226.52	376.50
Netherlands	115.98	189.49
Portugal	2.74	9.72
Spain	26.94	72.28
United Kingdom	875.31	1,019.75

Source: IMF, 1993, p. 39

Table 15 Spanish private banks among the 200 largest banks of the world (1992)

		Assets $ mil.	Net income $ mil.	Real profitability*
1	Dai-Ichi Kangyo Bank (Japan)	456,484	465	1.010
2	Fuji Bank (Japan)	454,745	523	1.014
3	Sumitomo Bank (Japan)	448,933	199	0.994
4	Sanwa Bank (Japan)	445,918	818	1.030
5	Sakura Bank (Japan)	437,952	557	1.018
8	Crédit Lyonnais (France)	352,013	−139	0.979
10	Deutsche Bank (Germany)	302,030	1,134	1.060
67	Bilbao Vizcaya	87,643	708	1.164
68	Central Hisp. Amer.	86,191	500	1.103
71	CBE	81,939	588	1.135
94	Banesto	61,753	161	1.022
97	Caixa	61,493	368	1.111
100	Santander	61,316	578	1.207
165	Caja de Madrid	32,192	255	1.166

Source: *Business Week*, 5 July 1993

*Real profitability: index of return on equity (= net income divided by average equity) adjusted for differing bank capital ratios, inflation, and tax rates.

7 Conclusions and epilogue

The international context of regime transition from authoritarian rule to parliamentary democracy has become one of the leading themes in the study of post-cold war international relations. The renaissance of liberal, economic and political, values during the 1980s and early 1990s, of which the 'New Great Transformation' in Central and Eastern Europe (Bryant and Mokrzycki 1994) is only one manifestation, points at the global nature of this process, on the one hand, and at the inextricable relation between structural changes in economics and politics, on the other. The study of interrelated changes at the levels of production and power and changes in world order structures from a Global Political Economy perspective can offer us a greater insight into, for instance, the crisis of the Keynesian welfare state in Western Europe and the collapse of the patronage state in Central and Eastern Europe. In fact, both phenomena are constituent parts of the same process of global restructuring after the decline of postwar American hegemony and the break-up of Soviet dominance, as indeed are the regime transitions in different regions of the world system during the last two decades. The different impact of transformative processes in individual countries or regions, and the integrating or disintegrating forces these processes unchain, can only properly be understood by referring to the different ways these countries or regions are (re-)incorporated into the global political economy.

In analysing regime transition in Southern Europe (Spain, Portugal and Greece), we stressed the striking similarities in the timing and content of the processes by which each country experienced an accelerated integration into the European, and world, capitalist system. When speaking of the developments in Southern Europe in the second half of the twentieth century, the combined processes of modernization and Westernization in these countries make it possible to compare them both with each other and with other groups of countries, notably the new democracies in Central and Eastern Europe.

'Modernization' refers to the process of relatively autonomous economic, social, and political development within the context of modern European state-building. The moment in world history this process of modernization takes place, and its content, are primarily based on historically determined, national factors. Yet, modernization also implies the long-term adoption of economic and political structures first introduced in England after the 1688 Glorious Revolution and then extended to the European continent through the process of Hobbesian state-building, starting in France after the French Revolution. In this context, it is worthwhile to recall the four elements on which, according to Gramsci, the study of the historical relationship between the modern French state originating in the Revolution and the other modern states of continental Europe should be based (Gramsci 1971: 114/115):

1 The revolutionary explosion in France.
2 European opposition to the French Revolution and its extension abroad.
3 War between France, under the republic and Napoleon, and the rest of Europe – initially, in order to avoid being stifled at birth, and subsequently with the aim of establishing a permanent French hegemony tending towards the creation of a universal empire.
4 National revolts against French hegemony, and birth of the modern European states by successive small waves of reform rather than by revolutionary explosions like the original French one. The 'successive waves' were made up of a combination of social struggles, interventions from above of the enlightened monarchy type, and national wars – with the two latter phenomena predominating.

The fourth element refers to Gramsci's concept of 'passive revolution', i.e. the gradual introduction 'from above' of a state/society configuration characterized by a high degree of internationalization, modernity and sociopolitical integration. Passive revolution is a defining characteristic of what we have called Hobbesian latecomer states (see Chapter 1). In resisting peripheralization by the heartland of capitalist development, these contender states succeed in achieving an autonomous, catch-up development, through revolutions from above, involving authoritarian patterns of political domination and the subordination of a weak, incipient civil society to the state-led project of economic modernization. Initially, the amalgamation of social and political power within the cupola of an emerging state class impedes the self-organization of domestic social forces, let alone the strengthening of a self-regulating civil society. Yet, in the course of the 'modernization from above', these 'progressive' social forces advance in a more or less surreptitious, 'molecular' fashion in the direction of the pattern prevailing in the heartland, and are eventually bound 'to surface and constitute [themselves] as a class' (van der Pijl 1994: 37; see also van der Pijl 1993: 239). Social transformation under authoritarian rule tends to unchain those forces which in the final stage of the Hobbesian catch-up process come to support democratic transition and full integration into the Lockeian heartland of capitalist development. We are dealing here with the two 'fundamental principles of political science' from which, according to Gramsci, the concept of passive revolution must be derived:

> 1. that no social formation disappears as long as the productive forces which have developed within it still find room for further forward movement; 2. that a society does not set itself tasks for whose solution the necessary conditions have not already been incubated.
>
> (Gramsci 1971: 106)

In short, and returning to our case study of Southern Europe, the transition from economic backwardness and economic nationalism to parliamentary democracy and EC membership in the course of the twentieth century would have been impossible without the process of Hobbesian state-building. Yet, economic development is not related to subsequent political modernization in a linear way. It is through the intermediate process of social transformation that the two processes are linked. In a study on the interrelationship of capitalist development and democracy in a number of countries, it was stated that 'industrialization transformed society in a fashion that empowered subordinate classes and made it difficult to politically exclude them' (Rueschemeyer *et al.* 1992: vii). To put it in other words:

> it is power relations that most importantly determine whether democracy can emerge, stabilize, and then maintain itself even in the face of adverse conditions. There is first the balance of power among different *classes and class coalitions*. This is a factor of overwhelming importance. It is complemented by two other power configurations – the structure, strength, and autonomy of the *state apparatus* and its interrelations with civil society and the impact of *transnational power relations* on both the balance of class power and on state-society relations.
>
> (ibid.: 5)

Our analysis of the social and political modernization in twentieth century Southern Europe started by and large from the same levels of analysis to explain the emergence and consolidation of democracy. In dealing with the 'impact of transnational power relations', we introduced the notion of Westernization.

'Westernization' refers to the process in which economic, social, and political development becomes increasingly dependent on external developments. In the course of the passive revolution, these external developments tend to fashion the way and extent in which Western (European) economic and socio-political structures are adopted. In the case of Southern Europe, the so-called internationalization of capital has been the mediating force between the processes of modernization and Westernization. Once state-led industrialization and economic nationalism came to conflict with the overall need for continuous economic growth, and with the further development of free enterprise, the state classes in Southern Europe were forced to open their respective national economies towards the world market and embark on a strategy of economic liberalization in the course of the 1950s. The resulting period of spectacular economic growth during the 1960s and early 1970s was not only accompanied by increasing external dependence on foreign investment and trade, but also accelerated the emancipation of the 'progressive' social forces in the three countries, first and foremost through transnational linkages with their counterparts in more advanced European countries. A more detailed study of developments in Spain during the twentieth century has shown the paramount importance of this transnationalization of economic and socio-political structures for the subsequent transition to – and consolidation of – democracy, on the one hand, and the full integration of Spain into the Common Market, on the other.

SPAIN'S ROAD TO MODERNITY

Without doubt, it is the Spanish state which has come to play an essential role in the economic development of Spain during the last hundred years. Apart from providing the legal framework in which private capital accumulation could take place under conditions of foreign protection (i.e. the turn to economic nationalism at the end of the nineteenth century), the state actively intervened in the process of industrialization by creating state monopolies (such as the state monopoly in the oil sector, CAMPSA, which came into existence after the nationalization of foreign companies in the 1920s), by promoting industries which the private sector had bypassed so far (exemplified by the role of the Instituto Nacional de Industria during the autarkic phase of the Franquist dictatorship), or, particularly in the course of the 1960s and 1970s, by socializing private losses in both the industrial and banking sectors.

In addition to these state interventionist practices, it was the authoritarian solution to the 'social problem', the 'vertebration' of Spanish society in a Hobbesian state configuration, and the state corporatist system of interest mediation during the Franquist dictatorship, which created the conditions for an accelerated capitalist development, which was relatively self-sustained until the 1960s. This is why the question of the excessive role of the Spanish state in economic development and discussions as to whether or not the protection of – and direct public participation in – nascent industries retarded the process of catching up with the most developed nations are of little historical relevance. As we saw in Chapter 2, it was the collision of interests between the powerful big landowners and the incipient industrial bourgeoisie in the Basque Provinces and Catalonia, the incapacity of the regenerationists to mediate between them, and the growing polarization between social classes, that eventually culminated in the Franquist 'revolution from above' after the Spanish Civil War. In fact, when faced with the prospect of social revolution, Franquism was the only option left for the dominant classes to 'save capitalism from the capitalists'. But in relegating their direct political power to the Hobbesian state, the dominant classes lost their control over the general direction of state intervention. State corporatism created the conditions for enhanced industrial development, the eventual economic liberalization and internationalization in the wake of the Stabilization Plan of 1959, and the subsequent transition to democracy, a sequence of structural transformations which the dominant forces of the Restoration oligarchy had tried to resist at the turn of the century.

During the Franquist dictatorship the balance of power among the dominant classes definitely changed to the detriment of the landed upper classes, which had traditionally been that social force most fiercely opposed to extending political inclusion to the dominated classes, and to the benefit of the financial and industrial bourgeoisie. The latter forces eventually came to support a transition to democracy in the course of the 1960s, mainly because economic and social modernization had altered the social class configuration in a substantial way. In particular the emergence of the new middle classes produced a more complex social stratification in which an ever-greater part of the Spanish population came to identify itself with institutions and ideologies that were alien to the ones prevailing in the extremely polarized socio-political system prior to the Civil War. This, together with a predominant inclination within the labour movement to accept the 'democratic route to a more equal society', established an almost nationwide consensus as to the general course and contents of the so-called *ruptura pactada*.

Part and parcel of this social and political modernization was the transformation of the state–society relation. State corporatism had offered the institutional framework for the deepening of capitalist relations of production, thereby unchaining those social forces, institutions and ideologies which in the end came to produce its internal erosion, and the subsequent transition to a system of interest mediation which we have labelled as societal corporatism. Using the twin categories of state and civil society, we described this process as the long-term strengthening of both. The strength of the post-Franquist state was said to depend on the extent to which it could adjust its comprehensive policy to the exigencies of transnationally mobile capital operating in a context of global neo-liberalism, without bourgeois civil society losing its self-sustaining social cohesion. In fact, we are dealing here with an exposition of the role of states in international relations which stresses the paramount importance of the coming into existence of a Lockeian heartland of transnational production in which patterns of social inequality and domination are no longer primarily shaped and institutionalized along national lines. It is from this view, emphasizing the transnational dynamics of global (and European) integration, that we elaborated the theoretical perspective of the present study.

We first outlined the three basic dimensions of what we called Atlantic Fordism: the postwar adoption of Fordist production methods; the concomitant macro-economic regulation within the context of the Keynesian welfare state; and the emergence of an *inter*national power configuration centred on common long-term strategies or world views dealing in an integrated way with such areas as labour relations, socio-economic policies, and the international socio-economic and political order. In the wake of the so-called crisis of Fordism of the early 1970s, a dramatic increase in the amount of transnationally mobile capital became the primary force behind a fundamental reshaping of international relations in the course of the 1970s and 1980s. A further globalization and regionalization of social and economic relations, on the one hand, and a progressive *trans*national power configuration between social forces and the emergence of transnational comprehensive concepts of control, on the other, became the most characteristic features of an emerging Lockeian heartland of transnational production. Within this Lockeian configuration the strength of a particular state is no longer related to the extent that it can 'maximize the conditions for profit-making by *its* enterprise within the world-economy' (as Wallerstein 1984: 5 suggests) but to the extent that it can meet the exigencies of transnationally mobile capital, a phenomenon which we referred to as the structural power of transnational capital. In other words, the strength of a state is related to its capacity to create an optimum macro-economic environment through government supply side intervention. This 'internationalization of the state', as such the reflection of the increasing structural power of transnational capital, particularly in the European context, has led to what some have called the 'hollowing out of the national state' (Jessop 1992: 11), referring to the growing importance of the subnational (regional or local) and supra-national levels of decision-making. Next to this, the transnational linkages between social and political institutions and associations, both formal and informal, that are not governmental in character, i.e. the so-called transnationalization of civil society, are another important feature of the Lockeian heartland of transnational production. Again, in the case of Southern Europe, these transnational linkages were of great importance in the smooth transition from dictatorship to democracy in the 1970s, and the subsequent integration of these countries in the European Community in the 1980s.

In the case of Spain, the large-scale introduction of Fordist structures took place in conjunction with the internationalization of capital after the opening up of the Spanish economy in 1959. The start of the period of democratic transition coincided with the crisis of Fordism and the declining hegemony of the United States. The period of Socialist rule in the 1980s and early 1990s, finally, coincided with the accelerated transnationalization of capital, the rise of global neo-liberalism, and the relaunching of the process of European integration. In the final part of this study (Chapters 3 to 6) we have analysed the Socialist government's comprehensive project, its foreign and macro-economic policies, and its relationship with the bastion of Spanish capitalism, i.e. private bank capital, in conjunction with this global process of restructuring.

The period of Socialist government from October 1982 to June 1993, referred to as the 'Socialist decade', can be roughly divided into three subperiods: the first, from 1982 to the general elections of 1986, was characterized by a dramatic moderation of the Socialists' policy objectives, manifested *inter alia* by the macro-economic emphasis on austerity and the party's pro-NATO stand; the second, from 1985/86 to early 1991, was characterized by rapid economic growth, the progressive adjustment to EC practices, the concentration of banking capital, but also by the first open confrontation with the trade unions in 1988 and the growing conflict between the Socialist government and the party apparatus. During this phase the PSOE obtained an absolute majority in parliament for the third consecutive time; and the third, from early 1991 to the general elections of June 1993, in which, in the wake of the Treaty of Maastricht, both the process of European integration and the Spanish economy re-entered a period of stagnation, and in which severe factional strife within the PSOE, in combination with a number of corruption scandals, came to affect both the government's authority and the viability of its European project.

THE FAILURE OF THE PROJECT

In Chapter 3 we first explained the rise to power of the Socialist party in late 1982 as one of the consequences of the long-term social modernization of Spain. The more complex social stratification resulting from the process of industrialization during the latter phase of Franquism, and particularly the growing strength of the so-called new middle classes, were the most important structural causes of the changing political landscape at the end of the period of democratic transition. In fact, the programmatic deradicalization of the PSOE, which began in the late 1970s, was clearly motivated by the Socialist party's attempt to catch these new middle-class votes. Next to this, the transnational party linkages with, among others, the German SPD, and particularly the contribution of Willy Brandt to the political formation of Felipe González, were important factors in the Spanish Socialists' 'Godesberg'.

These transnational linkages with the West European members of the Socialist International clearly influenced the specific contents and direction of the party's foreign policy objectives, and particularly its view of European co-operation. In fact, it was the unification of Europe which encompassed the 'cardinal and transcendent thought' underlying the hegemonic project of the PSOE in the early 1980s. In the course of the Socialist decade, all the constituent elements of this project were subordinated to the ambition to become one of the leading nations within the EC, and, at least rhetorically, to counteract at the supra-national, European level the predominant tendency of neo-liberal deregulation and free market integration. Only through a process of enhanced economic modernization, it was argued, could Spain catch up with the stronger European economies; and only on the basis of such a position of economic strength could the Spanish Socialist party attempt to reformulate and redirect the process of European integration. The primacy of short-term macro-economic adjustment over long-term strategies in practice worked to the benefit of the 'neo-liberals' in the Socialist government, grouped around the Minister of Economics and Finance, Carlos Solchaga, whose growing power in turn produced an ever-increasing tension and overt strife between the so-called Solchaguistas and the Guerristas within the party apparatus, on the one hand, and between the Socialist government and the trade unions, on the other.

In the post-Maastricht years 1992 and 1993 a number of developments were to give a final blow to the original project of the PSOE, and with it all the key role players of the previous period – with the exception of Prime Minister González – disappeared from the centre of power. Next to the deteriorating economic situation and three successive peseta devaluations, which not only showed the bankruptcy of the hard currency policy followed during the Socialist decade but also substantially weakened the position of Carlos Solchaga in government and *vis-à-vis* the party apparatus, the PSOE came to face two other major problems which in combination resulted in the decision to bring forward the general elections. First, a number of corruption scandals came into the open, implicating *inter alia* the party apparatus (for its alleged role in the irregular funding of the PSOE by individual companies) and the governor of the Bank of Spain, Mariano Rubio (for channelling confidential information to two of his closest friends). The latter scandal resulted in the resignation of Rubio as a first sign of the declining power of the group of 'beautiful people' (see *El País*, 15 March 1992). Second, in the course of 1992 the intra-party strife between the three principal factions of the PSOE, i.e. the Guerristas, Solchaguistas and the adherents of the 'radical democratic orientation' (the so-called *renovadores* or renewers) (see Chapter 3), was publicly exposed and reached such dimensions that González was eventually forced to reassert his authority, among other things by announcing in April 1993 his intention to bring forward the general elections, which were originally scheduled in the autumn. Despite the dramatic economic situation, the corruption scandals, and the disunity within the ruling party, and despite the unfavourable forecasts coming from the opinion polls, the PSOE succeeded in limiting its electoral decline to such an extent that the final results actually boiled down to a victory for the Socialists (see Appendix). In obtaining 159 seats out of the total number of 350 seats in parliament, the PSOE was the only party that could enter into a majority coalition with either the regional parties or with Izquierda Unida, given the fact that a coalition between the latter and the right-wing Partido Popular was out of the question. But in losing its absolute majority, the PSOE had closed a period of more than a decade, characterized by its undivided rule over a nation in which the winners and losers of the Socialists' European project had come to split up society, albeit in a new, transnational, setting. Paradoxically, this division into 'haves' and 'have-nots' might well form part of the explanation of the continuous democratic approval of the Socialists' policy and the ever-greater differentiation of income and living standards to which this policy boils down. As Zygmunt Bauman points out in reflecting on Western affluent democracies, 'the number of citizens who may reasonably expect a better deal from the free market than from any of its alternatives . . . now exceeds the number of those who cannot do well without state-managed corrections of the market'. Taking into account the relatively high number of abstentions, 'the first easily out-vote the second' (Bauman 1994: 26).

The general elections of June 1993 marked the end of a political cycle in two other respects. First, the two principal antagonists during the Socialist Decade, Carlos Solchaga and Alfonso Guerra, were progressively marginalized from political decision-making in the course of events. Solchaga was not eligible for reappointment as Minister of Economics and Finance and was succeeded by the former Minister of Agriculture, Pedro Solbes. Solchaga himself became the new leader of the Socialist group in parliament despite fierce resistance from the Guerristas. In June 1994 Solchaga had to resign as a result of the 'Rubio Case' (the financial malpractices of Mariano Rubio occurred when Solchaga was still Minister and politically responsible). Though he remained vice-secretary of the PSOE, Guerra was stripped of his main source of influence: particularly after the 33rd party congress of the PSOE in March 1994, the Guerristas had become a minority group within the executive organs of the party. With the overt approval of González, the so-called *renovadores* had finally obtained virtual control over the party apparatus.

Second, and due to the results of the general elections, González initially intended to form a coalition government with the Catalan nationalists of Jordi Pujol and, possibly, with the Basque nationalists of Javier Arzallus. Since Pujol refused to participate in a central government but was willing to ensure the necessary majority in Cortes for González' investiture as prime minister, a Socialist minority government was formed. Ever since, support for the central minority government has been made dependent on far-reaching concessions as to an ever-greater degree of home rule and fiscal autonomy for Catalonia. This situation has converted Pujol into a real powerbroker and one of the key figures in Spanish politics (see, for instance, *El Pais*, 11 September 1994). The results of the European elections in June 1994 further weakened the position of the PSOE. For the first time since 1982, the Socialists came out of the elections as the country's second party with 18 per cent of total vote, Partido Popular obtaining almost 24 per cent.

THE EUROPEANIZATION OF SPAIN'S FOREIGN AND ECONOMIC POLICY

The Socialists' foreign security policy, and particularly their volte-face with respect to Spain's membership of NATO, formed another example of the *de facto* tuning in of the government's decisions to mainstream global neo-liberalism and Atlanticism. As stated above, a recurrent theme in the foreign policy statements of the party's leadership was the belief that a united Europe could eventually come to play a progressive role in world politics. To this end, the process of European integration should be extended to the fields of foreign policy and security. In the short term the integration of Spain into NATO would strengthen the 'European pillar' as a first step to the creation of a genuine European defence. Two additional factors can explain the Socialist government's pro-NATO stand in the referendum of 1986. First, NATO membership could contribute to the modernization of the Spanish army and reduce its traditional role in domestic policy by occupying it with external defence. Second, Spain's membership of the Atlantic Alliance was explicitly linked to the country's entry into the Common Market.

Partly as a consequence of the extended relaunching of European integration and partly as a result of the end of the cold war, from 1986 onwards issues of foreign policy and security coordination were subordinated to issues of economic and monetary integration. While publicly taking a clear stand in the ongoing debates with regard to the course and future direction of European integration – that between 'Atlanticists' and 'Europeanists', that between those in favour of intergovernmental cooperation and those who support some kind of supra-nationalism, and that between those in favour of a widening of the EC and those who stress the need to deepen the present level of integration first – the Socialist government came to give priority to the policy of economic and monetary union as initiated during the European Council meeting at Madrid in June 1989 and finally agreed upon during the Maastricht summit in December 1991. As a consequence, the realization of the Socialist government's strategic objectives in the end was made dependent on meeting the so-called convergence criteria first, European unification becoming the legitimation of economic restructuring and macro-economic austerity at home.

Entry into the EC and the subsequent need for industrial restructuring and macro-economic convergence in the light of the so-called 'extended relaunching' of the process of European integration (i.e. the completion of the Single Market and EMU) were not the only reasons for the Socialist government's 'drift into neo-liberalism' (Gillespie 1993). Immediately after coming to power, the new government started to tackle the structural imbalances of the Spanish economy by implementing a restrictive monetary policy aimed at reducing inflation. In search of the reasons for this neo-liberal austerity course, we distinguished the following factors: first, even before their landslide victory in the 1982 elections, the Socialists had moderated their economic policy objectives in a successful attempt to attract middle-class votes; second, they took clear notice of the dramatic experiences of Socialist governments in France and Greece which had initially tried to pursue a stimulation policy; and third, the structural dependence on imports, particularly with respect to investment goods, the spectacular rise of transnationally mobile capital, and the successful implementation of an austerity policy in the countries at the top of the intercapitalist hierarchy, reduced the leeway in Spain to stimulate the economy.

This 'top-down' internationalization of austerity determined the margins within which the restructuring of Spanish industry could be macroeconomically steered in the face of the free movement of goods and capital in the Single European Market. In addition to the restrictive monetary policy, the Socialist government opted for a strong peseta policy. In fact, despite a substantial appreciation in the second half of the 1980s the government decided to incorporate the peseta into the Exchange Rate Mechanism of the EMS. The fixing of the Spanish currency at a relatively overvalued rate, it was argued, would increase import competition and hence force domestic industry to innovate, on the one hand, and would cheapen the imports of investment goods, on the other. In other words, monetary and exchange rate policies became the principal mechanisms in the forced restructuring of Spanish industry and in the optimization of investment and trade conditions for foreign capital through supply side government intervention. In the early 1990s, the next step in the process of European integration, i.e. the Maastricht agreements on monetary union and the related convergence criteria, was used as an additional ground to legitimize the policy of cutting budget deficits and reducing inflation. In this sense, the government's Convergence Plan of early 1992 formed the most extreme and explicit example of how the remainder of the social-democratic elements in the original project of the Spanish Socialists had been sacrificed to neo-liberal restructuring, and the ultimate proof of the structural power of transnational capital over the general direction of government policy during the Socialist decade. Yet the objective of macroeconomic convergence and the policy goals set in the Convergence Plan soon proved to be based on outdated evidence as the Spanish economy was struck by international recession.

The rapid deterioration of the Spanish economy started in 1991 and came openly to the fore in the post-Maastricht year. In the period between December 1991 and February 1993 a recurrent theme in the economic pages of the Spanish newspapers was the publication of even worse figures for unemployment, inflation, public deficit, and economic growth. In 1993, the Spanish economy experienced the sharpest decline in thirty years, with GDP falling by 1 per cent, pushing the unemployment rate to almost 24 per cent (OECD 1994: 9). Time after time, the Socialist government announced new restrictive measures in a more and more desperate effort to keep its adjustment policy alive. Only a couple of months after the presentation of the Convergence Plan, for instance, more recent macro-economic indicators had already outdated the assumptions underlying this plan, and sparked off additional surgeries, eventually leading to the presentation of the 'most restrictive budget of the last twenty years' in September 1992 (see *El País*, 30 September 1992).

Meanwhile, the entire edifice of the Socialists' exchange rate policy collapsed as a result of the monetary turmoil in the wake of the negative vote of the Danish electorate in the Maastricht referendum of June 1992. After massive speculation against the peseta, the Socialist government was forced to devalue its currency in the European exchange rate mechanism by 5 per cent on 17 September, and by another 6 per cent on 22 November. In defence of the peseta, the Bank of Spain used up 33.3 per cent of its reserves in the three months between August and December (see *El País*, 5 December 1992). Finally, in the middle of the electoral campaign, on 13 May 1993, the peseta was devalued by 8 per cent, despite a secret agreement between Helmut Kohl and González early in April to maintain the current rate at all costs, and notwithstanding the massive intervention of the Bundesbank in defence of the peseta (see *El País*, 2 May 1993 and 14 May 1993). A return to normal conditions in foreign exchange markets took place after August 1993, following the widening of the ERM bands.

As a result of international recovery, in 1994 the main macro-economic indicators improved considerably and the outlook for 1995 seems to confirm this trend (OECD 1994; *El País*, 24 September 1994), though Spain is still far from satisfying the conditions for EMU as the European Council of Ministers of Economics and Finance (Ecofin) recently affirmed (*El País*, 9 October 1994). For this reason, the adjustment policy has been vigorously continued in spite of the high social costs involved, particularly in the field of job destruction.

In October 1980 the opposition leader Felipe González commented that 'the democratic system of our country does not easily resist two millions of unemployed people' (quoted in Sotelo 1993: 12). After more than ten years of Socialist government, and after a total of more than 3 million unemployed had been reached, it was Jacques Delors who stated in February 1993 that the public opinion of a country with an unemployment rate of more than 20 per cent cannot easily endure the efforts necessary to meet the EMU convergence criteria. Regretting the fact that unemployment rates were not included in this list of criteria, he added that 'the entry of Spain into the European Monetary Union is nevertheless incompatible with a 20% unemployment rate' (*El País*, 12 February 1993).

However, rising unemployment did not destabilize the democratic system, nor did the figure of 3 million unemployed at the end of the

Socialist decade produce any substantial relaxation of the ambitious convergence plan of the Socialist government. On the contrary, immediately after the unexpected 'victory' in the elections of June 1993, González excluded Izquierda Unida from a coalition government in advance because of the party's opposition to the Treaty of Maastricht, and stipulated that the future partners would have to fulfil the condition of subscribing to the 'concrete European project entailed by the Treaty of the European Union and the entire convergence plan' (*El País*, 12 June 1993). Without doubt, the right-wing Catalan nationalists headed by Jordi Pujol were eager to subscribe to the neo-liberal underpinning of the Socialists' economic policy. In fact, their support of the central minority government was made dependent on continuous macro-economic austerity and adjustment. Apart from this political backing in parliament, it could be asked whether the policy of the present government still rests on concrete social interests.

CENTRES OF SOCIAL AND POLITICAL POWER IN SPAIN

We identified the group of so-called 'beautiful people' occupying central positions in government, the Bank of Spain, and in private and public banking, together with part of Spanish bank capital, foreign (European) capital, and the cadres of public enterprise, *inter alia* organized in the *Club de Empresarios*, as the most important economic and political forces underpinning the Socialist policy of neo-liberal restructuring. Through a complex network of personal friendships, party interests, partisan appointments, interlocking directorates, and financial ties, these forces were interconnected. More importantly, however, their articulation was based on a common view of domestic and European economic and political questions, and their cohesion was based on a common adherence to the Socialists' project of integrating Spain into the Lockeian heartland of transnational production. In an attempt to illustrate the impact of this power configuration on decision-making, we elaborated on the government's industrial policy and on its role in the mergers of the largest private and public banks.

The industrial policy of the Socialist government was from the very start directed at restructuring the public companies belonging to the state holding INI, aimed at reducing the 'surplus of staff' and at modernizing the production apparatus. In the course of the Socialist decade, this so-called industrial reconversion progressively boiled down to the closure of firms running at a loss, the sale of others to foreign capital, and the concentration of government efforts on the most viable industrial sectors. As to the latter, a strategy of intra-industrial specialization was accompanied by a strategy of transnationalizing public enterprise, either by selling part of the public share to foreign companies or through investments of individual public firms abroad.

The latter strategy was also applied to the powerful group of mixed banks, the so-called *siete grandes*. Next to the essential role of the state, *inter alia* through the creation of public companies, the development of Spanish banking from its origin in the wake of incipient industrialization in the second half of the nineteenth century to the mergers of the largest private banks in the late 1980s and early 1990s is one of the most important characteristics of the more general modernization of Spanish society. Founded as genuine mixed banks, and strengthened during the successive phases of banking concentration, the seven largest private banks came to play a predominant role in the country's long-term transformation from a pre-industrial to a modern mass consumer society in the course of the twentieth century. In particular the Bank Regulation Act of 1921, which *inter alia* impeded the further expansion of foreign banks while establishing the primacy of Spanish finance, and the period of *status quo* between 1936 and 1962, which worked to the benefit of the most substantial private banks, were responsible for the concentration of economic power in the hands of a small number of big banking consortia and the all-pervasive influence of a financial oligarchy, which extended its tentacles of involvement in industry through equity participation, interlocking directorates and credit. During the Franquist era, private banks exercised an enormous influence on political decision-making, primarily but not exclusively in the field of macro-economic and monetary issues. The way in which the stronghold of Spanish capitalism could effectuate its interests comes fairly close to what we have denominated as the behavioural power of capital (see Chapter 1). Once the crisis of the Franquist dictatorship loomed ahead in the late 1960s and early 1970s, new forms of interest mediation had to be developed which would be less based on state repression and more on societal consensus. To this end, comprehensive strategic views of such interrelated areas as macro-economics, and industrial and social policy; of the role of the state with respect to free enterprise and free market integration; and of international – economic and political – co-operation and integration, were elaborated in the cupola of both the *siete grandes* and the state bureaucracy. More particularly, it was the most enlightened elements, sympathetic to an accelerated incorporation of the Spanish economy into the Lockeian heartland of transnational production, and most vulnerable to the leading strategic orientations in Europe, who came to play an essential role in the formation of the Socialists' hegemonic project.

By taking the private banking mergers in the late 1980s as a point of departure, we argued that it was particularly the most dynamic and outward-looking section of private bank capital that came closest to, and most openly supported, the European ambitions of the Socialist government. More specifically, two Basque banks, Banco de Bilbao and Banco de Vizcaya, whose leaders were known for their proximity to politicians like González and Solchaga, came to initiate the merger process (in close co-operation with the group of 'beautiful people') which drastically reshaped the landscape of Spanish banking. The main objective of these government-induced banking mergers was the creation of a reduced number of big consortia in the orbit of the Socialist party strong enough to face free competition in the Single European Market and to stay in the forefront of the ongoing transnationalization of Spanish business in the 1990s.

After a tumultuous period of intrigues and open confrontations in the highest echelons of Spanish society, the bank most fiercely opposed to the forced concentration, Banesto, succeeded in keeping its independence. For the time being, as it soon turned out. In December 1993, the Bank of Spain took control of Banesto and, alleging gross mismanagement, removed Mario Conde as chairman of the bank's board. Four months later, Banesto was acquired for 2.2 billion dollars by Banco Santander. At present, Banco Santander is Spain's internationally most active bank, its offshore operations generating almost 50 per cent of earnings (see *Business Week*, 28 February 1994). In particular its growing involvement in Latin America points at a global rather than a European strategy. In a preliminary way, it may be stated that this last take-over (officially the result of Banco de Santander bidding higher than its main contender, Banco Bilbao Vizcaya) indicates that the Socialist government is looking for new allies in the likely event that the process of European integration is not moving in the direction of ever-greater economic and sociopolitical regionalization (see Holman 1995).

EUROPEAN UNION: DEEPENING OR WIDENING?

The amalgamation of the Socialist hegemonic project with the accumulation strategies and comprehensive world views of both the most internationalized section of domestic capital and foreign transnational capital points at a very essential difference between the aborted attempt to establish parliamentary democracy in Spain in the Second Republic and the successful democratic consolidation during the Socialist decade. It was the Hobbesian solution to the 'social problem' that sparked off a fundamental restructuring of social relations, manifested in the shift from an isolated, predominantly agrarian and highly invertebrated society to a progressively outward-looking industrial society. It was the opening up of the Spanish economy at the end of the 1950s and the subsequent 'internationalization of capital' in the setting of Atlantic Fordism that laid the economic foundation of the further modernization and Westernization of Spain. And it was the Socialist party that headed the accelerated integration of Spain into the Lockeian heartland of transnational production and finance in the 1980s. In short, it was first national and then international integration that accounted for Spain's transition to modernity in the course of the twentieth century. International integration has increased Spain's vulnerability to changing international realities and Spain's dependence on decisions made by others, or rather, has made Spain part and parcel of a global community on whose future course and direction its political leaders have no influence whatsoever. Until recently, these politicians seemed unaware of this reality, or at least that is what they pretended. As Carlos Solchaga stated two months before the general elections of June 1993,

> We have made a commitment to Europe and to economic and monetary union and we believe that Spain will, in 1997 or in 1999, be a member of the group of European nations that will redefine the role of Europe in the world's economy.
> (*Financial Times*, 2 April 1993)

At that time, the Socialist government had to face at least three serious problems: declining electoral support in the polls, economic recession, and a general stagnation of the process of European integration. This latter phenomenon may well lead to a new phase of 'Eurosclerosis' in which a ruinous 'convergence race' is the only thing left of the initial intentions laid down in the Single European Act. In a situation in which progress in the fields of *inter alia* Social Policy, European Policy Co-operation, Security Policy is virtually non-existent, European integration boils down to deregulation and the free movement of goods and capital. This in turn seems to confirm a more globalist approach to European integration, centred on a power configuration of the leading sectors of pan-European business and the governments of the major European powers. In this context, highly optimistic statements like the one by Carlos Solchaga, seem inappropriate for two reasons. First, it remains to be seen whether Spain can meet the EMU convergence criteria in due course, and if so, only at high social costs. In fact, while inevitably generating greater social cleavages at home and in risking major confrontations with both trade unions and the less competitive sections of Spanish business, the Socialist government's pursuance of its European ambitions may nevertheless result in Spain ending up on the wrong side of a future two-tier Europe. Such an outcome will almost certainly strengthen those forces in Spanish society who are not – or no longer – prepared to sacrifice their short-term interests for a far remote and highly dubious ambition, and, hence, spark off a re-nationalization of politics. Second, if Spain succeeds in becoming a full member of EMU, and if the Socialist party at that time is still in power, it most likely will have serious troubles to 'redefine the role of Europe' along the lines of its 'cardinal and transcendent thought'. In fact, at present the European Union seems to move away from supra-national integration as long as the main political actors tend to stress the primacy of widening over deepening. Though the member states decided to postpone a decision on the enlargement of the EU with Central and East European countries until after the Intergovernmental Conference of 1996, at the same occasion (during the meeting of the European Council in Essen in December 1994) they also agreed to start a discussion on the way in which both the Common Agricultural Policy and the structural funds can be rationalized in order to cope with a future enlargement. It comes as no surprise that net-receiving countries like Spain are not in a hurry to initiate such a discussion. Recent attempts by the Socialist government to obstruct the enlargement of the EU with the addition of former EFTA countries are an illustration of the fact that Spain is no longer the uncritical pro-European partner of olden days.

APPENDIX

Table 16 Results of the elections to the Congress, 6 June 1993

	Votes	%	Seats
PSOE	9,076,218	38.68	159
PP	8,169,585	34.82	141
IU	2,246,107	9.57	18
CiU	1,162,534	4.95	17
PNV	290,386	1.24	5
CC	206,953	0.88	4
HB	206,296	0.88	2
ERC	188,800	0.80	1
PAR	144,261	0.61	1
EA	129,263	0.55	1
UV	112,032	0.48	1

Source: *El País*, 8 June 1993

PSOE: Partido Socialista Obrero Español; PP: Partido Popular; IU: Izquierda Unida; CiU: Convergència i Unió; PNV: Partido Nacionalista Vasco; CC: Coalición Canaria; HB: Herri Batasuna; ERC: Esquerra Republicana de Catalunya; PAR: Partido Aragonés; EA: Eusko Alkartasuna; UV: Unió Valenciana.

Notes

1 INTRODUCTION: GLOBAL POLITICAL ECONOMY AND THE TRANSITION TO MODERNITY

1 By 'interstate dependence theory' Robert Bach is referring to that part of dependency literature which Cardoso has critically reviewed under the title 'The Consumption of Dependency Theory in the United States' (Cardoso, quoted in Bach 1980).
2 'Society does not exist independently of human activity (the error of reification),' Bhaskar continues. 'But it is not the product of it (the error of voluntarism)' (ibid.). An important implication of Bhaskar's conception is that society and individuals are ontologically separate. That is, no contradiction exists between intentional human activity, on the one hand, and the regularities and structural patterns of social systems, on the other, and there is thus no need to connect them dialectically (or rather, no reason can be found even to start such a project). Instead of regarding the relation between people and society as contradictory, a model of social activity should view human agency as one of the constituent elements in the operation of social systems. In other words, there is an ontological hiatus between society and people, which affects the very possibility of connecting them methodologically (ibid.).
3 Behavioural or

> direct aspects of business power and influence relative to labor, include its financial resources, expertise, contacts with governments, and control over much of the media. Business has a privileged ability to influence government, for example through lobbying.... In this type of conceptualization ... business (and capital) is viewed as a type of privileged vested interest in a more or less pluralist ... political system.
>
> (Gill and Law 1989: 480)

> The structural aspect of power is associated with both material and normative dimensions of society, such as market structures and the role of ideology, which may or may not be mutually reinforcing. The tenacity of normative structures is illustrated by how, in modern economies, consistently higher priority is given to economic growth relative to other goals, such as conservation.... At the heart of this notion are the ideas that private

property and accumulation are sacrosanct, and that without the private sector growth would be endangered.

(ibid.: 480–481)

4 For a critical review of these approaches, see Holman 1993a and 1993b.
5 It is important to note that Poulantzas' concept of the domestic bourgeoisie is not the same as that of the autochthonous or national bourgeoisie, i.e., a bourgeoisie that is really independent of foreign capital. In his opinion, this national bourgeoisie has ceased to exist in Spain, Portugal and Greece.
6 For some critics on this point, see: Giner and Salcedo 1976; Muñoz, *et al.* 1978: 269; Maravall 1982: 7–8; Kohler 1982: 233 (n.17); Lomax 1983: 124.
7 As to Portugal, before the influx of foreign capital took shape in the 1960s, a powerful oligarchy already existed, consisting of a few families who dominated the Portuguese private sector almost completely. For instance, the top ten families owned all the important commercial banks, through which they controlled a large part of the national economy (Baklanoff 1978: 108). This oligarchy was characterized by its very strong ties to the Portuguese state (Makler 1976) – a relationship of interdependence which, together with the direct economic power of the large financial–industrial family groups, makes the characterization of the latter as a '*comprador* bourgeoisie', as Poulantzas described them, very unrealistic (see Lomax 1983: 124ff.). Groups such as Companhia União Fabril, Champalimaud, and Espírito Santo have to be considered as integral parts of the Portuguese national bourgeoisie (see Clarence-Smith 1985).

Although at first sight the situation in Greece seems very different, the same conclusion can be drawn with regard to the supposed existence of a *comprador* bourgeoisie. There are at least two important differences between Spain and Portugal, on the one hand, and Greece, on the other. In the first half of the twentieth century a commercial bourgeoisie came into existence in Greece, strongly related to the massive influx of Greek diaspora merchants, while Spain and Portugal saw the dominance of a financial–industrial bourgeoisie. Very characteristic of the Greek commercial bourgeoisie was its reluctance to invest capital in industrial activities at home. This, together with a general lack of capital in the Greek economy, 'obliged (and still obliges) Greece to depend on foreign capital and technology to fill the gap' (Evangelinides 1980: 127).

A second important difference is that in Spain and Portugal bank capital remained in private hands and directly or indirectly controlled a great part of the industrial activities in these countries, while in Greece the financial institutions were (and are) to a large extent controlled by the state.

As to the first point, Mouzelis has made it clear that the intra-bourgeois conflict suggested by Poulantzas did not take place in Greece and that the two factions themselves did not exist. But even if they had existed, there is no reason to believe that their interests were in conflict.

> Given the close collaboration of autochthonous and foreign capital, and given the fact that foreign capital was mainly directed by the Greek banking and investment institutions into areas where Greek commercial capital was unwilling or unable to go, it seems obvious that such interests were more complementary than antagonistic.
>
> (Mouzelis 1976: 79)

As to the second point, any analysis that presents the Greek state as a mere puppet of the bourgeoisie, as Poulantzas did in assuming that a struggle for power between certain factions can lead more or less automatically to a change in political regime, does not take into account the structural dependence of the Greek national bourgeoisie on the state, *inter alia* by way of the public financial institutions. The historically strong power of the state apparatus has made the Greek indigenous bourgeoisie highly dependent on the state for its consolidation and growth. This also applies to foreign capital in Greece (ibid.: 80).

8 Here we deal with two of the most important concepts in Lipietz' theory, i.e., 'regime of accumulation' and 'mode of regulation'. The former refers to 'the fairly long-term stabilization of the allocation of social production between consumption and accumulation', the latter can be defined as 'the set of internalized rules and social procedures which incorporate social elements into individual behaviour' (Lipietz 1987: 14/15, 32ff.).

9 Why peripheral Fordism? First, this is a true Fordism in that it involves both mechanization and a combination of intensive accumulation and a growing market for consumer durables. Secondly, it remains peripheral in that . . . jobs and production processes corresponding to the 'skilled manufacturing' and engineering levels are still mainly located outside these countries. Its markets represent a specific combination of consumption by the local middle classes, with workers in the Fordist sectors having limited access to consumer durables, and exports of cheap manufactures to the centre. Growth in social demand (which means *world* demand) for consumer durables is thus anticipated, but at the national level it is not institutionally regulated or adjusted to productivity gains in local *Fordist* branches.

(Lipietz 1987: 78–79)

10 From a personal communication of Arrighi in which he comments on the early work of Frank, quoted in Frank 1979: 6–7.

11 [Unless] increased productivity in the producer-goods sector offsets the rising technical composition of capital, the proportion of immobilized assets will become dangerously high; and unless increased productivity in the consumer-goods sector balances the rise in mass purchasing-power, the share of wages in total value-added will climb to the detriment of profit.

(Lipietz 1982: 35)

12 Note that Keyder in his contribution to the volume edited by Arrighi (1985) is referring to international Keynesianism, and the postwar hegemony of the United States in the international system. Although it may be doubted that such a system of international Keynesianism ever existed, we believe that Keyder's remarks apply to Keynesianism at the national level.

13 In considering the state/society complex as the basic entity of international relations, and elaborating on Cox' assumption 'that there exist a plurality of forms of state, expressing different configurations of state/society complexes' (Cox 1986: 205), it was Kees van der Pijl who first developed this ideal–typical distinction between Lockeian heartland (after the author of the *Two Treatises of Government*) and Hobbesian outer rim (after the author of the *Leviathan*) (see van der Pijl 1989). The former category *inter alia* refers to the transnational spread of civil society (including its ruling class dimension), as a result of which particular state functions are parcelled out over several states and quasi-state structures are created, reflecting

the international socialization of state functions. In the course of the expansion of this Lockeian state/society complex during the *Pax Britannica*, and its further growth during the *Pax Americana*, only a small number of countries successfully resisted peripheralization. These so-called Hobbesian latecomer states only succeeded in achieving an autonomous, catch-up development through revolutions from above, involving authoritarian patterns of political domination, bureaucratic centralization and the subordination of civil society to the state-led plan of modernization.

> Yet the state classes of various stripe also have to reckon with domestic social forces developing surreptitiously, 'molecularly' in the direction of the pattern prevailing in the heartland; if only as a consequence of the very transformations that are being wrought by the revolutions from above.... At some point (and here, the political orientation of the state class and the stringency of state control are of course crucial determinants) this social stratum is bound to surface and constitute itself as a class.
>
> (van der Pijl 1994: 37)

In fact, as will be shown in the next chapters, the process of Hobbesian state-building under Franquist rule was a precondition for the development of a genuine class society in Spain, and for the subsequent incorporation of the latter into the Lockeian state/society complex.

14 It should be remembered that the establishment of stable parliamentary democracies in Spain, Portugal, and Greece was a precondition of their entry into the Common Market. At the same time, proponents of EEC membership within these countries defended their position by arguing that accession would help to stabilize and consolidate democracy in Spain, Portugal, and Greece.

2 THE MAKING OF CONTEMPORARY SPAIN: SOCIO-ECONOMIC AND POLITICAL MODERNIZATION IN THE TWENTIETH CENTURY

1 On the emergence of a Catalan industrial bourgeoisie in the eighteenth century, see Jutglar 1984: 93ff. The expansion of the Catalan textile industry in the mid-nineteenth century is treated in Harrison 1978: 58ff.; see also Nadal 1975: 188ff. For the emergence of heavy industry in the Basque Provinces, see Nadal 1975: 155ff., and Tamames 1980: 496–497. The role of foreign investment is treated in Tortella Casares 1983: 99ff.; on foreign investment and mining, see Harvey and Taylor 1987; on railway construction, see Tortella Casares 1982: 163ff. Finally, the foreign finance of Spanish capitalism in the nineteenth century is treated in Costa 1983.

2 One of the leading Spanish economic historians, Jordi Nadal, argues,

> In 1930, ... Spain is, of course, a country with more industry than in 1874 or 1833, but also more behind than in both years.... Everyone knows, in fact, that the problems of backwardness and development are relative, and should be raised in terms of international ranking. In this sense, the failure of a century of Spanish industrialization still seems indisputable to me.
>
> (Nadal 1985: 101)

3 For a survey of the debate on the causes of retarded industrialization, see the prologue by Gabriel Tortella in Prados de la Escosura 1988, and the introductory chapter of the same book; see also Carreras 1988: 81–83.
4 It was the Catalan finance minister Laureano Figuerola, for instance, who worked out the rather revolutionary free-trade budget of 1869 (see Jutglar 1984: 201; see also Costas 1983). It is not difficult to understand that at the time most finance ministers were in favour of some kind of free trade. After all, the agricultural exports provided the Spanish state 'with most of its income and the economy as a whole with its purchasing power abroad' (Carr 1982: 278). It was in this sense that Figuerola defended his budget:

> The nature of Spanish exports has not varied for fifty years. We sell what we sold, though we sell more. Minerals and agriculture earn our purchasing power abroad. The whole of the manufacturing industry does not provide 5 per cent of our exports.
> (quoted in Carr 1982: 279)

5 Carlos Marichal, for example, describes the debates in the Spanish congress in early 1842, confronting the commercial interests of the Andalusian wine exporters, closely related to British capital, and the interests of Catalan manufacturers. The representative of the latter interests in the Cortes, Gil Sanz, characterized the ideas of his opponent, Sánchez Silva, as similar 'more to those of a defender of Great Britain than to those of a Spanish legislator', and he warned him that his free-trade project would convert Spain into an economic colony of England and into a predominantly agrarian nation depending on the export of primary products in exchange for foreign (and mainly British) industrial products (quoted in Marichal 1980: 232). Where this could lead to was already indicated in a letter from the British ambassador in Madrid to the Foreign Secretary in London, in 1837. If he received sufficient support from London, he wrote, he would succeed in his attempt to 'portugalize' Spain (ibid.: 235). For an analysis of Portuguese dependence on Great Britain from the seventeenth century onwards, and, hence, for an insight into what the British ambassador had in mind, see the work of Sandro Sideri (Sideri 1970).
6 According to Carr, the adoption of the ideas of this minor German philosopher by the founding father of Spanish Krausism, Julián Sanz del Río, was the result of an intellectual 'vacuum which could be filled by nonsense provided it was not French in origin. German Krausism, by what must be considered an intellectual accident, became for an isolated intellectual world a means of reunion with the stream of European thought' (Carr 1982: 301).
7 The leading political and social echelons at the turn of the century combined their project of Hispanicization with a renewed cultural and economic orientation towards Latin America. The loss of the last colonies to the United States, the so-called Great Disaster of 1898, actually gave the campaign against secular, materialistic capitalism and imperialism an additional impetus. Spain, perhaps with the sole exception of England, was one of the first European countries to experience in a direct way the rising hegemony of the United States in the international system at the end of the nineteenth century (on the Spanish-American war, and particularly its perception in Spanish society, see Serrano 1984). In this context, a politico-ideological and cultural movement came into existence which is usually labelled as Hispano-Americanism (or Hispanism).

As a common denominator, the adherents of this movement shared an 'unassailable faith in the existence of a transatlantic Hispanic family, community, or race' (Pike 1971: 1). But apart from this fundamental agreement, the traditional Spanish oligarchy and the Basque and Catalan bourgeoisie had different intentions in stimulating Hispano-Americanism. Traditionalists used it mainly for domestic socio-political purposes inasmuch as it represented a world-view akin to social imperialism. To them, the Hispano-Americanist identity reflected a common desire to make the Hispanic world safe from the influence of the United States and from secularism and materialism. In the Spanish context at the turn of the century, this implied a strong resistance to the full introduction of capitalism and a fierce defence of traditionalism based on the preservation of Catholic values. On the other hand, the Basque and Catalan industrialists were eager to create new markets in the New World. Instead of compensating for the loss of the overseas colonial markets by increasing working-class purchasing power at home, they argued, Spain should undertake a massive campaign to open outlets in the now independent, Spanish-speaking republics. To this end, a successful promotion of the idea of a transnational Hispanic community (i.e. primarily directed at the people and leaders of Spanish America) was essential (see Pike 1971; see also Blinkhorn 1980). In this respect, the peripheral bourgeoisie was prone to those regenerationists whom Pike includes under the heading of liberal Hispanists (Pike 1971).

8 As Shlomo Ben-Ami concludes:

> The irony was that he, who had seized power, in the first place, in order to defend an antiquated social system against its enemies on the left, soon realized that the best defence Spanish capitalism could hope for lay in a certain degree of social change, however controlled and limited. This was a 'revolution from above' that came to avoid that from 'below'. In the process he alienated both the defenders of stagnation, who were expected to pay for the regime's social emphasis, and the champions of a real, far more radical change of the social structure. Entangled in this predicament, he stepped deep into oblivion.
>
> (Ben-Ami 1983: 401)

In fact, Ben-Ami speaks of a *révolution manquée* since, in shattering the foundations of the restoration regime, Primo de Rivera failed to build an Estado Novo, therewith creating a 'dangerous vacuum of power' (ibid.: 399).

9 I am following the definition by Philippe Schmitter as a point of departure, according to whom corporatism is a system of interest representation,

> in which the constituent units are organized into a limited number of singular, compulsory, noncompetitive, hierarchically ordered and functionally differentiated categories, recognized or licensed (if not created) by the state and granted a deliberate representational monopoly within their respective categories in exchange for observing certain controls on their selection of leaders and articulation of demands and supports.
>
> (Schmitter 1974: 93–94)

For a critique of this definition, see Jessop 1979.

10 On state interventionism during the first two decades of the Franquist regime, see the comprehensive study by Clavera *et al.* 1978; see also González-

González 1979; ch. 2, García Delgado 1986, and Velasco Murviedro 1984. One example of the regime's attitude towards industrial development is offered by the creation of the state holding Instituto Nacional de Industria in 1941, modelled on the Italian IRI (see especially Schwartz and González 1978). The impact of this first phase of autarky on the postwar economic development of Spain has been subjected to different interpretations. Spokesmen for the regime, on the one hand, were always eager to affirm the strong links between the efficient way in which the regime administered the industrialization of the Spanish economy and its very successful development. Franquism constituted the necessary precondition for economic growth, it was argued. On the other hand, there are those who strongly believe that the Spanish economic miracle of the 1960s took place despite the Franco regime. Stressing the fascist elements in the first years of the regime (1939–1942), it was the failures related to the economic policy of the regime, they argue, that made a subsequent economic liberalization mandatory. In this sense, the influx of foreign capital, goods and persons contributed in a decisive way to the successful modernization of Spain, again, despite the Franco regime (see for example Esteban 1978: 147ff.). In other words, the lack of international competition and the excessive role of the regime in economic planning are held responsible for all the negative elements in the postwar process of economic development, while external factors account for the positive elements after the economic liberalization of 1959. A comparison can be made with the debate on the causes of Spain's being a 'late joiner', and particularly with the stand that the turn to protectionism in the 1890s had a negative impact on economic development in the following decades (see Tortella Casares 1983: 148–157). In both cases, however, and apart from the fact that *a posteriori* speculation on the possible positive effects of an alternative direction is at best highly hypothetical, it is difficult to see how politicians could have acted differently in both cases. Though clearly inspired by fascist ideologies, the reality of economic isolation left the Franquist regime no alternative but to embark on autarky.

11 As indicated earlier, the regenerationist position in this debate was defended by intellectuals recruited from the politically marginal middle classes. The absence of a social stratum strong and large enough to bridge the gap between the two Spains, i.e. between two polarized classes – 'the large class of those who worked with their hands and the small class of those who did not' (Brenan 1976: 88) – was one of the most important causes of the Spanish Civil War. Ironically, the social cohesion of the Spanish bourgeoisie in the 1960s coincided with the emergence of the so-called new middle classes, which eventually came to play a decisive role in the process of democratic transition and in the deradicalization of the Socialist party during the late 1970s (see Chapter 3).

12 As a matter of fact, the political climate of the late 1970s and early 1980s was in several respects the opposite of that of the 1930s, as was illustrated by the frustrated coup of February 1981. 'Spanish society of the eighties was in no mood for military government. Spain had changed profoundly during the long years of Franco's authoritarian rule. Those who wished to turn the clock back were a nostalgic minority' (Graham 1984: 4).

13 See Gunther *et al.* 1988: 75. The German Friedrich Ebert Foundation initiated discussion circles between representatives of the PSOE and captains of

industry, on the one hand, and contacts between the Socialist trade union UGT and the employers' organization CEOE, on the other (see Kohler 1982: 43).

3 OPERATION EUROPE: THE HEGEMONIC PROJECT OF THE PSOE

1 Joaquín Sánchez de Toca, *Del Poder Naval en España y su Política Económica para la Nacionalidad Ibero-Americana*, 1898; quoted in Pike 1971: 63–64.
2 Since we are primarily interested in the period of democratic consolidation after the Socialists' rise to power in October 1982, this chapter will only pay attention to the previous period of democratic transition inasmuch as it is necessary for an understanding of post-1982 developments. On the different phases of the period of democratic transition (1976–1982), and for a conceptualization of the notions of transition and consolidation, see for example Caciagli 1986: 3–14, and Maravall and Santamaria 1989.
3 On the growth of the PSOE during the 1976–1982 period, the social composition of its electorate and of its affiliation, see Tezanos 1983; 1989b; see also Caciagli 1986: ch.6, and Maravall 1982: part 3. On the UCD, see Caciagli 1989; 1986: ch.7. On the right-wing Alianza Popular, see Montero 1989, and García Cotarelo and López Nieto 1988. The PCE is treated, for instance, in González Hernández 1989. On social class and the Spanish party system, see Gunther *et al.* 1988: ch. 5. On the basis of this research it could be stated that, in the course of the period of democratic transition, the PSOE has taken advantage like no other party of the changing electoral composition resulting from the socio-economic developments in the 1960s and 1970s. This is evident in the fact that the party drew its support in the 1982 elections from almost all social strata.
4 The resignation of Alfonso Guerra as vice-premier was the final outcome of a public scandal that came to be known in Spain as *el caso Guerra*. The brother of Alfonso Guerra, Juan Guerra, had used a government office in Sevilla to promote his own private activities. Using the name of his famous brother, he succeeded in enriching himself through all kinds of lucrative projects, including land speculation, mediation in real estate transactions and public contracts.
5 Serra became one of the confidants of Felipe González in the course of the 1980s (see *El País*, 10 March 1991). In particular his tactful diplomacy as Minister of Defence, and his success in reorganizing and modernizing the Spanish army, substantially increased his prestige both inside and outside the party. Though he had carefully avoided participating in the prolonged intraparty confrontations between the major 'sensibilities', he certainly belonged to the right-wing of the PSOE. His affirmation that the PSOE should direct its efforts at the Spanish citizen and not at a particular social class, his statements in defence of the government's economic policy, and his self-affirmation as the sole mediator between the party and the government, had proved his independence *vis-à-vis* the Guerristas in the party apparatus.

It has frequently been reported that an additional reason for the appointment of Serra as vice-premier was his contact with the regional parties in parliament. Faced with the possibility of a loss of votes in the 1993 elections, the Catalan Serra could prepare a future coalition with the Basque and Catalan nationalist parties (*El País*, 23 June 1991).

4 THE NATO REFERENDUM AND BEYOND: FROM GREAT POWER AMBITION TO SMALL POWER REALITY

1 In 1965, Felipe González studied for some time in Louvain, where he experienced the treatment to which Spaniards were subjected. In a letter to his girl friend, he wrote:

> Lots of bars in Brussels have a sign which says: no entry for Spaniards, Africans and Latinamericans. . . . The railway stations are packed with Spaniards who spend hours and hours in a state of disorientation. They're . . . in the saddest human and spiritual misery.
> (Guerra 1984: 30)

Patrick Camiller comments:

> Over the next twenty years this formative experience, in which economic and national oppression were so closely intermingled, would be progressively emptied of social content and condensed into a single political ambition: to make Spain a West European Nation, *just like the rest.*
> (Camiller 1986: 7)

To a large extent, this explains the offensive strategy of the Socialist government during the 1980s with respect to the process of European integration.

2 Apart from the above mentioned general priority, the maintenance of special relationships with Latin America and the Middle East had been a constant in foreign policy ever since the late 1940s. Initially started as an attempt by Franco to partially overcome the consequences of international isolation by seeking support outside the Western world, these special relationships became fully integrated cornerstones of Spanish foreign policy.

Next to this, the improvement of bilateral relations with a number of countries on the basis of specific issues has been and still is another priority in Spanish foreign policy (see Armero 1978, 1989). Diplomatic contacts with Great Britain on the Gibraltar question; with Morocco and Algeria on the Western Sahara, and on the Spanish enclaves in North Africa, Ceuta and Melilla; with France, initially with respect to North Africa, later on the question of Basque terrorism and the entry of Spain into the Common Market (see Macdonald 1988).

3 Quoted in Rodríguez 1988: 71. For the original Spanish text, see Armero 1989: 248.
4 For a survey of the NATO debate in the Spanish press, see the collection of newspaper articles written by about one hundred 'opinion leaders' over the period 1979–1986 in CIDOB 1986.
5 This ambivalent position of the CP was affirmed in a declaration on the NATO referendum in December 1985. For the complete text of this declaration, see *España y la OTAN* 1986: 278–280.
6 The position of the UGT was a more complicated one. Having strong historical ties with the PSOE, and having not yet broken off this special relationship (this rupture would eventually take place after the general strike of December 1988, see the next chapter), the leadership of the Socialist trade union did not want to participate actively in the campaign against NATO membership. In order to avoid open confrontation with the PSOE, the UGT retained its anti-NATO posture, but did not intend to spend 'one single peseta to promote the campaign

against NATO' as its leader Nicolás Redondo affirmed (see *Cambio 16*, 10 February 1986).

7 It is not at all evident that this argument was more than mere rhetoric. Two counter-arguments can be raised against the validity of the link between NATO membership and the democratization of the Spanish army. First, history has proved that membership is perfectly compatible with the presence of authoritarian regimes, or even with military insurrection, as the coups in, for example, Greece and Turkey have shown. As Pedro Vilanova has stated, 'the argument that the entry of Spain into NATO will democratise its Army is groundless. Portugal was a member of NATO from the beginning without the dictatorship of Salazar and Caetano being in the least affected' (Vilanova 1983: 162). At an early stage in the debate, Fernando Morán expressed similar views (see Morán 1980: 102–103). Second, if this argument was so essential for the Socialist government, the conditionality clause in the referendum, according to which the participation of Spain in the Atlantic Alliance would not include its incorporation in the integrated military structure, introduced an important qualification.

8 Article 30 of the Single European Act contains the treaty provisions concerning European cooperation in the field of foreign policy. Section 6 of article 30 runs as follows:

6.a. The High Contracting Parties consider that closer cooperation on questions of European security would contribute in an essential way to the development of a European identity in external policy matters. They are ready to coordinate their positions more closely on the political and economic aspects of security.

b. The High Contracting Parties are determined to maintain the technological and industrial conditions necessary for their security. They shall work to that end both at national level and, where appropriate, within the framework of the competent institutions and bodies.

c. Nothing in this Title shall impede closer cooperation in the field of security between certain of the High Contracting Parties within the framework of the Western European Union or the Atlantic Alliance.

9 In October 1991, France and Germany announced the creation of a military unit of 35,000 soldiers as the 'kernel' of a new (West) European defence organization. This unified corps, which implies the continuation and extension of the 'mixed brigade' that both countries created in 1990, should be subsumed under the WEU. In direct response to this initiative, the United Kingdom, the United States, and the NATO headquarters in Brussels expressed their fierce opposition, while countries like the Netherlands, Portugal and Denmark were more cautious in their rejection. Spain, Belgium, Greece and, to a lesser extent, Italy backed the Franco-German proposals enthusiastically.

10 In general, and despite considerable diplomatic efforts by the Socialist government, it must be concluded that the Spanish presidency did not produce spectacular results in the fields of external relations and EPC. Moreover, Spain could only marginally convert its own foreign policy priorities into specific decisions at Community level. However, perhaps this is not the main advantage of the presidency in the first place. It is rather the opportunity to represent the twelve member states on the world stage (in the framework of EPC) that gives the presidency an added value, inasmuch as it offers a means to stress the

distinctive features of the member state in question (see Regelsberger 1989). In this sense, the 'Spanish semester' seems to have had the desired effect, though the exact degree is difficult to measure. For a more extensive evaluation of the Spanish presidency during the first half of 1989, see Holman 1989.

11 It is interesting to note that the party's programme for the years 1986–1990, elaborated prior to the 1986 elections, started from the primacy of domestic policy issues, and still referred to the process of European integration as a challenge to the Spanish economy and an opportunity for Spain to strengthen its position in the world (see PSOE 1986). In the electoral programme of 1989 the last vestiges of a state-centric view of world politics were dropped; European unification was presented as the principal 'mobilizing reference' for the future of Spanish society (see PSOE 1989a).

12 Part of this agreement was the clause allowing Britain to opt out of the third and final phase of the EMU. In a separate protocol attached to the EMU treaty, Britain is given the right not to join the single currency.

13 The Spanish representatives in the committee were the president of the Spanish Central Bank, Mariano Rubio, and the former socialist Minister of Economics and Finance, Miguel Boyer. Both members were known for their proximity to Carlos Solchaga.

14 In the post-Maastricht discussion on the concept of subsidiarity, Spain defended the broadest possible interpretation. In opposing the British attempt to curtail the powers of the EC institutions, the Socialist government delivered a memorandum to the Council of Ministers which defended an even more federalist stand than that of the Commission (see *El País*, 31 October 1992).

5 SOCIALIST ECONOMIC POLICY AND EUROPEAN INTEGRATION: THE INTERNATIONALIZATION OF DOMESTIC POLITICS

1 The relative decline of the industrial sector in the Spanish economy is shown in the following table. However, the regressive evolution of the industrial sector, measured by a decrease of 6.5 per cent in its contribution to the GNP over the period 1970–1985, is not exclusively due to a process of de-industrialization, but also to a process of tertiarization.

Table 17 Sectoral structure of GNP (in %)

Years	Agriculture	Industry	Services
1970	10.7	42.0	47.3
1977	8.7	39.8	51.5
1985	6.0	35.5	58.5

Source: Vázquez 1990: 84

2 Quotation marks are used when speaking of 'positive outcomes' because the label 'positive' is a subjective one – curtailing inflation, for instance, always implies fixing (or increasing) income differentials – and because it remains to be shown that 'outcomes' are the actual result of intentional policy measures.
3 In 1988, for instance, the rise of total employment by 2.9 per cent was due to an increase in employment in the non-agricultural private sector by 5 per cent and an increase of employment in the public sector of 2.8 per cent (exclusively due to the general government sector, compensating a decline in public enterprises), while the agricultural labour force continued to shrink (in fact, it declined by 37 per cent between 1977 and 1988) (OECD 1989: 16).
4 A closer look at the geographical origin of Spanish imports points to the dominant role of intra-EC trade in the development of the Spanish trade balance after 1985 (OECD 1991: 102).
5 The balance of payments statistics indicate that the structural trade deficit was more than compensated by services (especially tourism and net transfers) in combination with the influx of long-term capital, resulting in continuously rising basic balance surpluses after 1982 (Table 4).
6 With respect to the strong employment growth in the second half of the 1980s, it must be added that the loosening of labour market regulations and the various employment promotion programmes have facilitated this trend in a more than marginal way. However, in the case of the Vocational Training and Job Opportunities Plan, finance came mainly from the European Social Fund, and labour market liberalization has resulted in a rise in temporary and part-time workers as well as low-paid apprenticeships (see OECD 1991; and Economic and Social Committee 1989).
7 It goes without saying that developments in the direction of a European Single Market, and a European Monetary (and Political) Union, form a paradigmatic case in point, but the process of transnationalization is certainly not confined to the twelve member states of the European Community. Here the distinction between globalization and regionalization as alternative material outcomes and strategic projections becomes relevant. Both strategies transcend the strict national interest articulation of previous periods in the history of world capitalism, though the concept of regionalization points to the 'relocation' of this 'primacy of the endogenous', and the reintroduction of the essentials of a genuine trade policy for that matter, at a regional level. In the latter case, the analogy with the process of nation-building and the coming into existence of integrated, national markets is obvious.

The energetic way in which the Spanish government is liberalizing and deregulating its national economy in relation to the economies of the other member states seems to contradict its fierce opposition to a swift opening up of the Common Market towards Eastern Europe (see also Chapter 4). Apart from the fear of obtaining less foreign capital, either in the form of direct investment or through the structural funds of the EC, the Socialists seem to fear short-term competition from third countries which may indirectly affect the restructuring process of Spanish industry, either indirectly because products from Eastern Europe may replace Spanish exports to the EC countries, or because foreign companies may divert their labour-intensive production to countries with even more competitive and flexible factor (i.e. labour) markets. Both tendencies

230 *Notes*

might deteriorate the Spanish factor (i.e. capital) markets, and hence affect the adjustment of domestic industry to European standards.

8   This diagram is adopted from an unpublished manuscript by Gerd Junne (Amsterdam 1979), with the kind permission of the author.

9   The argument developed here is based on Holman 1992. For a more detailed analysis of the competing strategies and their eventual amalgamation, the reader is referred to this article. See also the section on p. 162.

10 The reader will note that we have relied heavily on a recent categorization by Jeffry Frieden (Frieden 1991). Nevertheless, our subdivision differs in two respects: first, Frieden's sub-category of export-oriented producers of tradeable goods (i.e., national enterprises producing primarily for the international market) has been split up into import-competing producers of goods for the European market and 'export-competing' producers of goods for the world market; and second, instead of Frieden's sub-categories of producers of non-tradeable goods and services, and international traders and investors, we use the subcategory of global financial institutions.

11 For a survey of the major aspects related to foreign direct investment in Spain, see the various contributions in Bajo Rubio and Carrascosa Morales 1991.

12 See, for instance, the early studies published by the Spanish Institute of Economic Studies in Madrid: on the competitive capacity of Spanish industry and the commercial impact of full membership ESADE 1979, and Melo and Monés 1982; the impact on the Spanish agricultural sector is analysed in Camilleri (ed.) 1984. See also the analysis of the general situation of Spanish industry on the eve of EC membership and its capacity to adapt to new conditions in Noelke and Taylor 1980. See, finally, the special issue of *Cinco Días* (1980) for a discussion of the advantages and disadvantages of European integration.

13 Bearing in mind that the completion of the Single Market implies first and foremost the removal of all kinds of non-tariff barriers to intra-Community free trade, these most affected sectors were selected on the basis of a number of indicators: the level of non-tariff barriers and the dispersion of prices for identical products between member states (measuring the level of fragmentation of the EC market) and the rate of penetration of imports (measuring the share of domestic demand accounted for by imports). These forty sectors where non-tariff barriers impeded intra-Community trade represented about 50 per cent of industrial value added in the Community. They were classified in four different groups according to their level of intra-Community trade and the level of price dispersion that identical products display across member states

   1 Industries in high-tech public-procurement markets (telecommunications, computers, medical equipment, etc.) characterized by a low level of price dispersion and a high degree of intra-Community trade due to the presence of multinationals in these industries, but also characterized by an even higher level of extra-Community trade due to a productivity disadvantage of European firms in comparison with their American and Japanese competitors.

   2 Industries in traditional public-procurement and regulated markets divided into a subgroup of industries with a low level of intra-Community trade and a high level of intra-Community price dispersion (like energy-generating plant and railway equipment).

3 A subgroup (including industries like shipbuilding and electrical engineering) with a low level of intra-Community trade but a limited price dispersion due to extra-Community imports.
4 Those industries still affected by technical, administrative or fiscal barriers to intra-Community free trade and hence characterized by significant price dispersion (including mass consumer products like white goods, televisions, textiles and clothing, and certain capital goods [machinery] and intermediate goods) (Commission of the European Communities 1990: 3).

14 For an analysis of the Spanish industrial structure during the crisis period of 1978–1984, see Segura *et al.* 1989; the structural weaknesses of Spanish industry are extensively analysed in Bueno Campos (ed.) 1987, and Buesa and Molero 1988. The impact of full EC membership on Spanish industry is, *inter alia*, dealt with in Velarde Fuertes 1992, Bueno Campos 1989, and Arroyo Ilera 1990 (ch.4). The winners and losers of the completion of the internal market are analysed per industrial sector and per member state in Ewbank Preece 1990.

15 The values are European Commission forecasts as of November 1991. The long-term interest rate of Greece is taken from *The Economist*, 14 December 1991, p. 30. Inflation: annual percentage change in the GDP price deflator. Government balance: net lending (+) or net borrowing (−) of general government as a percentage of GDP. Debt: gross debt of general government as a percentage of GDP.

16 The fifth column (currency) refers to the criterion of respecting the normal fluctuation margins of the ERM of 2.25 per cent. In December 1991, this excluded Portugal and Greece because they were outside the EMS, and Spain and Great Britain because they still had margins of 6 per cent.

17 Following the inter-industry scenario, less developed member states (like Spain, Portugal, and Greece) 'increase their specialization in those sectors where they currently enjoy comparative advantages'. More particularly, in this first scenario the completion of the Single Market will allow these countries to increase their exports of mainly labour-intensive products (such as clothing and footwear). Such specialization in traditional, low-demand growth industries carries significant risks, since their markets are facing increasing competition from developing countries and Eastern Europe. Under the intra-industry scenario,

> the structure of industrial production converges towards that found in the more developed countries of the Community. . . . It is assumed that the southern States will progressively transform their current industrial specialization patterns notably by seeking to strengthen their positions in high-tech industries where higher rates of demand growth can be expected.
> (Commission of the European Communities 1990: 6)

18 For a discussion of the neo-corporatist agreements after 1977 (and until 1986) see the contributions to Zaragoza (ed.) 1988, and Pérez Yruela and Giner (eds) 1988. See also Pérez Díaz 1987.

19 For a survey of the main positions in the nationwide debate shortly before and after the general strike, see the selection of contributions to *El País* in Juliá (ed.) 1989.

6 MERGING INTO EUROPE: PRIVATE BANK CAPITAL AND THE SOCIALIST GOVERNMENT

1 The reader will notice that the notion of the *siete grandes*, i.e. the group of the seven largest private banks in Spain, is a very arbitrary and sometimes even confusing one. It was originally used to refer to the concentration of economic power in the hands of the seven largest banks: Banesto, Banco Central, Banco Hispano Americano, Banco de Bilbao, Banco de Vizcaya, Banco Santander, and Banco Popular. However, the notion has become less accurate as a result of recent takeovers and mergers. In fact, at the time of writing (late 1994) there are 'only' four largest left and accordingly we should speak of the *cuatro grandes*, that is, if we exclude the public banks and the (Catalan) savings banks. In the following pages we will continue to use the notion of the *siete grandes*, not as a quantitative term but as a historical and qualitative indication of the concentration of economic power within a small group of private banks.

2 Time after time Spanish bankers have stressed the paramount importance of this 'German system' of big banks having great power over industry. Banco Central's former president Villalonga stated in 1962 that 'the industrialization of the country would have been impossible without the existence of a great, national and regional, banking sector characterized by its mixed banks' (quoted in Muñoz 1970: 45–46). His successor Alfonso Escámez stated in 1975 that

> in order to develop the economy, Spain had only two possible paths to follow: on the one hand, development could be left entirely to the state, entailing nationalization and total concentration of the economy in the hands of the State; on the other hand, there were the banks. . . . Spain had no industrial tradition at the time, remember. It was the banking system that rendered possible the industrial development of Spain.
> (*The Banker*, April 1975: 430)

And Banesto's president Jaime Gómez-Acebo stated in 1969 that

> it is impossible to imagine the modern industry without a sizeable, efficient and competent banking organization. Comments which stress the different interests of these economic sectors have their origin in a lack of knowledge about the function of the industries and of the banker: to him corresponds the mission, so vital for the economy, to collect inactive funds and to lend them for their beneficial mobilization.
> (*Actualidad Económica*, 3 May 1969)

For other statements stressing the same point, see also Roldán *et al.* 1973, II: 244ff.

3 In reaction to the 1962 Regulation Act, Banesto created an industrial bank called Bandesco, the Banco Central founded the Banco de Fomento, the Banco de Bilbao founded the Banco Industrial de Bilbao, the Banco de Vizcaya founded Induban, the Banco de Santander founded Banco Intercontinental, and the Banco Popular founded Eurobanco. The Banco Hispano Americano was already related to the Banco Urquijo.

4 Participants in Bandesco included Morgan Guaranty Trust, International Finance Corporation, Barclays Bank, Banco Comerciale Italiana, Rothschild Frères, and Deutsche Bank. Participants in Vizcaya's Induban included

Westminster Foreign Bank, Crédit Lyonnais, Worms & Co., Dresdner Bank, Algemene Bank Nederland, and Cie. Financière de Suez (see Muñoz 1970: 164; see also González Temprano *et al.* 1981: 105).

5 Looking more closely at these foreign direct investments in Spain during the 1960s and early 1970s, the following conclusions can be drawn (Muñoz *et al.* 1978: 131–136):

 1 The regional distribution of foreign direct investments (FDI) shows that Madrid and Barcelona accounted for almost two-thirds of total FDI.
 2 In general terms, FDI in Madrid were directed at constituting new companies with 100 per cent foreign capital or with a very high foreign participation, whereas in Barcelona the phenomenon of joint ventures with a less decisive foreign participation was more common.
 3 If we look at the origin of FDI in combination with their regional distribution, a tendency can be discerned of American FDI focusing particularly on Madrid and European FDI on Barcelona. More particularly, between 1966 and 1971 American FDI were three times higher in Madrid than in Barcelona; West German FDI, on the other hand, were three times higher in Barcelona than in Madrid. This difference made some commentators speak of a '*Madrid norteamericano*' and a '*Cataluña Europea*' (quoted in ibid.).
 4 Closely related to the above point, foreign companies in Cataluña were more inclined to co-operate at the executive level with national individuals, whereas American firms in Madrid tended to exclude the 'national element' from their highest executive ranks.
 5 In distinguishing FDI producing for the home market and export-oriented FDI, the former could particularly be found in Madrid, whereas the latter were more typical of the Barcelona area.

6 It has frequently been suggested that the obstruction from part of the Spanish business community was one of the factors that led to the early resignation of Suárez in January 1981. On the other hand, several important names in Spanish banking, mainly active in Banesto, were said to have been involved in the abortive coup of 23 February 1981 (see Graham 1984: 92, 105; and Rivases 1988: 29).

7 'Best' being defined *inter alia* on the basis of the following attributes:

> The bank must be profitable: it must have high return-on-equity and, to a lesser extent, return-on-asset figures. It must be managed tightly and cost-effectively with a low cost-to-income ratio. It must fund itself at the keenest possible rates and lend (or generate fee income) in ways that produce the highest possible return and therefore a high net interest margin.
> (*Euromoney*, December 1990)

8 In the remainder of this chapter we will primarily concentrate on the Banco de Bilbao and the Banco de Vizcaya, on the one hand, and Banesto, on the other, being the three banks (and after the merger of Bilbao and Vizcaya, the two banks) most opposed to each other as regards their relationship with the Socialist government and their corporate strategies. We will also pay attention to the Banco Central and the Banco Hispano Americano, especially where their role in the concentration process is concerned, but less so to the smallest members of the *siete grandes*, the Banco de Santander and the Banco Popular

Español, not only because of their small size but also because of their marginal role in the banking mergers. These two banks are only referred to when national and international ranking by profits, efficiency, etc., is at stake (the role of Santander in the 1994 takeover of Banesto will be dealt with in Chapter 7). Similarly, we will only focus our attention on the Spanish (and mainly Catalan) savings banks and public banks with regard to their role in the concentration process during the 'Socialist decade'. Finally, we will not deal with either the minor private banks like the Banco March (controlled by the March family, which went through a spectacular expansion during the Socialist decade); nor with the blind organization, ONCE, which gathered its wealth through the lucrative lottery business, and played a certain role in the attempted merger between the Banco Central and Banesto; nor, finally, with private financiers like Javier de la Rosa (related to the Kuwait Investment Office) and '*los Albertos*', two cousins who became public figures for a time because of their turbulent marriages with the Koplowitz sisters, on the one hand, and, more importantly, their attempt to control the Banco Central through their company Cartera Central, on the other (see García-Abadillo and Fidalgo 1989).

9 For the Gramscian notion of 'organic intellectual', see Gramsci 1983; see also Gill 1990: 51ff.
10 In comparing the role of Sánchez Asiaín with the one Adolfo Suárez played during the period of democratic transition, the editorial of *El País* stated that 'when the time is ripe for studying the economic transition from a protectionist regime to the Single Europe of 1993, it will turn out that one of the most distinguished protagonists is a banker: José Angel Sánchez Asiaín' (*El País*, 21 January 1990).
11 In 1991, the board of directors of the *Club de Empresarios* included Jesús Prieto, president of Mercasa; Julián García Valverde, former president of RENFE and then Minister of Health; Federico de Lora, general manager of INI; José Luis Alvarez Margaride, president of Thyssen Boeticher; Javier Alvarez Vara, president of CASA; Guillermo de la Dehesa, former member of the Socialist government and then director of Banco Pastor; Luis Delso Heras, president of Trasmediterránea; Antonio López García, president of Amper; and Cándido Velázquez Gaztelu, president of Telefónica (see the Club's magazine *Empresa y Futuro*, April 1991).
12 His rise to the top of Banesto ... led to his photograph appearing more often in gossip magazines than it did in the financial press. A snappy dresser with an engaging manner, he endows the 'get-rich-quick' fever sweeping Spain with that touch of elegance needed to avoid offending social sensibilities. Conde is a new kind of Spanish capitalist who not only knows how to earn it but also how to spend it.

(*International Management*, March 1989: 25)

13 Another statement by Conde clearly illustrates the kind of businessman he had in mind:

Twenty years ago the dominant culture was the culture of the North. We all admired the Swedish model, which was nothing but a society based on security, a society of civil servants. Now, another model, another culture, is imposed: the culture of initiative. . . . Now, the individual reaffirms itself in opposition to the state. This is the model of the South. I am a representative of this culture.

(quoted in *El Globo*, 4 December 1987)

14 In the aftermath of the abortive takeover by the Banco de Bilbao, Mario Conde restructured Banesto's board of directors by appointing nine new members. Three of them were known for their close links with the Guerristas (see *Cambio 16*, 28 December 1987; and *El País*, 17 December 1987).
15 Percentages include both commercial and savings banks. In 1991, foreign assets as a percentage of total assets amounted to 8.02 per cent as regards commercial banks and 1.96 per cent as regards savings banks.

Bibliography

Actualidad Económica see relevant reference.
Albarracin, J. (1991) 'La Política de los Sindicatos y la Dinámica del Movimiento Obrero', in M. Etxezarreta (ed.) op. cit., pp. 401–425.
Alcaide, C. (1992) 'El Plan de Covergencia', *El País Negocios*, 12 April, p. 7.
Alcaide Inchausti, J. (1990) 'Evolución de la Economia Española en 1990', *Situación* (Servicio de Estudios del Banco Bilbao Vizcaya), no. 3, pp. 5–31.
Alonso, J. A., et al. (1982) 'La Integración en la CEE: Líneas de Coherencia y Especializacion del Sistema Productivo Español', *Investigaciones Económicas*, no. 17, pp. 127–149.
Alonso Olea, M. et al. (1992) *España y la Unión Europea. Los Consecuencias del Tratado de Maastricht* (Barcelona: Círculo de Lectores and Plaza & Janés).
Amigot, M. (1990) *Neguri* (Barcelona: Tibidabo).
Amodia, J. (1977) *Franco's Political Legacy: From Fascism to Facade Democracy* (London: Allen Lane).
—— (1990) 'Personalities and Slogans: The Spanish Election of October 1989', *West European Politics*, vol. 13, no. 2, April, pp. 293–298.
Andréu, J.M. (1983) 'La Banca Extranjera en España: Pasado, Presente y Futuro', *Situación*, no. 1, pp. 32–50.
Armero, J.M. (1978) *La Política Exterior de Franco* (Barcelona: Planeta).
—— (1989) *Política Exterior de España en Democracia* (Madrid: Espasa-Calpe).
Arrighi, G. (1985) 'Fascism to Democratic Socialism: Logic and Limits of a Transition', in G. Arrighi (ed.) *Semiperipheral Development: The Politics of Southern Europe in the Twentieth Century* (Beverly Hills: Sage), pp. 243–279.
Arroyo llera, F. (1990) *El Reto de Europa: España en la CEE* (Madrid: Editorial Síntesis).
Artus, J.R. and Young, J.H. (1979) 'Fixed and Flexible Exchange Rates: A Renewal of the Debate', *IMF Staff Papers*, vol. 27, pp. 654–698.
Axt, H.J. (1984) 'On the Way to Self-Reliance? PASOK's Government Policy in Greece', *Journal of Modern Greek Studies*, vol. 2, no. 2, pp. 189–208.
Bach, R.L. (1980) 'On the Holism of a World-Systems Perspective', in T.K. Hopkins and I. Wallerstein (eds) *Processes of the World-System* (Beverly Hills: Sage), pp. 289–310.
Bajo Rubio, O. and Carrascosa Morales, A. (eds) (1991) *Inversión Extranjera en*

España: Análisis y Política, special issue of *Información Comercial Española*, Nos. 696–697, August/September.
Baklanoff, E.N. (1978) *The Economic Transformation of Spain and Portugal* (New York: Praeger).
Banco de Bilbao (1982) *Una Historia de la Banca Privada*, special issue of *Situación*, no. 3 (Bilbao: Servicio de Estudios del Banco de Bilbao).
Banco de España (1990) *Cuentas Financieras de la Economía Española (1980–1989)* (Madrid: Banco de España).
Banesto (1991) *Discurso del Sr. Presidente del Banco Español de Credito ante la Junta General de Accionistas*, 25 May (Madrid: Grupo Banesto).
The Banker see relevant reference.
Barbé, E. (1981) *España y la OTAN. La Problemática Europea en Materia de Seguridad* (Barcelona: Laia).
Bauman, Z. (1994) 'After the patronage state: a model in search of class interests', in C. Bryant and E. Mokrzycki (eds) op. cit., pp. 14–35.
Ben-Ami, S. (1983) *Fascism from Above: The Dictatorship of Primo de Rivera in Spain, 1923–1930* (Oxford: Clarendon Press).
Berend, I.T. and Ránki, G. (1982) *The European periphery and industrialization, 1780–1914* (Budapest: Akadémiai Kiadó).
Berges, A., Ontiveros, E. and Valero, F.J. (1990) *Internacionalización de la Banca. El Caso Español* (Madrid: Espasa-Calpe).
Bhaskar, R. (1979) *The Possibility of Naturalism: A Philosophical Critique of the Contemporary Human Sciences* (Brighton: Harvester Press).
Blaisse, M. (1991) 'Spain – Between Ambition and Reality', *European Affairs*, vol. 5, no. 3, June/July, pp. 56–62.
Blinkhorn, M. (1980) 'Spain: the "Spanish Problem" and the Imperial Myth', *Journal of Contemporary History*, vol. 15, no. 1, January, pp. 5–25.
Braudel, F. (1986) *The Mediterranean and the Mediterranean World in the Age of Philip II* (London: Collins).
Brenan, G. (1976) *The Spanish Labyrinth: An Account of the Social and Political Background of the Spanish Civil War* (Cambridge: Cambridge University Press).
Bryant, C.G.A. and Mokrzycki, E. (eds) (1994) *The New Great Transformation? Change and Continuity in East-Central Europe* (London and New York: Routledge).
Bueno Campos, E. (ed.) (1987) *La Empresa Española: Estructura y Resultados* (Madrid: Instituto de Estudios Económicos).
—— (1989) 'La Empresa. Estrategias de la Empresa Española y la Europa de 1993', in S.M. Ruesga (ed.), *1993. España ante el Mercado Unico* (Madrid: Ediciones Pirámide), pp. 147–161.
Buesa, M. and Molero, J. (1988) *Estructura Industrial de España* (Madrid: Fondo de Cultura Económica – Paideia).
Business Week see relevant reference.
Cacho, J. (1988) *Asalto al Poder. La Revolución de Mario Conde* (Madrid: Temas de Hoy).
Caciagli, M. (1986) *Elecciones y Partidos en la Transición Española* (Madrid: Centro de Investigaciones Sociológicas, Siglo XXI).
—— (1989) 'La Parábola de la Unión de Centro Democrático', in J.F. Tezanos *et al.* (eds) op. cit., pp. 389–432.

Calvo Sotelo, L. (1990) *Memoria Viva de la Transición* (Barcelona: Plaza & Janes/*Cambio 16*).
Cambio 16 see relevant reference.
Camiller, P. (1986) 'Spanish Socialism in the Atlantic Order', *New Left Review*, no. 156, March/April, pp. 5–36.
Camilleri, A. (ed.) (1984) *La Agricultura Española ante la CEE* (Madrid: Instituto de Estudios Económicos).
Canosa, R. (1945) *Un Siglo de Banca Privada (1845–1945). Apuntes para la Historia de las Finanzas españolas* (Madrid: Nuevas Gráficas).
Carande, R. (1965) *Carlos V y sus Banqueros. La vida económica en Castilla (1516–1556)*, 3 volumes (Madrid: Sociedad de Estudios y Publicaciones).
Carr, R. (1982) *Spain: 1808–1975* (Oxford: Clarendon Press), 2nd edition.
Carreras, A. (1988) 'La industrialización Española en el marco de la historia económica Europea: ritmos y caracteres comparadas', in J.L. García Delgado (ed.), *España. Economía* (Madrid: Espasa-Calpe), pp. 79–115.
Casilda Béjar, R. (1992) *Sistema Financiero Español. Banca y Caja de Ahorro ante un Entorno Competitivo* (Madrid: Alianza Editorial).
Cavero, J. (1990) *Poderes Fácticos en la Democracia* (Madrid: Espasa-Calpe).
Cezanne, W. and Möller, H. (1979) *Die Europäische Union als Währungsunion?* (Baden-Baden: Nomos).
CIDOB (1986) *El Debat sobre l'OTAN* (Barcelona: CIDOB, Materials de Debat – Secció d'Estudis sobre Pau i Conflictes).
Cinco Días (1980) *España ante la CEE* (Madrid: special issue of the daily newspaper *Cinco Días*), May.
Clarence-Smith, G. (1985) *The Third Portuguese Empire 1825–1975: A Study in Economic Imperialism* (Manchester: Manchester University Press).
Clavera, J. et al. (1978) *Capitalismo Español: de la Autarquía a la Estabilización (1939–1959)* (Madrid: Cuadernos para el Diálogo).
Commission of the European Communities (1990) *The impact of the internal market by industrial sector: the challenge for the Member States* (special edition of *European Economy and Social Europe*).
—— (1991) *Annual Economic Report 1991–92: Strengthening Growth and Improving Convergence*, European Economy, no. 50, December.
Conde, M. (1990) 'El Papel del Empresario en la Situación Económica Actual', Lecture at the University of Santiago de Compostela, 15 November (Madrid: Banesto).
—— (1991) 'Alternativas Industriales de España ante la C.E.E.', Lecture at the University of Deusto, 18 April (Madrid: Grupo Banesto).
Confederación Española de Organizaciones Empresariales (1981) *La Empresa Española ante la Adhesión al Mercado Común* (Madrid: CEOE), 2 volumes.
Correljé, A.F. (1990) 'The Liberalization of the Spanish Oil Sector: Strategies for a Competitive Future', *Eurices Paper*, no. 90 – 1 (Rotterdam: Centre for International Energy Studies).
Costa, J. (1984) *Oligarquía y Caciquismo, Colectivismo Agrario y Otros Escritos* (Madrid: Alianza) (selected by R. Pérez de la Dehesa).
Costa, M.T. (1983) *Financiación Exterior del Capitalismo Español en el Siglo XIX* (Barcelona: Universidad de Barcelona).
Costas, A. (1983) 'El viraje del pensamiento político-económico español a mediados del siglo XIX: la "conversión" de Laureano Figuerola y la formulación del librecambismo industrialista', *Moneda y Credito*, no. 167, pp. 47–70.

Cox, R. (1983) 'Gramsci, Hegemony and International Relations: An Essay in Method', *Millennium: Journal of International Studies*, vol. 12, no. 2, pp. 162–175.
—— (1986) 'Social Forces, States and World Orders: Beyond International Relations Theory', in R.O. Keohane (ed.), *Neorealism and its Critics* (New York: Columbia University Press).
—— (1987) *Production, Power, and World Order: Social Forces in the Making of History* (New York: Columbia University Press).
Dehesa, G. de la (1990) 'The Spanish Economic Transition to a Full Market Economy', paper for the conference 'The Transition to a Market Economy in Central and Eastern Europe', OECD, Centre for Co-operation with the European Economies in Transition, Paris, 28–30 November.
—— (1992) '¿Existe alguna alternativa a la convergencia?', *El País*, 20 June, p. 38.
Deubner, C. (1982) *Der unsichere 'Europäische Konsens' in den iberischen Ländern. Der Beitritt zur EG als soziales und innenpolitisches Problem in Portugal und Spanien* (Baden-Baden: Nomos).
Díaz Herrera, J. and Tijeras, R. (1991) *El Dinero del Poder. La Trama Económica en la España Socialista* (Madrid: Cambio 16).
Díaz-Varela, M. and Guindal, M. (1990) *A la Sombra del Poder* (Barcelona: Tibidabo).
Donges, J.B. (1990) 'Similitudes y Diferencias con el Entorno Europeo', in J.L. García Delgado (ed.), *op. cit.*, pp. 559–580.
Economic and Social Committee (1989) *The Economic and Social Situation in Spain*, (appendix to the report of the Section for Economic, Financial and Monetary Questions on the Economic Situation in the Community in mid-1989), CES 526/89 (+ Tables and Graphs), Brussels, 19 June.
The Economist see relevant reference.
Elliot, J.H. (1989) *Spain and its World, 1500–1700: Selected Essays* (New Haven and London: Yale University Press).
—— (1990) *Imperial Spain, 1469–1716* (London: Penguin Books).
Elorza, A. (1990) 'La Organización y las Ideas (En Torno al Próximo Congreso del PSOE). *El País*, 31 October 1990, p. 22.
Empresa y Futuro see relevant reference.
ESADE (1979) *La Industria Española ante la CEE* (Madrid: Instituto de Estudios Económicos).
Escudero, M. (1991) 'La Pluralidad de Sensibilidades en el PSOE', *Sistema*, no. 102, pp. 19–30.
España y la OTAN. Textos y Documentos (1986), edition prepared by C. del Arenal and F. Aldecoa (Madrid: Tecnos, Colección 'Relaciones Exteriores de España').
Esteban, J.M. (1978) 'La política económica del Franquismo: una interpretación', in P. Preston (ed.), *España en crisis: La evolución y decadencia del régimen de Franco* (Mexico and Madrid: Fondo de Cultura Económica), pp. 147–180.
Etxezarreta, M. (1991) 'Introducción. La Economía Política del Proceso de Acumulación', in M. Etxezarreta (ed.) op. cit., pp. 31–92.
—— (ed.) (1991) *La Reestructuración del Capitalismo en España, 1970–1990* (Barcelona/Madrid: Icaria & Fuhem).
Euromoney see relevant reference.
Evangelinides, M. (1980) 'Transnational Integration and National Disintegration', *The Greek Review of Social Research*, vol. 38, pp. 121–140.

Ewbank Preece (1990) *Winners and Losers in the New Europe: A Multi Client Study* (Brighton and Redditch: Ewbank Preece and Jarrett Associates).
Fernández Marugan, F. (1992) 'La Década de los Ochenta: Impulso y Reforma Económica', in A. Guerra and J.F. Tezanos (eds) *La Década del Cambio. Diez Años de Gobierno Socialista, 1982–1992* (Madrid: Sistema), pp. 135–194.
The Financial Times see relevant reference.
Foweraker, J. (1987) 'Corporatist Strategies and the Transition to Democracy in Spain', *Comparative Politics*, vol. 20, no. 1, Oct., pp. 57–72.
Frank, A.G. (1979) *Dependent Accumulation and Underdevelopment* (New York: Monthly Review Press).
Frieden, J.A. (1991) 'Invested Interests: the Politics of National Economic Policies in a World of Global Finance', *International Organization*, vol. 45, no. 4, Autumn, pp. 425–451.
Fuentes Quintana, E. (1988) 'Tres Decenios de la Economía Española en perspectiva', in J.L. García Delgado (ed.) op. cit., pp. 1–75.
—— (1990) 'De los Pactos de la Moncloa a la Constitución (julio 1977–diciembre 1978)', in J.L. García Delgado (ed.) op. cit., pp. 23–34.
—— (1992) 'La Hacienda Pública de la Democracia Española y la Integración Europea', in M. Alonso Olea *et al.*, op. cit., pp. 139–168.
Futuro see relevant reference.
García-Abadillo, C. and Fidalgo, L.F. (1989) *La Rebelión de los Albertos* (Madrid: Temas de Hoy).
García Cotarelo, R. and López Nieto, L. (1988) 'Spanish Conservatism, 1976–87', *West European Politics*, vol. 11, no. 2, April, pp. 80–95.
García Delgado, J.L. (1986) 'Estancamiento industrial e intervencionismo económico durante el primer Franquismo', in J. Fontana (ed.) *España bajo el Franquismo* (Barcelona: Crítica), pp. 170–191.
—— (ed.) (1988) *España. Economía* (Madrid: Espasa-Calpe).
—— (ed.) (1990) *Economía Española de la Transicion y la Democracia* (Madrid: Centro de Investigaciones Sociológicas).
García Fernández, J. (1990) 'Política Empresarial Pública, 1973–1988', in P. Martín Aceña and F. Comín (eds) *Empresa Pública e Industrialización en España* (Madrid: Alianza Económia y Finanzas), pp. 217–250.
García San Miguel, L. (1980) *Las Clases Sociales en la España Actual* (Madrid: Centro de Investigaciones Sociológicas).
García i Segura, C. (1985) 'La Política Exterior del PSOE durant la Transició Política Espanyola. De la Clandestinitat a la Constitució (1971–1978)', part I, *Afers Internacionals*, no. 7, pp. 47–66.
—— (1986a) 'La Política Exterior del PSOE durant la Transició Política Espanyola. De la Clandestinitat a la Constitució (1971–78)', part 2, *Afers Internacionals*, no. 8, pp. 63–73.
—— (1986b) 'La Política Exterior del PSOE durant la Transició Política Espanyola. De la Clandestinitat a la Constitució (1971–78)', part 3, *Afers Internacionals*, no. 9, pp. 43–61.
Giddens, A. (1979) *Central Problems in Social Theory: Action, Structure and Contra- dictions in Social Analysis* (London: Macmillan).
—— (1981) *A Contemporary Critique of Historical Materialism* (London: Macmillan).
Gill, S. (1990) *American Hegemony and the Trilateral Commission* (Cambridge: Cambridge University Press).

—— (1993) 'Introduction', in S. Gill (ed.) *Gramsci, Historical Materialism and International Relations* (Cambridge: Cambridge University Press).
Gill, S. and Law, D. (1989) 'Global Hegemony and the Structural Power of Capital', *International Studies Quarterly*, vol. 33, pp. 475–499.
Gillespie, R. (1993) 'Programa 2000: the Appearance and Reality of Socialist Renewal in Spain', *West European Politics*, pp. 78–96.
Giner, S. and Salcedo, J. (1976) 'The Ideological Practice of Nicos Poulantzas', *Archives Européennes de Sociologie*, vol. 17, no. 2, pp. 344–365.
Giner, S. and Sevilla Guzman, E. (1980) 'From despotism to parliamentarism: class domination and political order in the Spanish state', in R. Scase (ed.), *The State in Western Europe* (London: Croom Helm) pp. 197–229.
—— (1984) 'Spain: from corporatism to corporatism', in A. Williams (ed.) *Southern Europe Transformed: Political and economic change in Greece, Italy, Portugal and Spain* (London: Harper and Row).
El Globo see relevant reference.
Gómez Uranga, M. (1991) 'La Internacionalización de la Industria Española: un Proceso Acelerado', in M. Etxezarreta (ed.) op. cit., pp. 465–500.
González i Calvet, J. (1991) 'Transformación del Sector Público e Intervención en la Economía', in M. Etxezarreta (ed.) op. cit., pp. 177–237.
González-González, M.J. (1979) *La económia política del Franquismo (1940–1970). Dirigismo, mercado y planificación* (Madrid: Tecnos).
González Hernández, J.C. (1989) 'El Partido Comunista de España en el Proceso de Transición Política', in J.F. Tezanos *et al.* (eds) op. cit., pp. 543–585.
González Ledesma, F. *et al.* (1977) *Las Elecciones del Cambio* (Barcelona: Plaza & Janés).
González Temprano, A., Sánchez Robayna, D. and Torres Villanueva, E. (1981) *La Banca y el Estado en la España Contemporánea (1939–1979)* (Madrid: Espejo).
Graham, R. (1984) *Spain: Change of a Nation* (London: Michael Joseph).
Grahl, J. and Teague, P. (1989) 'The Cost of Neo-Liberal Europe', *New Left Review*, no. 174, March/April, pp. 33–50.
—— (1990) *The Big Market: The Future of the European Community* (London: Lawrence and Wishart).
Gramsci, A. (1983) *Selections from the Prison Notebooks* (New York: International Publishers).
Guerra, A. (1984) *Felipe González. De Suresnes a la Moncloa* (Madrid: Novatex).
—— (1986) 'Sobre el Referéndum', *El País*, 12 January, p. 11.
Guillén, A. (1990) 'The emergence of the Spanish welfare state: The role of ideas in the policy process', *International Journal of Political Economy*, vol. 20, no. 2, Summer, pp. 82–96.
Gunther, R., Sani, G. and Shabad, G. (1988) *Spain after Franco: The Making of a Competitive Party System* (Berkeley and Los Angeles: University of California Press).
Harrison, J. (1978) *An Economic History of Modern Spain* (New York: Holmes & Meier).
Harvey, C. and Taylor, P. (1987) 'Mineral wealth and economic development: foreign direct investment in Spain, 1851–1913', *Economic History Review*, 2nd ser. XL, no. 2, pp. 185–207.
Holman, O. (1989) 'Het Spaanse Voorzitterschap van de Europese Gemeenschappen', *Internationale Spectator*, vol. 43, no. 10, October, pp. 627–633.

Bibliography

—— (1992) 'Introduction. Transnational Class Strategy and the New Europe', in O. Holman (ed.), *European Unification in the 1990s: Myth and Reality, International Journal of Political Economy* (Special Issue), vol. 22, no. 1, Spring, pp. 3–22.

—— (1993a) 'Internationalization and Democratisation: Southern Europe, Latin America and the World Economic Crisis', in S. Gill (ed.) *Gramsci, Historical Materialism and International Relations* (Cambridge: Cambridge University Press), pp. 213–236.

—— (1993b) *Integrating Southern Europe: EC Expansion and the Transnationalisation of Spain*, Academic Dissertation (University of Amsterdam).

—— (1995) *A Short History of Spanish Banking* (Amsterdam: Amsterdam International Studies).

Holman, O. and Poot, K. (1983) 'Europese Monetaire Integratie, Struktuurpolitiek en Bezuinigingsbeleid in Frankrijk', *Tijdschrift voor Politieke Ekonomie*, vol. 6, no. 4, pp. 57–84.

Huneeus, C. (1985) *La Unión de Centro Democrático y la Transición a la Democracia en España* (Madrid: Centro de Investigaciones Sociológicas, Siglo XXI).

IMF (1993) *International Financial Statistics* (Washington, DC.).

El Independiente see relevant reference.

International Management see relevant reference.

Jessop, B. (1979) 'Corporatism, Parliamentarism and Social Democracy', in P. Schmitter and G. Lehmbruch (eds) *Trends Towards Corporatist Intermediation* (Beverly Hills: Sage), pp. 185–212.

—— (1983) 'Accumulation Strategies, State Forms, and Hegemonic Projects', *Kapitalistate*, no. 10/11, pp. 89–111.

—— (1992) 'Changing Forms and Functions of the State in an Era of Globalization and Regionalization', paper presented to EAPE Conference, Paris, 4–7 November.

Julía, S. (ed.) (1989) *La Desavenencia. Partido, Sindicatos y Huelga General* (Madrid: El País – Aguilar).

Jutglar, A. (1984) *Historia Crítica de la Burguesía en Cataluña* (Barcelona: Anthropos).

Kalecki, M. (1971) 'Political Aspects of Full Employment', in *Selected Essays on the Dynamics of the Capitalist Economy* (Cambridge: Cambridge University Press).

Keesings Historisch Archief see relevant reference.

Keyder, C. (1985) 'The American Recovery of Southern Europe: Aid and Hegemony', in G. Arrighi (ed.) *Semiperipheral Development: The Politics of Southern Europe in the Twentieth Century* (Beverly Hills: Sage), pp. 135–148.

King, R. (1984) 'Population Mobility: Emigration, Return Migration and Internal Migration', in A. Williams (ed.) *Southern Europe Transformed: Political and Economic Change in Greece, Italy, Portugal and Spain* (London: Harper and Row), pp. 145–178.

Kohler, B. (1982) *Political Forces in Spain, Greece and Portugal* (London: Butterworth).

Laclau, E. (1977) *Politics and Ideology in Marxist Theory: Capitalism, Fascism, Populism* (London: Verso).

Lancaster, T.D. (1989) *Policy Stability and Democratic Change: Energy in Spain's Transition* (University Park & London: The Pennsylvania State University Press).

Linde, L.M. (1990) 'La Profundización de la Crisis Económica', in J.L. García Delgado (ed.) op. cit., pp. 35–57.
Lipietz, A. (1982) 'Towards Global Fordism?' *New Left Review*, no. 132, pp. 33–47.
—— (1987) *Mirages and Miracles: The Crises of Global Fordism* (London: Verso).
Lipietz, A. and Leborgne, D. (1990) 'How to avoid a two-tier Europe', *Labour and Society*, vol. 15, no. 2, pp. 177–199.
Lomana, G. (1987) *El Ciclón Socialista (1982–1986: Primera Legislatura Socialista)* (Barcelona: Plaza & Janés).
Lomax, B. (1983) 'Ideology and Illusion in the Portuguese Revolution: The Role of the Left', in L.S. Graham and D.L. Wheeler (eds) *In Search of Modern Portugal: The Revolution and its Consequences* (Madison: University of Wisconsin Press), pp. 105–134.
López-Claros, A. (1988) *The Search for Efficiency in the Adjustment Process: Spain in the 1980s*, Occasional Paper no. 57 (Washington: International Monetary Fund).
López-Morillas, J. (1981) *The Krausist Movement and Ideological Change in Spain, 1854–1874* (Cambridge: Cambridge University Press).
Lyrintzis, C. (1984) 'Political Parties in Post-Junta Greece: A Case of "Bureaucratic Clientelism"?', in G. Pridham (ed.) *The New Mediterranean Democracies: Regime Transition in Spain, Greece and Portugal* (London: Frank Cass), pp. 99–118.
MacDonald, G.D. (1988) 'European Community Enlargement and the Evolution of French-Spanish Co-operation', in F.G. Gil and J.S. Tulchin (eds) *Spain's Entry into NATO: Conflicting Political and Strategic Perspectives* (Boulder & London: Lynne Rienner), pp. 72–92.
Makler, H.M. (1976) 'The Portuguese Industrial Elite and its Corporative Relations: A Study of Compartmentalization in an Authoritarian Regime', *Economic Development and Cultural Change*, vol. 24, no. 3, pp. 495–526.
Maluquer de Motes, J. (1987) 'De la crisis colonial a la guerra europea: veinte años de economía española', in J. Nadal, A. Carreras, and C. Sudrià (eds) *La economía española en el siglo XIX. Una perspectiva histórica* (Barcelona: Ariel), pp. 62–104.
Manifiesto del Programma 2000 (1991) (Presentation by W. Brandt, F. González and A. Guerra) (Madrid: Sistema).
Mao Tse-Tung (1977) *Five Essays on Philosophy* (Peking: Foreign Languages Press).
Maravall, J. (1978) *Dictatorship and Political Dissent: Workers and students in Franco's Spain* (London: Tavistock).
—— (1982) *The Transition to Democracy in Spain* (London: Croom Helm).
Maravall, J. and Santamaría, J. (1989) 'Transición Política y Consolidación de la Democracia en España', in J.F. Tezanos *et al.* (eds) op. cit., pp. 183–249.
Marichal, C. (1980) *La Revolución Liberal y los Primeros Partidos Políticos en España: 1834–1844* (Madrid: Catedra).
Marquina Barrio, A. (1986) *España en la Política de Seguridad Occidental, 1939–1986* (Madrid: Servicio de Publicaciones del EME, Colección 'Ediciones Ejercito').
—— (1989) 'The Bases in Spain', in T. Veremis and Y. Valinakis, *U.S. Bases in the Mediterranean: The Cases of Greece and Spain* (Athens: Eliamep, Occasional Papers and Monographs, no. 7), pp. 43–73.
Martín, C. (1990) 'Spain', in: Commission of the European Communities, *The*

impact of the internal market by industrial sector: the challenge for the Member States (Special edition of *European Economy and Social Europe*), pp. 203–223.

Martínez Alier, J. (1985) 'Viejas ideologias y nuevas realidades corporativistas', *Revista Española de Investigaciones Sociológicas*, no. 31, Julio/Sept., pp. 119–142.

Martínez Alier, J. and Roca, J. (1987–88) 'Spain after Franco. From Corporatist Ideology to Corporatist Reality', in P. Mattick, Jr. (ed.) *Politics and Economics in Southern Europe: Limits of Change in Spain, Greece, and Portugal*, International Journal of Political Economy, vol. 17, no. 4, Winter, pp. 56–87.

Martínez Cuadrado, M. (1983) *La burguesía conservadora (1874–1931)* (Madrid: Alianza Universidad).

Martínez González-Tablas, A. (1979) *Capitalismo Extranjero en España* (Madrid: Cupsa).

Melo, F. and Monés, M.A. (1982) *La Integración de España en el Mercado Común. Un Estudio de Protección Arancelaria Efectiva* (Madrid: Instituto de Estudios Económicos).

Mercado see relevant reference.

Ministerio de Trabajo y Seguridad Social (1985) *Acuerdo Económico y Social, 1985–86* (Madrid).

Molero, J. (1992) 'German Investment in Spain: Strategies and Behaviour of German Industrial Subsidiaries', in J. van Dijck and A. Wentink (eds) *Transnational Business in Europe* (Tilburg, Tilburg University Press), pp. 162–188.

Monod, J., Gyllenhammar, P. and Dekker, W. (1991) *Reshaping Europe: A Report from the European Round Table of Industrialists* (Brussels: ERT), September.

Montero, J. R. (1989) 'Los Fracasos Políticos y Electorales de la Derecha Española: Alianza Popular, 1976–1987', in J.F. Tezanos *et al.* (eds) op. cit., pp. 495–542.

Moore, B. (1981) *Social Origins of Dictatorship and Democracy* (Harmondsworth: Penguin Books).

Moral Santín, J.A., Carballo, R. and Temprano, A.G. (1981) 'La Formacion del Capitalismo Industrial en España (1855–1959)', in R. Carballo *et al.* (eds) *Crecimiento Económico y Crisis Estructural en España (1959–1980)* (Madrid: Akal), pp. 11–64.

Morán, F. (1980) *Una Política Exterior para España. Una Alternativa Socialista* (Barcelona: Planeta).

—— (1984) 'Principios de la Política Exterior Española', *Leviatán*, no. 16, verano, pp. 7–19.

—— (1990) *España en su Sitio* (Barcelona: Plaza & Janés/*Cambio 16*).

Morodo, R. (1984) 'Etapas del estado totalitario Franquista: dictatura constituyente, cristalización y evolución institucionales', *Revista de Política Comparada*, nos. 10/11, pp. 345–357.

Mouzelis, N. (1976) 'Capitalism and Dictatorship in Postwar Greece', *New Left Review*, no. 96, pp. 57–80.

—— (1978) 'Class and Clientelistic Politics: The Case of Greece', *Socio- logical Review*, vol. 26, pp. 471–497.

Moya, C. (1984) *Señas de Leviatán. Estado nacional y sociedad industrial: España 1936–1980* (Madrid: Alianza Universidad).

Muñoz, J. (1970) *El Poder de la Banca en España* (Madrid: ZYX).

—— (1978) 'La Expansión Bancaria entre 1919 y 1926: La Formación de una Banca "Nacional"', *Cuadernos Económicos de ICE*, no. 6, pp. 98–162.

Muñoz, J., Roldán, S., García Delgado, J.L. and Serrano, A. (1974) *La Economía Española 1973* (Madrid: Cuadernos para el Diálogo).
Muñoz, J., Roldán, S. and Serrano, A. (1978) *La Internacionalizacion del Capital en España, 1959–1977* (Madrid: Cuadernos para el Diálogo).
Myro, R. (1988a) 'La Industria: Expansión, Crisis y Reconversión', in J.L. García Delgado (ed.) op. cit., pp. 197–230.
—— (1988b) 'Las Empresas Públicas', in J.L. García Delgado (ed.) op. cit., pp. 471–497.
Nadal, J. (1975) *El fracaso de la Revolución industrial en España, 1814–1913* (Barcelona: Ariel).
—— (1985) 'Un siglo de industrialización en España, 1833–1930', in N. Sanchez-Albornoz (ed.) *La modernización económica de España, 1830–1930* (Madrid: Alianza Universidad), pp. 89–101.
Nash, E. (1983) 'The Spanish Socialist Party since Franco', in D.S. Bell (ed.) *Democratic Politics in Spain: Spanish Politics after Franco* (New York: Praeger), pp. 29–62.
Nieto de Alba, U. (1984) *De la Dictadura al Socialismo Democrático. Análisis sobre el cambio de modelo socioeconómico en España* (Madrid: Unión Editorial).
Noelke, M. and Taylor, R. (1980) *Spanish Industry and the Impact of Membership of the European Community* (Brussels: European Research Associates).
NRC Handelsblad see relevant reference.
O'Donnell, G. and Schmitter, P. (1986) *Transitions from Authoritarian Rule: Tentative Conclusions about Uncertain Democracies* (Baltimore and London: Johns Hopkins University Press).
OECD (1983) *Economic Surveys: Greece* (OECD: Paris).
—— (1984a) *Economic Surveys: Spain* (OECD: Paris).
—— (1984b) *Economic Surveys: Portugal* (OECD: Paris).
—— (1989) *Economic Surveys: Spain (1988/1989)* (OECD: Paris).
—— (1991) *Economic Surveys: Spain (1990/1991)* (OECD: Paris).
—— (1992) *Economic Surveys: Spain (1991/1992)* (OECD: Paris).
—— (1993a) *Economic Surveys: Spain (1992/1993)* (OECD: Paris).
—— (1993b) *Bank Profitability: Financial Statements of Banks (1982–1991) (statistical supplement)* (OECD: Paris).
—— (1994) *Economic Surveys: Spain (1993/1994)* (OECD: Paris).
Ontiveros, E. and Valero, F.J. (1988) 'El Sistema Financiero. Instituciones y Funcionamiento', in J.L. García Delgado (ed.) op.cit., pp. 367–430.
Ortega, A. (1991) 'Spain and the European Security Puzzle', *European Affairs*, vol. 5, no. 3, June/July, pp. 68–71.
Ortega y Gasset, J. (1984) *España Invertebrada. Bosquejo de algunos pensamientos históricos* (Madrid: Espasa-Calpe) (first published in 1921).
Overbeek, H. (1990) *Global Capitalism and National Decline: The Thatcher Decade in Perspective* (London: Unwin Hyman).
—— (1992) 'Caught Between Europe and the Atlantic: Britain's European Policy under Margaret Thatcher', in C. Polychroniou (ed.) *Perspectives and Issues in International Political Economy* (Westport, London: Praeger), pp. 133–149.
El País see relevant reference.
Paramio, L. (1992) 'Los Sindicatos y la Política en España, 1982–1992', in A. Guerra and J.F. Tezanos (eds) *La Decada del Cambio. Diez Años de Gobierno Socialista, 1982–1992* (Madrid: Sistema), pp. 521–538.

Payne, S. (1987) El Régimen de Franco 1936–1975 (Madrid: Alianza Universidad).
Pensamiento Político de Franco (1975) Volume I and II (systematization by A. del Río Cisneros) (Madrid: Ediciones del Movimiento).
Pérez de la Dehesa, R. (1984) 'Prólogo', in J. Costa, *Oligarquía y Caciquismo, Colectivismo Agrario y Otros Escritos* (Madrid: Alianza Universidad), pp. 7–14.
Pérez Díaz, V. (1984) 'Políticas económicas y pautas sociales en la España de la transición. La doble cara del neocorporatismo', in J. Linz (ed.) *España: un presente para el futuro. Tomo I: La sociedad* (Madrid: Instituto de Estudios Económicos), pp. 21–55.
—— (1987) *El Retorno de la Sociedad Civil. Respuestas sociales a la transición política, la crisis económica y los cambios culturales de España 1975–1985* (Madrid: Instituto de Estudios Económicos).
Pérez Henares, A., Malo de Molina, C.A. and Curiel, E. (1989) *Luces y Sombras del Poder Militar en España* (Madrid: Temas de Hoy).
Pérez Royo, J. (1988) 'Repercussions on the Democratic Process of Spain's entry into Nato', in F.G. Gil and J.S. Tulchin (eds) *Spain's Entry into Nato: Conflicting Political and Strategic Perspectives* (Boulder & London: Lynne Rienner), pp. 20–28.
Pérez Yruela, M. and Giner, S. (eds) (1988) *El Corporatismo en España* (Barcelona: Ariel).
Picciotto, S. (1991) 'The Internationalisation of the State', *Capital and Class*, vol. 43, Spring, pp. 43–63.
Pike, F.B. (1971) *Hispanismo, 1898–1936: Spanish Conservatives and Liberals and their Relations with Spanish America* (Notre Dame: University of Notre Dame Press).
—— (1972) 'Capitalism and Consumerism in Spain in the 1960s: What Lessons for Latin American development?', *Inter-American Economic Affairs*, vol. 26, no. 3, pp. 3–43.
—— (1973) 'Capitalism and Consumerism in Spain of the 1890s: A Latin Americanist's View', *Inter-American Economic Affairs*, vol. 26, no. 4, Spring, pp. 19–47.
—— (1974) 'The New Corporatism in Franco's Spain and Some Latin American Perspectives', in F.B. Pike and T. Stritch (eds) *The New Corporatism: Social–Political Structures in the Iberian World* (Notre Dame and London: University of Notre Dame Press), pp. 171–209.
Polanyi, K. (1957) *The Great Transformation: The Political and Economic Origins of Our Time* (Boston: Beacon Press).
Pollack, B. (1987) *The Paradox of Spanish Foreign Policy: Spain's International Relations from Franco to Democracy* (London: Pinter Publishers).
Portero, F. (1989) *Franco Aislado. La Cuestión Española (1945–1950)* (Madrid: Aguilar Maior).
Poulantzas, N. (1976) *The Crisis of the Dictatorships, Portugal, Greece, Spain* (London: New Left Books).
Prados de la Escosura, L. (1988) *De Imperio a nación. Crecimiento y atraso económico en España (1780–1930)* (Madrid: Alianza Universidad).
Preston, P. (1984) 'Fear of Freedom: The Spanish Army after Franco', in C. Abel and N. Torrents (eds) *Spain: Conditional Democracy* (London: Croom Helm), pp. 161–185.

Preston, P. and Smyth, D. (1984) *Spain, the EEC and Nato* (London: Routledge and Royal Institute of International Affairs).

PSOE (1986) *Por Buen Camino. Para seguir avanzando*, Programa 1986/1990 (Madrid: PSOE).

—— (1989a) *España en Progreso*, Programa Electoral 1989 (Madrid: PSOE).

—— (1989b) *Con Fuerza en Europa*, Manifiesto Europeo – 89 (Madrid: PSOE).

—— (1990) *Resoluciones del 32 Congreso Federal* (Madrid: PSOE).

Regelsberger, E. (1989) 'Spanien und die EPZ – Kein Enfant terrible', *Integration*, no. 2, April, pp. 72–82.

Rivases, J. (1988) *Los Banqueros del PSOE* (Barcelona: Ediciones B).

Rodríguez, E.A. (1988) 'Atlanticism and Europeanism: Nato and Trends in Spanish Foreign Policy', in F.G. Gill and J.S. Tulchin (eds) *Spain's Entry into Nato: Conflicting Political and Strategic Perspectives* (Boulder & London: Lynne Rienner Publishers), pp. 55–71.

Rodríguez Antón, J.M. (1990) *La Banca en España. Un Reto para 1992* (Madrid: Pirámide).

Rodríguez López, J. (1989) 'El Período de la Transición Política desde la Perspectiva del Análisis Económico', in J.F. Tezanos, *et al.*, (eds) op.cit., pp. 117–147.

Rojo, L.A. (1987) 'La Crisis de la Economía Española, 1973–1984', in J. Nadal, *et al.*, (eds) *La Economía Española en el Siglo XX. Una Perspectiva Histórica* (Barcelona: Ariel), pp. 190–200.

Roldán, S., García Delgado, J. L. and Muñoz, J. (1973) *La Formación de la Sociedad Capitalista en España. 1914–1920* (Madrid: Confederación Española de Cajas de Ahorro), Volumes I and II.

Roldán Jiménez, A. (1985) 'Adhesión de España a la CEE: Consecuencias para la Banca Española', *Situación*, no. 1, pp. 47–57.

Rueschemeyer, D., Stephens, E.H. and Stephens, J. D. (1992) *Capitalist Development and Democracy* (Cambridge: Polity Press).

Ruiz Martín, F. (1970) 'La Banca en España hasta 1782', in Banco de España *El Banco de España. Una Historia Económica* (Madrid: Banco de España), pp. 3–196.

Sánchez-Albornoz, N. (1985) 'Castilla. El neoarcaísmo agrario', in N. Sánchez-Albornoz (ed.) *La modernización económica de España, 1830–1930* (Madrid: Alianza Universidad), pp. 287–298.

Sánchez Asiaín, J.A. (1987) *Reflexiones sobre la Banca. Los Nuevos Espacios del Negocio Bancario* (Madrid: Real Academia de Ciencias Morales y políticas).

—— (1992) 'El Sistema Financiero Español ante la Unión Económica Europea', in M. Alonso Olea *et al.*, op. cit., pp. 111–135.

Sandholtz, W. and Zysman, Z. (1989) '1992: Recasting the European Bargain', *World Politics*, vol. 42, October, pp. 95–128.

Sarasqueta, A. (1985) *Después de Franco, La OTAN* (Barcelona: Plaza & Janés).

Schlupp, F. (1980) 'Modell Deutschland and the International Division of Labour', in E. Krippendorff and V. Rittberger (eds) *The Foreign Policy of West Germany* (Beverly Hills/London: Sage), pp. 33–101.

Schmitter, P. (1974) 'Still the Century of Corporatism?' in F.B. Pike and T. Stritch (eds) *The New Corporatism: Social–Political Structures in the Iberian World*, pp. 85–131 (Notre Dame and London: University of Notre Dame Press).

—— (1991) 'The European Community as an Emergent and Novel Form of

Political Domination', *Estudio/Working Paper 1991/26*, Centro de Estudios Avanzados en Ciencias Sociales, Fundación Juan March, Madrid, September.

Schwartz, P. and González, M.J. (1978) *Una historia del Instituto Nacional de Industria (1941–1976)* (Madrid: Tecnos).

Segura, J., et al. (1989) *La Industria Española en la crisis, 1978–1984* (Madrid: Alianza Economía y Finanzas).

Serrano, C. (1984) *Final de Imperio. España, 1895–1898* (Madrid: Siglo XXI).

Share, D. (1985) 'Two Transitions: Democratization and Evolution of the Spanish Left', *West European Politics*, vol. 8, no. 1, pp. 82–103.

Shubert, A. (1980) 'Oil Companies and Governments: International Reaction to the Nationalization of the Petroleum Industry in Spain: 1927–1930', *Journal of Contemporary History*, vol. 15, October, pp. 701–720.

Sideri, S. (1970) *Trade and Power: Informal Colonialism in Anglo-Portuguese Relations* (Rotterdam: Universitaire Pers).

Sotelo, I. (1993) 'Una política socialdemócrata de empleo', in *El País*, 27 February, pp. 11–12.

—— (1984) 'Poder Institucional y Hegemonia Social', *Leviatán*, no. 16, pp. 47–56.

Split, P. (1982) 'De Annales-school. Een inleiding', *Te Elfder Ure*, no. 31, December, pp. 328–378.

Tamames, R. (1966) *La Lucha contra los Monopolios* (Madrid: Tecnos).

—— (1977) *La Oligarquía Financiera en España* (Barcelona: Planeta).

—— (1978) *Estructura Económica de España* (Madrid: Alianza Universidad), Tomo I.

—— (1980) *Estructura Económica de España* (Madrid: Alianza Universidad), Tomo II.

—— (1986) *The Spanish Economy: An Introduction* (New York: St Martin's Press).

Termes, R. (1992) *Antropología del Capitalismo. Un Debate Abierto* (Barcelona: Plaza & Janés/Cambio 16).

Tezanos, J.F. (1983) *Sociologia del Socialismo Español* (Madrid: Tecnos).

—— (1989a) 'Modernización y Cambio Social en España', in J.F. Tezanos et al. (eds) op. cit., pp. 63–116.

—— (1989b) 'Continuidad y Cambio en el Socialismo Español: el PSOE durante la Transición Democrática', in J.F. Tezanos et al. (eds) op. cit., pp. 433–493.

Tezanos, J.F., Cotarelo, R. and de Blas, A. (eds) (1989) *La Transición Democrática Española* (Madrid: Sistema)

Thomas, H. (1977) *The Spanish Civil War* (London: Hamish Hamilton).

Tiempo see relevant reference.

Torrero, A. (1989) *Estudios sobre el Sistema Financiero* (Madrid: Espasa-Calpe).

Tortella Casares, G. (1970) 'El Banco de España entre 1829–1929. La Formacion de un Banco Central', in Banco de España, *El Banco de España. Una Historia Económica* (Madrid: Banco de España), pp. 261–313.

—— (1982) *Los Origenes del Capitalismo en España. Banca, Industria y Ferrocarriles en el siglo XIX* (Madrid: Tecnos).

—— (1983) 'La Economía Española, 1830–1900', in M. Tuñón de Lara (ed.) *Historia de España. Tomo VIII: Revolución Burguesa, Oligarquía y Constitucionalismo (1834–1923)* (Barcelona: Labor), pp. 11–167.

—— (1985) 'Producción y productividad agraria, 1830–1930', in N. Sánchez-Albornoz (ed.) *La modernización económica de España, 1830–1930* (Madrid: Alianza Universidad), pp. 63–88.

Bibliography 249

Tortosa, J.M. (1985) *El 'Cambio' y la Modernización. OTAN, CEE y Nuevas Tecnologías* (Alicante: Instituto Juan Gil-Albert).
Treaty on European Union (1992) (text of the Maastricht Treaty) (Luxembourg: Office for Official Publications of the EC).
Trevithick, J.A. (1980) *Inflation: A Guide to the Crisis in Economics* (London: Penguin Books).
Tsoukalis, L. (1981) *The European Community and its Mediterranean Enlargement* (London: Allen & Unwin).
Tuñón De Lara, M. (1982) *Medio Siglo de Cultura Española, 1885-1936* (Barcelona: Bruguera).
Tusell, J. (1988) 'The Transition to Democracy and Spain's Membership in Nato', in F.G. Gil and J.S. Tulchin (eds) *Spain's Entry into Nato. Conflicting Political and Strategic Perspectives* (Boulder & London: Lynne Rienner), pp. 11-19.
Urwin, D. (1991) *The Community of Europe: A History of European Integration since 1945* (London: Longman).
Usera, L. de (1974) 'International Banking Activity in Spain', in various authors, *International Economics and Banking: To Lars-Erik Thunholm* (Stockholm: University of Stockholm), pp. 197-210.
Valdueza, R. (1982) *Die spanische Gewerkschaftsbewegung unter Franco* (München: Minerva).
Van der Pijl, K. (1984) *The Making of an Atlantic Ruling Class* (London: Verso).
—— (1988) 'Concepts of Control in International Relations', Department of International Relations, University of Amsterdam, (unpublished manuscript).
—— (1989) 'Ruling Classes, Hegemony, and the State System: Theoretical and Historical Considerations', *International Journal of Political Economy*, vol. 19, no. 3, pp. 7-35.
—— (1991) 'German Reunification and World Politics', *Sheffield Papers in International Studies*, no. 7, University of Sheffield.
—— (1993) 'Soviet Socialism and passive revolution', S. Gill (ed.) *Gramsci, Historical Materialism and International Relations* (Cambridge: Cambridge University Press), pp. 237-258.
—— (1994) *Transnational Historical Materialism: An Outline*, unpublished manuscript (University of Amsterdam).
Vázquez, J.A. (1990) 'Crisis, Cambio y Recuperación Industrial', in J.L. García Delgado (ed.) op. cit., pp. 81-117.
Velarde Fuertes, J. (1969) *Sobre la Decadencia Económica de España* (Madrid: Tecnos).
—— (1992) 'Los Sectores Productivos Españoles ante el Reto Comunitario de los Años Noventa', in M. Alonso Olea *et al.*, op. cit., pp. 171-215.
Velasco Murviedro, C. (1984) 'El "ingenierismo" como directriz básica de la política económica durante la autarquía (1936-1951)', *Información Comercial Española*, no. 606, Febr., pp. 97-106.
Vellas, F. (1979) 'Ford Fiesta Spain: A Case Study of International Investment and Trade', *Journal of World Trade Law*, vol. 13, no. 6, Nov.-Dec., pp. 481-494.
Vilanova, P. (1983) 'Spain: the Army and the Transition', in D.S. Bell (ed.) *Democratic Politics in Spain: Spanish Politics after Franco* (London: Frances Pinter), pp. 147-164.
—— (1985a) 'El PSOE: España y la Seguridad Europea', in H. Portelli, *et al.*, *Socialdemocracia y Defensa Europea* (Barcelona: Ariel), pp. 9-27.

Bibliography

—— (1985b) 'Limites et Possibilités en Politique Extérieure: le Cas de l'Espagne', paper for the Workshop on Socialist Governments in Southern Europe, ECPR Joint Sessions, March 25–30, Barcelona.

Vilar, S. (1986) *La Década Sorprendente, 1976–1986* (Barcelona: Planeta).

Viñas, A. (1981) *Los Pactos Secretos de Franco con Estados Unidos. Bases, Ayuda Económica, Recortes de Soberanía* (Barcelona: Grijalbo).

Viñas, A., et al., (1979) *Política Comercial Exterior en España (1931–1975)* (Madrid: Banco Exterior de España), 3 volumes.

Wallerstein, I. (1974) *The Modern World-System I. Capitalist Agriculture and the Origins of the European World-Economy in the Sixteenth Century* (New York: Academic Press).

—— (1984) *The Politics of the World Economy* (Cambridge: Cambridge University Press).

Wolfe, A. (1981) *America's Impasse: The Rise and Fall of the Politics of Growth* (New York: Pantheon).

Zaragoza, A. (ed.) (1988) *Pactos Sociales, Sindicatos y Patronal en España* (Madrid: Siglo XXI).

Index

agriculture: employment in 18, 75, 130; industrial interests, conflict with 46; modernization, slowness of 45, 51; protectionism and 44; transition from pre-capitalist agrarian economic structure 40, 215
Alianza Popular 175, 188, 189
army: coup attempt of 1981 111; coup of 1923 52–3; NATO membership and 111, 210; PSOE and 78, 82, 111
Atlantic Fordism: adoption of Fordist production methods 16–19, 206; authoritarian rule as impediment to 29; changing world order structures and the power of transnational capital 21–30; concepts of control and 6, 21–6; dimensions of 16 *ff*; generally 6, 16; integration of Southern Europe and 26–30; macro-economic regulation and the welfare state 19–21
autarcky 44, 45, 53, 56, 64, 170, 203
authoritarianism: Atlantic Fordism, impeding 29; economic elites and 58; political deradicalization and 74; regenerationism as ideological foundation of 46–52; social transformation and 202; state corporatism and 55
Aznar, José María 189

balance of payments crises 56
banking: American banks 171; 'aristocracy' 169; assets 197–8; Bank RegulationAct 1921 169, 214; Basque banks 176, 177, 184–5, 193 *ff*, 215; 'beautiful people of the PSOE' and 182–3, 208, 213, 215; branch offices 169, 170, 172; Central Bank 169; *Club de los Siete* 173–5, 192; commercial banking 171; Commercial Law of 1885 169; competitiveness 162, 166, 179, 180, 184, 194, 196; concentration 83, 170, 171, 172–3, 183, 187, 192–9, 206, 214; Conde, Mario 190–2, 194, 195, 215; *Consejo Superior Bancario* 173; Credit and Banking Regulation Act 1962 170–1; crisis 179; democratization and 173–5; divisions 192–3; dominant position in economy 11, 166, 168–9, 170, 171, 172–3, 214; EC membership and 179; expansion of 169, 175–6; foreign banks 11, 12, 40, 169, 170, 171–2, 179, 186–8, 196, 197, 214; founding capital 176–7; Franquist regime, relationship with 177; government intervention in 166–7, 179, 192–9; government policies, influence on 173, 174, 184–5; historical background 167–75; industrial banking 40, 83171; industrialization and 11, 12, 169, 170, 176, 177; international comparisons 180, 181, 197, 198–9; Madrid banks 176, 177; management 178, 194; mergers

167, 180, 184, 192–8, 214–15;
mixed banking 169, 170–1, 214;
monopolization 170, 173;
neo-liberals and 185, 196;
oligarchic character of 11, 170,
173, 214; profitability 178, 180,
181, 197; PSOE and 179 *ff*, 215;
regional origins 176; Sánchez
Asiaín, José Angel 184–5; *siete
grandes* 167, 170, 171, 172–3,
175–9, 180, 214; Single European
market and 180, 185; 'Socialist'
bankers 184; state intervention and
177–8, 184–5; *status quo* period
1936–1962 169–70, 214; takeovers
170, 172, 187, 192, 194; Toledo,
Pedro 184, 185
Boada, Claudio 183
Boyer, Miguel 87, 109, 111, 182, 183
bourgeoisie: Basque 40, 43, 44, 50,
52, 61, 66, 176, 204; Catalan 40,
43, 44, 50, 52, 61, 66, 204;
concepts of control and 22–6, 61–2,
63, 178, 192; democratization and
62–3, 65, 67, 188, 204; domestic/
comprador conflict 10–12;
economic policy and 137;
fractionation of 178–9, 192–3;
Franco, under 61–2, 178;
hegemony of 22, 68; interests of
compromised by Fordism 17;
interests of, safeguarding 29, 61–3;
labour co-operation with 62;
national, creation of 178; Newly
Industrializing Countries, in 15;
transnational 24, 33, 40, 63, 64, 68,
83

Calvo Sotelo, Leopoldo 76, 101
capital: *see* banking;
internationalization of capital
capital goods 132–3, 139–41, 142
Catalan nationalists 209, 213
Catholic Church: corporate ideologies
in 56; ideological basis of Franquist
state, as 36, 41; PSOE and 78
CCOO *see* trade unions
CEOE (Confederación Española de
Organizaciones Empresariales):
NATO membership and 107–8,
189; identity crisis 189–90;
opposition to economic policy 164,
190; political persuasions of 188–9
class polarization 41, 51–2, 53, 56, 204
clientelism: bureaucratic 79–80, 81,
88; generally 41, 65–6
Club de Empresarios 186, 213
Coalición Popular 107
collective bargaining 57
Common Market: *see* European
Community membership
Communist Party 57, 106, 107 174
competitiveness: banking 162, 166,
179, 180, 184, 194, 196; industrial
126, 133, 135, 139, 149, 150–1,
156, 157–8, 159, 161, 166, 183, 191
concepts of control: EC
political/economic decision-making
and 144 *ff*; generally 22–6, 33–4,
59, 63; hegemonic 22, 59–60, 175;
internalization of 22–3, 63;
internationalization of 22–3, 63;
mediating role of 6, 35; Spanish
differences 59; state, role of 22–3,
63; transnationally effective 144,
205
concertación social 128
Conde, Mario 190–2, 194, 195, 215
Costa, Joaquin 49–50, 51, 52
crisis of the dictatorships 4, 9–12, 28
Cuevas, José María 189, 190
currency convertability 56
current account deficit 133–4, 138

de Azcarate, Gumersindo 48–9
deflationary policies 77
democracy: worldwide spread of 3,
200
democratization: banking community
and 173–5; bourgeoisie and 62–3,
65, 67, 188, 204; death of Franco
and 61, 73; Eastern Europe 3, 26,
200; EC membership and 65, 67;
economic elites and 58, 61;
Fordism and 16 *ff*, 28; generally 3,
4; international context of 58–9;
internationalization, through 65;
interstate dependency approach to

9–16; Lipietz, Alain, on 12–16; opposition to 47, 61; political deradicalization and 74; Poulantzas, Nicos, on 9–12; societal corporatism and 55–60, 66–7; trade union support for 73, 204
dependent industrialization 9–10
domestic market: development of 18, 45

Eastern Europe: democratization 3, 26, 200; European Union membership 26–7, 117, 119–20, 210, 217
economic growth in Southern Europe 4, 17
economic liberalization: generally 4, 11, 17, 27–8, 40, 47, 53, 203, 215; impact of 57, 58 reasons for 56–7; society and 57
economic nationalism 45, 46, 50, 52, 135, 177, 190, 202, 203
economic policy: adjustment policy 77, 80–1, 83–4, 126–7, 134, 137, 147; austerity policy 77, 92, 125, 127, 141, 142–3, 146, 147, 164, 206, 210–11; contradictory interpretations of 127–8; deflationary 77; EC membership and 147–56; EMU and *see* European Monetary Union; external restraints and 136–47; foreign pressure on decision-making 146; Guerra, Alfonso, and 87–8; hypothetical options 80–1; international economic crisis and 77, 125–6; intra-party conflict 88, 90, 92; macro-economic *see* macro-economic policies; middle class influence on 136–7, 145–6; moderate impact of PSOE 5, 145–7; 'political business cycle' 137; public spending 81, 83, 90, 156, 164; shortcomings of 86; Single European Market and *see* Single European Market; stimulation 77, 80, 137, 138, 141–2, 156, 210; three central objectives of 126–7; trade unions' response to 127
EFTA: EC membership and 120

elections: *see* general elections
emigration: role played by 17
employment increases 130–1
employment policies 77–8, 130
Escudero, Manuel 85, 87, 90
estate system 36, 39, 41
European Council presidency: priorities of programme 114–15
European Community membership: banking and 179; democratic prerequisite for 65, 67; Eastern European 26–7, 117, 119–20, 210, 217; economy, impact on 148–56; EFTA states 120; generally 29–30, 96, 149, 207; NATO membership and 100–1, 111–13; opposition to Spanish membership from France etc 78, 112; PSOE and 78, 80–1, 82, 122, 207; strong state, representing 38; studies of 149–51; ultimate goal, as 5, 67; widespread support for 78
European integration: general framework of 143 *ff*, 216–17 globalist approach to 165, 216; socio-economic actors 144–5; *see also* European Monetary Union; European Political Union; Single European Market
European Monetary Union: criteria for 152–3, 212, 216; decision-making 152–3; generally 115, 116, 117, 118, 119; macro-economic convergence and 147, 148–9, 152–6, 210, 211, 216; *plan de convergencia* 155–6, 211, 212, 213; social policy and 91; two-tier 153–5, 216–17;
European Political Union: generally 116, 117, 118, 119, 120; social policy and 91
Europeanization: generally 80, 92, 96, 102; regenerationism and 47–8, 50, 51, 57; widespread support for 78; *see also* foreign policy
'Euro-Thatcherism' 116
exchange rates 138–9
Exchange Rate Mechanism 138, 153, 161

254 *Index*

exports 131–4, 141, 151

Falangists 56
Felipismo 82
Fordism: co-existence with other forms of organisation 18; crisis of as basis for change 6, 12–16, 205; introduction of 16–17; Lipietz, Alain, on 12–16; 'peripheral' 13, 14, 15; Southern European differences 18–19; *see also* Atlantic Fordism
foreign investment: dependence on 28; EC 144–5; early industrialization and 42; high technology, in 159; influence of 11, 12, 17; liberalization of 38; manufacturing, in 159; US 144, 171
foreign policy: contradictory situation affecting 78–9; 'decalogue' 104–5; domestification of 98–9; EC membership *see* European Community membership; EC presidency and 114–15; economic factors influencing 98, 99; EMU and 115, 116, 117, 118, 119; European Political Union and 116, 117, 118, 119, 120; generally 77, 98; historical background 97–8; international recognition, quest for, and 97, 99, 122; NATO membership *see* NATO membership; offensive strategy 99; Programme 2000 and 122–4; secondary power, Spain as 96–7, 123; security objectives 98, 99, 111, 112–13, 210 *see also* NATO membership; Single European Market and 96, 114, 115; Socialist International influence on 65, 207; special relationships with Latin America/Middle East and 98; Third Worldism and 98, 102, 108–9; Transition Programme 101–2
foreign trade 126
Fraga, Manuel 107, 175, 188, 189
France: economic stimulation policies 77, 141–2, 210; modernization of Europe and 201

Franco, Francisco: death of 61; decisive role of regime 40, 53; generally 53
free trade 44

general elections: 1977 76; 1979 76; 1982 76, 77, 79; 1993 208–9, 217; summary of results 1977–1989 95
general strike of 1988 78, 128, 164
Germany: hegemony of 120–1
giro social 78, 89
global class formation 24
global economy of transnational production 134–5
global political economy: transition to modernity and 3–6
global system as a social structure 8
González, Felipe: authoritarian leadership of 85; bankers, relationship with 184; Brandt, Willy, influence of 65, 77, 84, 207; NATO membership and 110; unquestioned leadership of 84, 103
Greece: economic stimulation policies 77, 142, 210; integration into international capitalist system 4–5
Gross Domestic Product 129
Gross National product 148
Guerra, Alfonso: Boyer, Miguel, confrontation with 87, 88; bureaucratic clientelism strategy of 79–80, 81, 88; economic policy and 87–8; marginalization of 209; NATO membership and 108, 109–10; neo-liberals, confrontation with 87–90, 108, 207 party organisation, control of 79, 85, 87, 89, 209; resignation of 88, 90

hegemony: American 16, 24, 26, 29, 81, 200; French 201; generally 22, 59–60, 175; German 120–1; PSOE project *see* Socialist party (PSOE); world hegemony 24; *see also* concepts of control
high technology industries 81, 159
Hispanicization 47, 50, 51, 57
Hobbesian state-building 24, 34, 39, 60, 66, 83, 143, 201, 202

import substitution 17, 44
imports 131–4, 151
industrial reconversion: dual strategy, as part of 157, 159; employment levels and 157, 213; generally 81, 126–7, 147, 151, 211, 213; multinationalization 157, 158, 213–14; privatization *see* privatization; profitability and 157, 158, 159–60; public sector 156–60;
industrialization: de-industrialization 126, 128, 157; dependent 9–10; employment in industry 18, 75; European Community membership and 5; late industrialization 42–52; Lipietz, Alain, on 12–16; post-World War I expansion 52; Poulantzas, Nicos, on 10–12; reindustrialization 126–7, 147, 148–9
inflation: capital goods industry and 141; economic liberalization, influencing 56; EMU and 152, 155; exchange rate adjustments and 138–9; reduction as policy objective 77, 126, 128, 129, 133, 134, 147, 155, 210; severity of 125, 211
Instituto Nacional de Industria (INI): employment, reduction of 157, 213; profitability 158, 159–60; reconversion of companies 128, 156–60, 213–14; subdivision of 160
interest mediation: *see* state corporatism
interest rates: EMU and 153, 155; increase in 131; lowering as economic stimulus 156
international Fordism: *see* Atlantic Fordism
international organisations: Spanish membership of 56
international relations: traditional theory of 3, 5; transnational perspective of 3, 6
internationalization of capital: concepts of control and 6, 22–5, 28; Fordism, spread of, and 16–17; link between modernization and Westernization, as 28, 203, 215–16

interstate dependency: Lipietz, Alain, on 12–16 Poulantzas, Nicos, on 9–12 social change and 6, 7–16
Izquierda Unida 208, 213

Keynesianism: Atlantic Fordism and 19–21, 58; full employment, establishing 137
Krausism 48–50

labour costs 129–30
labour market deregulation 155
labour relations: *see* trade unions
Latin America: debt crisis 115; democratization of 3, 26, 55; special relationship with 98
liberal political and economic values: renaissance of 3, 26, 200
liberalization *see* economic liberalization
Lipietz, Alain: social change, on 12–16
Lockeian heartland of transnational production 24, 27, 39, 43, 68, 83, 93, 180, 196, 202, 205, 206, 213, 214, 216

Maastricht Treaty 96, 114
macro-economic policies: beneficiaries of 83, 161–2; EC membership, impact of 147 *ff*; EMU and *see* European Monetary Union; generally 19–21, 83, 92, 186; Moncloa Pacts and 163; necessity of 126–7; neo-liberal, whether 148; reindustrialization and 148–9; social dialogue and 163; social policy and 91, 123, 126; sink or swim strategy 135; structural imbalances and 128–36; supply side orientation 134, 135, 186
Marxism: PSOE and 76–7, 84
middle classes: influence on economic policy 136–7, 145–6; rise of 41, 75, 146, 204, 207; support for PSOE 75–6, 83
mixed economies 19–21
modernization: competing ideologies of 64–5; generally 4, 6, 43, 200–2; meaning of 27, 201; PSOE and 80;

resistance to 50
Moncloa Pacts 55, 162–3
monetary policy 81, 83, 128, 130, 131, 134, 147, 156, 210, 211
monetary union *see* European Monetary Union
Morán, Fernando 108–9
multinationalization of companies 157, 158

nationalism: economic 45, 46, 50, 52, 135, 177, 190, 202, 203; generally 41; supra-national Europeanism versus 102; weak state, in 36
NATO membership: abstentions in referendum 106, 107; ambiguity of PSOE 103–4, 110, 112; army and 111; CEOE and 107; *Club de los Sieste* support for 107–8; Coalición Popular and 107; conditionality clauses of referendum 106, 110; debate on 107–8; 'decalogue' and 104–5, 110; deradicalization of PSOE and 101–4, 106 *ff*; EC membership and 100–1, 111–13; Europeanization of Atlantic Alliance and 98, 99, 111, 112–13; factionalism within PSOE and 108, 109–10; foreign policy aim, as 98; Guerra, Alfonso, and 108–10 Morán, Fernando, and 108–9; opposition to 78, 106; PSOE and 78, 80, 82, 98, 101 *ff*, 209–10; referendum on 100 *ff*; Serra, Narcís, and 109, 111; Transition Programme and 101–2; UCD policy on 101, 103; United States etc support for 78–9 volte-face of PSOE 106–113, 209
neo-liberals: banking and 185; economic policy and 81, 86, 147, 148, 158–9; Guerristas, conflict with 87–90, 108, 207; *see also* Solchaga, Carlos
neutrality 102

Opus Dei technocrats 56, 57, 59, 64
Ortega y Gasset, José 52

particularism: effects of 44, 52; Franco and 53, 178; generally 36, 41, 51
Partido Popular: business links of 81; European elections of 1994 and 209; opposition to economic policy 164; political alternative to PSOE, as 189
passive revolution 201–2
peseta: appreciation of 131, 134, 138; devaluation of 163, 207, 212; ERM, incorporation into 211
poderes facticos 36, 78, 82
political deradicalization 74
political opposition 188–92
political regionalization 143, 145, 165, 205
Portugal: integration into international capitalist system 4–5, 200
Poulantzas, Nicos: social change, on 9–12
Primo de Rivera, Miguel: coup of 1923 52–3
privatization: EMU and 155; industrial policy, as part of 128; substantial 158
private capital: primary motor of economic recovery, as 157
productivity: Fordism and 16, 17, 18, 19, 21; late industrialization and 45; modernization, as prerequisite to 157; neutralization of 133; social dialogue and 129; unit labour costs and 130
profitability of companies 129, 157, 158
Programme 2000 89–90, 122–4
protectionism 42, 43, 44–5, 46, 50, 81, 176, 190
PSOE (Partido Socialista Obrero Español): *see* Socialist party (PSOE)
public sector *see* Institute Nacional de Industria
public spending *see* economic policy
Pujol, Jordi 209, 213

redundancies 130
regenerationism 46–52

religion as ideology 36, 41
Rubio, Mariano 183, 208
ruling class: creation of single 61
ruptura pactada 62–3, 73, 204
rural depopulation 75

Sánchez Asiaín, José Angel 184–5
Serra, Narcís 109, 111
service sector employment 18, 75
Single European Market: banking and 180, 185; conflicts as to 116; economy, impact on 149–56; industrial sectors, impact on 159; intra-party tensions and 91; macro-economic convergence and 147, 210; national decision-making and 116, 152; PSOE policy and 80; second phase of Europeanization of foreign policy, marking 114; secondary role of Spain 96, 115; support for 115–16
social change: explanation for 7–9; external influences on 8–9; interstate dependency as explanation for 6, 9–16; understanding 6
Social Charter 115
social-democratization: Fordism and 20–1; European Community membership and 5; generally 73–4, 84, 136
social unrest 74
Socialist International 187, 207
socialist parties in Southern Europe: legitimization of 4–5
Socialist party (PSOE): bureaucratic clientelism and 79–80, 81; corruption scandals 88, 208; deradicalization of 65, 76–7, 78, 85, 101–4, 106 *ff*, 136, 145, 206, 207; economic policy of *see* economic policy; electoral stability of 79, 81, 136; factional strife within 84 *ff*, 206, 207, 208; financing of 65, 187–8; foreign capital and 187–8; foreign policy of *see* foreign policy; Guerristas versus neo-liberals 87–90, 206, 207, 208; hegemonic project of 80, 81 *ff*, 91–2, 188, 206 *ff*; hypothetical policy options of 80–1; ideology of 65, 84–6; international economic crisis and 77; internationalization of politics and 82, 83, 92; institutional power of 79–80, 81; Italian Socialist Party (PSI) and 188; Marxism and 76–7, 84; middle class support for 75–6, 83; NATO membership and *see* NATO membership; neo-liberal wing *see* neo-liberals; opposition to 188–92; *poderes facticos* and 78, 82; Programme 2000 89–90, 122–4; radical democratic orientation of 86, 87; rationalist economic orientation of 86; reformist political orientation of 85–6; renewal, orientation of 86, 87; scandals 88, 208; 'sensibilities' within 85–7; 'social liberals' *see* neo-liberals; 'technocrats' *see* neo-liberals; transnationalization of 65; UCD weakness and 76
socialization of private losses 158
societal corporatism 41, 55–60, 73
society: changes in social stratification 75; conflicts within 7; emancipation of 35, 58; major developments in Spanish society 40–1; regenerationism and problems of 46–52; rural depopulation, effect of 75; state, relationship to 34, 35–9, 67–8, 204–5; transnationalization of 65, 82
Solchaga, Carlos: banking and 183, 184, 185; economic policy and 81, 86, 88, 128; Guerristas, conflict with 88–90, 207, 208; marginalization of 209; resignation of 209
Spain: integration into international capitalist system 4–5, 92, 200; major developments in recent history 40–1; peculiarities of Spanish case 35–42; state strength/weakness 36–9;
Spanish Civil War 40, 41, 53
Stabilization Plan of 1959 11, 38, 40, 44, 56

state: corporatism *see* state corporatism; economy, role in 43, 45, 46, 48, 49, 83, 128, 177, 203–4 *see also* industrial reconversion; internationalization of 25–6, 134, 205–6; social structure, as 8; society, relationship to 34, 35–9, 67–8, 204–5; weak and strong 36–9
state corporatorism: concept of 54–5; concepts of control distinguished 60; social dialogue 163; transition to societal corporatism 41, 55–60, 66–7, 204–5
steel industry 158
Suárez, Adolfo 62, 63, 76, 101, 188
superpower politics: demise of 3, 26
supra-national institutionalism 117, 119, 120, 143, 145, 165, 180, 206, 207, 210, 217

technocrats: *see* neo-liberals
textile industry 42, 44, 158
Thatcher, Margaret 116
theoretical perspective 3–30
Toledo, Pedro 78, 184, 185
tourism: dependence on 28; role played by 17
trade deficit 126, 131–4, 135, 138, 148
trade patterns 139–40
trade unions: *concertación social* 128; democratization, support for 73; disciplinary action on leaders by PSOE 164; economic policy and 127; general strike of 1988 78, 128, 164; *giro social*, call for 78, 163; Keynesian economic policy and 19; Moncloa Pacts 162–3; NATO membership, opposition to 107; relationship with PSOE 77–8, 82, 83–4, 89, 148, 163–5, 206; social dialogue with 128, 162–3; state corporatism and 54–5, 163
transnational dynamics of global integration 5–6

UCD (Uníon de Centro Democrático) 62–3, 76, 126, 175, 188, 189
UGT *see* trade unions
unemployment 77, 84, 125, 128, 130–1, 137, 148, 211–13
United States: banks 171; hegemony of 16, 24, 26, 29, 81, 206; military bases 100, 102; pressure on Franquist regime 56; support for Spanish NATO membership 79
universal suffrage 33

Vertical Syndicate 55, 57–8

wage restraint 128, 129, 130, 133
wage rises: EMU and 155; Fordism and 16, 17, 18, 19, 21; late industrialization and 45; social dialogue and 130
welfare state: contradictions of 27; dimension of Fordism, as 19–21
Western European Union 98, 105, 113
Westernization: generally 35, 40, 43, 46, 200, 203; internationalization of capital and 29; meaning of 27, 203
workers: victims of PSOE policies, as 83–4
world time 35, 58